Key Themes in
...cial Work

...ves

...hardlow

He ...
Before them: a ...
shiny, metal plate pl...

305
                    DARKTAN (CONT'...
          Huh! Strange.

The other rats, gathered behind him, have wide eyes. ...
Darktan is worried, everyone is worried.

Darktan examines the trap, smells it.

306
                    DARKTAN (CONT'D)
          Reminds me of a Prattle and Johnson
          little snapper, but those are not
          round like this one. (sniffs)
          Eeh... And there's no extra safety
          catch.
307
                    (beat)
          I think we need... Mister Clicky.

A gasp from the rats.

308
                    CLAN RATS
                    (in unison)
          Huuuh! Mir. Clicky... Yes, Mr.
          Clicky...

A CLOCKWORK WINDING sound. The rats part, revealing a SHINY,
METALLIC RAT. It has a dented body and glassy eyes, and short
string tail, chopped off by a trap. However, it can't get
killed, because it is a mechanical, wind-up cat toy --
MISTER CLICKY rattles his way through the rats.

On his back, a KEY whirs and turns. Rats pat him, encourage
him, urging him on --

309
                    NOURISHING
          Hey Oy, Good luck, Buddy!

310
                    FARMHOUSE
          It's Showtime, Mr. Clicky!

311
                    PEACHES
          Go, Mister Clicky, you can do it!

Mr. Clicky stops. Darktan frowns. But Mr. Clicky doesn't
budge, even whirs back a little, to the disdain of Darktan.

312
                    DARKTAN
          On the double, soldier. What are
          you waiting for? Time to do your
          duty.

First published in 2001 by:
Russell House Publishing Ltd.
4 St. George's House
Uplyme Road
Lyme Regis
Dorset DT7 3LS

Tel: 01297-443948
Fax: 01297-442722
e-mail: help@russellhouse.co.uk

British Library Cataloguing-in-publication Data:
A catalogue record for this book is available from the British Library.

ISBN: 1-898924-69-4

Typeset by The Hallamshire Press Limited, Sheffield

Printed by Bath Press, Bath

Russell House Publishing

Is a group of social work, probation, education and youth and community work practitioners and academics working in collaboration with a professional publishing team. Our aim is to work closely with the field to produce innovative and valuable materials to help managers, trainers, practitioners and students. We are keen to receive feedback on publications and new ideas for future projects.

From beginning to end we have held to the blueprint of 'mediations'. In this sense, the proposed models may be seen as contributing to the crucial ongoing debate between the right to universality and the demand of historical difference.

Ricoeur (1995: p 12)

Also by Adrian Adams, Peter Erath and Steven M. Shardlow as part of the same series of books:

Adams, A., Erath, P., and Shardlow, S.M. (Eds.) (2000). *Fundamentals of Social Work in Selected European Countries*. Lyme Regis: Russell House.
Shardlow, S.M., and Cooper, S. (2000). *A Bibliography of European Studies in Social Work*. Lyme Regis: Russell House.

Contents

Acknowledgements   vii

The Authors   viii

Preface   x
Adrian Adams, Peter Erath and Steven M. Shardlow

Introduction   xii
Adrian Adams, Peter Erath and Steven M. Shardlow

Chapter 1
Comparing Social Work from a European Perspective: 1
Towards a Comparative Science of Social Work
Peter Erath, Juha Hämäläinen and Horst Sing

Chapter 2
The Role of Social Policy in Social Work   5
Pauli Niemelä and Juha Hämäläinen

Chapter 3
Theory in Social Work   15
Peter Erath and Juha Hämäläinen

Chapter 4
Research in Social Work   27
Ivana Loučková and Adrian Adams

Chapter 5
Ethical Aspects of Social Work—A Common Set of Values and   39
the Regulation of Practice: England an Example
Steven M. Shardlow

Chapter 6
The Increasing Importance of Law to Social Work Practice: UK an Example   47
Belinda Schwehr

Chapter 7
Social Work and Economic Policy: The Netherlands an Example   57
Geert van der Laan

Chapter 8
Social Work and the Third Sector: The Example of the German Welfare State   69
Wolfgang Klug

Chapter 9
Social Alarm and Public Reassurance: The Italian Example   77
Rino Fasol and Franco Fraccaroli

Chapter 10
Social Work Education and Training: The Spanish Experience   85
Jordi Sabater

Chapter 11
Social Work as a Career: Choice or Accident? The French Example   95
Emmanuel Jovelin

Postscript   103
Adrian Adams, Peter Erath and Steven M. Shardlow

References   105

Index   113

Figures and Tables

Table   2.1: Idealised Models of Welfare State Systems   6
Figure 2.1: Subjects in the Provision of Welfare Services   9
Figure 2.2: Dimensions of Welfare Regimes   9
Table   2.2: Models of Social Policy, from Residual to Institutional and   11
        from 'Legitimistic' to 'Solidaristic' as Applied to Finland
Figure 3.1: Social Work Theories Located within a Framework of Different
        Helping Perspectives   16
Figure 3.2: Social Work Theories within a Framework of Traditional Knowledge Forms   18
Table   5.1: Braye and Preston-Shoot's Categorisation of Values   40
Figure 5.1: Supporting the Quality Agenda   45
Figure 8.1: The Three Sectors of Welfare   69
Figure 8.2: Function, Role and Location of Welfare Institutions in Germany   70
Figure 8.3: The Role of Welfare Organisations   73
Table 10.1: The Syllabus   91

Acknowledgements

A large number of people are involved in the production of any book, this is no exception. Many of the names go unrecorded but we would like to thank all who have been involved, in particular those who have translated chapters, and the staff at Russell House who have been enthusiastic and helpful as this book and the project of which it forms a part have developed. We would like to extend our thanks to the following who have influenced the development of the ideas in this book: Oldřich Chytil, Willi Fischges, Evelyne Tully, Francesco Villa and Montse Feu. Individual authors have been influenced by many others, too numerous to mention, to all of them we offer our thanks.

We also wish to thank the European Union without whose financial support this book would not have been possible. The EU has provided the opportunity for us to come together as a group, through mobility programmes and to build good working relationships.

We wish to make the following specific acknowledgements:

- *To the Guardian for permission to reprint the cartoon, Clare in the Community.*

- *To the Department of Heath for permission to reprint the figure: Supporting the quality agenda.*

As ever, the editors and the authors of the book gratefully acknowledge the help of others but accept responsibility for the books contents—including any mistakes!

The Authors

Adrian Adams is Senior Lecturer in Social Work at Canterbury Christ Church University College, England. Previously he has worked as a social worker and as a Social Work Education Advisor for the Central Council for Education and Training in Social Work (CCETSW). Current research and teaching interests are in the role and contribution of social work in community care. He is editor of Kent Journal of Practice Research, an annual publication, sponsored by the Kent Consortium for Education and Training in Social Work Education.

Peter Erath is Professor of Social Work Theory in the Department of Social Work at the Catholic University of Eichstaett, Germany. He has previously worked as a teacher in the field of special education. He is a member of the German Society for Social Work and has been head of several research projects with large welfare organisations in Bavaria. He was co-ordinator of the European Module Project, 'Social Security Systems and Social Work Theories'. Current research and teaching interests are in the area of social work theories, social work with young people and comparative social work.

Rino Fasol is a Researcher at the Dipartimento di Sociologia e Ricerca Sociale and Professor of Organization of Social Services at the Corso di diploma in Servizio sociale of the Universita' degli Studi di Trento, Italy. His current research interests are in the field of the organisation of the social and health care systems at national and local level.

Franco Fraccaroli is Professor of Work and Organisational Psychology at the Faculty of Educational Science of the University of Genova, Italy. His current research interests are in the work and organisational socialisation processes and in the social psychology of health.

Juha Hämäläinen is Professor of Social Work (special area Social Pedagogy), Head of Department of Social Sciences at the University of Kuopio, Finland. He is interested in theoretical questions concerning social work, especially the development of ideas.

Emmanuel Jovelin is Doctor of sociology and diplomate of political sciences. He is a researcher and Professor in Sociology at the Social Institute of Lille-Vauban at the Catholic University of Lille, France. He has published 'Devenir travailleur social aujourd'hui, vocation ou repli?' Ed. L'harmattan, 1999.

Wolfgang Klug is Professor of Social Work (Methods) in the Department of Social Work at the Catholic University of Eichstaett, Germany. He has previously worked as a head of a centre of social aid. His special areas of research are: adult education, management of social organisations, quality management. He is a member of the German Society of Social Work (Community of research) and the German Association of Social Work (Community of practitioners). In 1999, he was elected as the Dean of his department.

Geert van der Laan is Professor of Social Work in the Department of General Social Sciences at the University of Utrecht, Netherlands. He is conducting research on 'Street Children' in Romania. He is Chairman of the One Europe Foundation and Member of the editorial board of the European Journal of Social Work.

Ivana Loučková is Associate Professor of Social Work Studies at the Medico-Social Faculty, Ostrava University, Czech Republic. Her teaching areas are theory and methodology of social sciences, social research and social work research, quantitative and qualitative data analysis and statistics. She is interested in the cultivation of research and developing social workers' skills in social interactions and in working with values and ethics questions.

Pauli Niemelä is Professor of Social Policy with particular reference to social work and Dean of the Faculty of Social Sciences at the University of Kuopio, Finland. He is a permanent expert used by the Social and Health Ministry (the National Research and Development Centre for Welfare and Health). His particular interests include human security/insecurity and coping methods, health and social policy, social ethics, social work in public health and the inter-generational questions.

Jordi Sabater is Professor of Social Policy and Social History at the Social Work School of the Ramon Llull University, Barcelona, Spain. He also has been professor at the Social Sciences School and the Social Education School and now is doing research on the evolution of social work in Spain. Current research and teaching interests are in the areas of social work education and comparative social policy in Europe. He has published several books about social movements and social policy in Catalonia.

Belinda Schwehr is a Senior Solicitor-Advocate at Rowe and Maw, a firm of lawyers based in London, England. She has a background as a barrister and an administrative law lecturer in several university law schools. She specialises in the law of adults' social services, mental health, and NHS law and fertility issues. She has lectured widely in her field, and has trained over fifty local authorities in the UK about the legal developments that have occurred in social services since the early 1990s. Her special interest is the impact of European Convention law and the UK's Human Rights Act on social work policy and practice.

Steven M. Shardlow is Professor of Social Work at the University of Salford, and Editor-in-Chief of the *Journal of Social Work*. Previously he has worked as a social work practitioner and manager in both field and residential work. He has been involved in international social work, particularly in Europe through development work, consultancy and research. Current research and teaching interests are in the following areas: professional ethics; comparative social practice in the social professions; professional social work education and practice— especially practice learning. He has published widely in these fields and his work has been translated into several languages.

Horst Sing is Professor of Political Science in the Department of Social Work at the Catholic University of Eichstaett, Germany. He is responsible for the 'Studienschwerpunkt interkulturelle/internationale Sozialarbeit' of the faculty and is Director of the 'Institut fuer vergleichende Sozialarbeitswissenschaft und interkulturelle/internationale Sozialarbeit' (ISIS), Eichstaett. Current research and teaching interests are in the area of International and Intercultural Social Work, especially in the Third World under different aspects of globalisation.

Preface

Adrian Adams, Peter Erath and Steven M. Shardlow

This book is the result of three years of co-operation by a multinational group, sponsored by the Socrates programme of the European Union. The initial aim of the group was to develop a common module on Theories and Models of Social Security Systems and Social Work Practice in Europe and then integrate this module into the curricula of their respective educational institutions. Inevitably, in such a time consuming and demanding project, not all European countries could be included; nevertheless, the group does include representatives from the range of different models of social security systems across Europe. One result of the work of the group has been to produce three books. First, a book that explores the historical and political contexts of social work in several European countries—*Fundamentals of Social Work in Selected European Countries*. Second, this book, which both builds upon the foundations laid by the first book and provides further critical analyses of key themes in social work across Europe that may be read either independently or jointly with the first book. Third, a bibliography of materials published in English about social work in Europe—*Bibliography of European Studies in Social Work*. These publications are intended to complement each other to promote an understanding about social work across Europe, and to encourage the development of better practice through the sharing of ideas.

During this programme of work, there has been an active exchange of lecturers and students from the participating universities within a framework of a student and staff mobility programme; with the texts, that comprise the contents of this book, emerging from a process of continuous development, discussion and refinement by the group. These texts have been devised to form the basis of lectures and seminars for social work students with an interest in the European dimension of social work and who undertake visits abroad as part of their studies. However, the texts are not solely aimed at students. Practitioners, managers and policy makers within the various countries within Europe cannot afford to ignore the ways in which social work practice is developing

across Europe. Hence, this book is intended to inform current debates about policy and practice and to help in the creation and exchange of ideas about new and innovative practice.

In the course of eight seminars, each lasting several days, during which the group discussed and debated the ideas that came to form the content of these texts, a number of shared themes emerged that shaped the construction of this book. These Key Themes, presented here, emerged from the rich source of fundamental issues that surround and inform the practice of social work and from which the different orientations towards what constitutes social welfare in Europe have emerged. The themes that we have selected are 'key' in the sense that they demonstrate constructions of social work that are neglected in any one national approach. Through this selection of papers, which examine the relationships that arise between social policy, theory, research, ethics, law, market forces, non-governmental enterprises, social alarm and reassurance, education and training, and individual career choices, we hope to generate a more thorough understanding of the limits to, and possibilities for, practising social work.

By reference to a range of comparative and often competing political, cultural and intellectual traditions, our ambition is to contribute to a process that seeks to overcome the dichotomies that arise within welfare regimes. For example, between social structure and human agency, collective solidarity and individual liberty, subjectivity and objectivity, morality and instrumentalism. Further, we seek to demonstrate the possibility that through a synthetic process of engagement between social work practitioners and social work clients, a communicatively orientated form of ethical practice may be arrived at beyond the reach of any single social system of regulation and administration.

The eleven separate chapters presented here, each offer an example of a key theme that contributes to the emergent trajectory of social work in Europe. Also collectively, the book demonstrates a shared belief by the author group of the necessity of contrasting and counter balancing the Anglo-American positivist model of welfare, that privileges individualism and is legitimated by reference to criteria of economy and effectiveness, with the humanistic and hermeneutic tradition that privileges solidarity and critical reflection.

Editing Principles

This book is published in English, since increasingly within Europe, English is the language of international communication. This places those, for whom English is not a first language and who read this book, at some disadvantage. With this in mind, the editors have sought to avoid unnecessary complexity of language and to provide explanations wherever this seems to be helpful.

Translation from other languages into English in a specialised field such as social work is problematic. There are many terms that have no direct and meaningful translation. According to Cooper and Pitts (1993), within the field of European social work there are a number of different vocabularies, each internally consistent and where terms derive meaning by virtue of reference to other terms. This presents enormous difficulties in translating *meaning* rather than words. We have tried to provide explanations for such terms but also have tended to leave these translated words to stand for themselves (for example, the term

'activation'—see Chapter 7). Hence, we hope that the book will introduce both new terms and ideas into the specialised language of social work, as expressed in English.

Those who write English as a second language bring an additional richness and vitality to the language, often introducing ideas and modes of expression that reflect their own linguistic background. We have tried to preserve this richness in the material included in this book yet also striven to ensure grammatical consistency and correctness.

The English language presents other problems: for example, it is difficult to refer to both men and women in an all-inclusive way when using the single pronoun. Using *he/she* or *(s)he* is clumsy, so we have tended wherever possible to use the plural form *they*: even if this sometimes strains the grammar a little.

There is another vexed question: spelling. There are two kinds of English, the American and the British. This book uses British English, as this is the form of English grounded in Europe.

References

Adams, A., Erath, P., and Shardlow, S.M. (Eds.) (2000). *Fundamentals of Social Work in Selected European Countries*. Lyme Regis: Russell House Publishing.

Shardlow, S.M., and Cooper, S. (2000). *A Bibliography of European Studies in Social Work*. Lyme Regis: Russell House Publishing.

Introduction

Adrian Adams, Peter Erath and Steven M. Shardlow

As national welfare state systems increasingly loose their influence in the face of emergent global and local imperatives and processes, social work remains suspended between competing interests and purposes.

> The most important phenomenon in Europe today is the slow withering away of the nation-state. The nation-state was a unique institution in history which united economic management, political authority and cultural hegemony. Today, economic management is moving away from the nation-state because of the globalisation of the economy. The nation-state is no longer an economic system, self-contained or self-sufficient. As far as the cultural hegemony is concerned it moves downwards from the state: the movement is not upwards like the economy, but downwards towards social movements, communities, ethnic groups and so on. What is left in the nation-state is just pure political authority without it being supported by economic management and cultural hegemony.
>
> (Bauman in Cantell and Pedersen, 1992: p 133)

Within this uncertain scenario, we propose that the role of the social work practitioner and educator is to offer an informed, rational and critical voice, which presents a challenge to the instrumentalism of the bureaucratic and economic systems of society. By so doing, social work would assert its legitimate role in seeking to both expose and alleviate oppression, distress and unmet need, and advocating on behalf of the interests of socially excluded people. Accordingly, we argue that the future legitimacy and accountability of social work rests upon its capacity to re-claim and re-articulate its core principles and purpose.

The themes explored in this book promote a re-examination of the assumptions and associations through which social work is constructed. Social work, whilst epistemologically grounded in the empiricism and hermeneutics of the social sciences, is also historically grounded in normalising and regulating discourses (Foucault, 1970)—that is, the imperatives and policies of the political and economic systems of society, and ontologically grounded in the moral-practical activity of the 'lifeworld' (Habermas, 1984 and 1987). In the following chapters, these themes

will be further explored. However, we do not propose that reference to the array of social theories or methods of enquiry in the social sciences can alone overcome the complexities of practice. Rather they are contextual and informative to the immediate nature and experience of contingent practice and the transformative power and resilience of social agency and self-consciousness (Gadamer, 1975).

Through the themes explored we hope to argue and demonstrate that:

- The interests of social work rest upon its capacity to recognise and engage with both the strategic and technical actions that emanate from social systems and the heterogeneous, moral and practical concerns that arise in the life world.

- Rather than pursue its current preoccupation with teleological forms of evidence, which offer the false promise of a gain in control at the expense of a loss of meaning, social work should recognise and work with uncertainty and diversity.

- Social workers reject constructions of the social as primarily determined by notions of structure and system and return to a focus upon practice and action and a reflective relation to their own affective and practical natures.

In short, we argue that social work within the wider European, rather than a narrow national perspective, provides access to new sources of meaning and validity by reference to which social workers may not only act in a self-critical attitude but reach out beyond their own national constructions of what constitutes social work.

Such an orientation requires a fundamental shift in reference away from social work's traditional source(s) of authority and towards emergent, organic, social movements that are grounded in arguments and forms of action that expose and challenge the dialects of normalising institutions. Such a shift is, we argue, both possible and necessary in order to counter current tendencies towards either the uncritical acceptance of the colonisation of moral and practical concerns by the economic and political systems, or the adoption of mere relativism in an increasingly pluralistic, subjectivist and fragmented post modern society. If social work is to resist and overcome these tendencies, what is most pressing is that it can articulate a credible philosophy, by reference to an expanding range of applicable norms, a widening of latitude for interpretation; an increase in reasoned justification and a capacity for accepting the differentiation of individual identities.

The need for a strong philosophical position in social work arises from the absence of any guiding theory of practice in relation to its sphere of activity: the promotion of personal autonomy. We suggest that social work requires a more fully developed philosophy, theory and model of practice. A practice characterised by a performative attitude of a participant in interaction: that is one that embodies the full range of social relations, symbolic meanings and strategic purposes within cultural contexts and dispositions (Bourdieu, 1977).

Such a practice, that represents both situated and structured action, would constitute the marking, expression and improvisation of pertaining social relations and forms of social exchange. As such, it would incorporate both the certainties of norms and rules and the potentiality and ambiguities of interpretation and strategy. Social work if it is to survive must operate as an authoritative, competent, strategic application of the symbolic order through the schematic and improvised performance of practice and the reflexivity and reciprocity of social exchanges.

This is a serious challenge to social work. It assumes that social work does not merely adapt to or accommodate the revisions imposed upon it by the changing relationship between global, national, and regional boundaries and divergent forms of social exchange, organisation and regulation. Rather, it takes upon itself the responsibility for giving an account of itself. Such an account implies a willingness to revisit and confront its own history, declare its aspirations and seek to realise them in action. Furthermore it requires an affirmation of an identity of its own, which also implies a risk, for in reclaiming authorship of its own future it risks the repudiation of the dominant teleological authority of the state in favour of the vulnerability and fragile association of the excluded.

This book is linked with the previously published book *Fundamentals of Social Work in Selected European Countries*. The two books have been designed to be read independently, although readers of this book may find that the detailed accounts of the development of social work contained within *Fundamentals of Social Work in Selected European Countries* may be helpful in providing additional information and analysis about the specifics of social work within given countries.

In this book, *Key Themes in European Social Work* we have tried to identify what we (not just the editors but all of the authors) believe to be some of the major issues facing social work across Europe. We have taken these issues and located them often within one counry to provide an example of how that county has responded to these key themes. These themes were identified over a period of several years of joint work through a Socrates programme. The themes identified were:

- The development of a science of comparative social work.
- Exploring the interaction of social work and social policy.
- Theory in social work: its nature, form and application.
- Developing a research minded approach to social work practice.
- Professional ethics and the regulation of social work practice.
- Applying the law to social work.
- The nature of the relationship between economic developments and social work.
- The engagment and importance of third sector (voluntary bodies or other non-state bodies) in social work.
- Public concerns about social work practice and expectations that social workers will exercise control over some groups in society.
- Educating social workers.
- Social work careers.

Hence, the methodology adopted in this book is innovative in comparative social work studies taking as it does a series of Key Themes. As each chapter in this book provides an example of an exploration of these themes in respect of at least one country. Many other books either focus upon a theme which is compared across several countries. We as editors invite you, the reader, to make these comparisons with your own county.

Comparing Social Work from a European Perspective: Towards a Comparative Science of Social Work

Peter Erath, Juha Hämäläinen and Horst Sing

Introduction

Comparative studies of social work in Europe, with some notable exceptions, (see, for example, Cannan, Berry and Lyons, 1992; Lorenz, 1994; Trevellion, 1996; Hetherington, Cooper, Smith and Wilford, 1997; Shardlow and Payne, 1998; and Chamberlyne, Cooper, Freeman and Rustin, 1999) are still rare. It is only recently that scholars and students have begun to identify and discuss those common and unique features on the landscape of practice such as: the range of knowledge; sources; theoretical models; and educational programmes that are found in different countries across Europe. In this chapter we will outline some of the key comparative issues that have been undertaken and discuss some of the current difficulties that remain with regard to the different levels, forms and methods through which comparisons can be made. We suggest that the potential for arriving at a comprehensive approach to a comparative social work science is as yet undeveloped and uncertain. However, as an endeavour, the attempt to develop such an approach provides an opportunity for analysis, debate and evaluation of both traditional assumptions and emergent (re-)constructions of social work.

Purpose in the comparative analysis of social work

We propose that the value of comparative social work studies lies in the opportunity offered for the development of an international and inter-cultural perspective through which to examine, analyse and interpret social work. The objects of such studies being those salient similarities and differences within the theoretical foundations, the practice forms and organisational arrangements of social work in different countries. All of these elements require systematic analysis in order to create a wide-scale rather than a purely localised theory of social work. Such a comparative analysis of social work would offer an opportunity for the exchange of experiences and understandings at an international level and release social work from the narrow horizons of national constructions and traditions. As such the development of comparative social work studies offers not only a more comprehensive framework for approaching and conceptualising social work; but also exposes the social conditions and cultural structures within which social work knowledge and action is made possible within different national state welfare regimes.

However, comparisons between different national social policies and social work forms are complicated when analysed in juxtaposition with processes and developments that arise at a global level (Deacon et al., 1997: p 53). Here, global considerations simultaneously affect local comparisons between social welfare systems, policies and social work traditions in different countries. For example, according to Deacon, a globalised economy brings welfare regimes into competition with each other and requires the development of supranational systems of social regulation. Currently, there are relatively few services and activities that can serve as an example of what can be called international social work. However, the speed of globalisation processes has exposed the lacunae in welfare, particular for those individuals and groups whose national status is uncertain, contested or fragile. There is an increasing need for international expertise in developing new forms of social work of a cross- and international character (Lyons, 1999: p 1). Comparative social work analysis and studies has an important contribution to make in this emergent field.

Issues of scope in comparative studies

Whilst there are now established theoretical and practical arguments for developing comparative studies, the question arises as to which aspects of social work in different countries are worthy of comparative study and research. That social work both as institution and profession is constructed through national economic, political and legal systems and cultural practices is not in question.

(see for example, Adams *et al.*, 2000: p 138). However, from a comparative perspective, what is important is the extent to which national conditions essentially shape the purpose, interests and forms of social work. Comparative studies serve to expose both those conditions and relationships under which social work arises and the inherent possibilities and constraints to transcend these same conditions. In selecting from such a broad range of potential sources, the focus of attention in comparative studies falls upon those dimensions which highlight how different national configurations emphasise or exclude particular ideological, theoretical or practical understandings of and responses to welfare needs and problems. As such, comparative studies provide insights into the role of social work relative to other social institutions in the governance of everyday life and the consequent expectations of the State's function, capacity and orientation towards and away from competing discourses and explanatory systems of causality.

From this perspective it becomes possible to identify particular dimensions that are suitable for comparative study, both in their own right, and in terms of the relationships that can be discerned between them and their impact upon different constructions and understandings of social work. These dimensions are:

- The national welfare system, whether orientation towards liberal—individualistic or corporatist—collective regimes, upon and to which social work refers.

- The national infrastructure and legislative framework, that is the wider system of social security, aid and assistance.

- The cultural determinants, that is the traditions and milieu that give symbolic meaning and shape to everyday social relations and the strategic purpose of institutional regimes and discourses.

- The social groups identified as the target of social work intervention by reference to dominant definitions, classifications and perceptions of social problems and needs.

- The organisational arrangements of social work per se, and its connection with other forms of welfare services, in particular educational and health services.

- The responsibilities and tasks applied to social work in respect of selected problems or needs and the subsequent selection and application of particular methods in social work practice.

- The system of social work education: its academic level, duration, teaching methods; and the content and structure of studies and practical instruction. The theoretical base is grounded in the philosophical, ethical, anthropological natural and social sciences considered relevant and necessary to social work.

Issues of method in comparative studies

Whilst it is possible to both justify and identify the need for, and dimensions of, comparative studies of social work, the development of the necessary methodological rigour required of a legitimate discipline is more problematic.

Firstly, comparative studies require as pre-requisites not only the identification of which phenomena and relationships are to be the objects of comparison, but also to confront the questions of how comparability is understood and to be achieved. Hence, before comparing one dimension with another, one needs to know not only what phenomena or relationships are to be compared but also the 'level of theoretical integration' (Heckhausen, 1972: p 84) at which the process of comparison will occur. In other words, comparative studies must satisfy a number of fundamental questions, for example:

- From which point of view are the objects that are to be compared with each other defined?

- Which of their constituent dimensions are sufficiently comparable and commensurable?

- Can what is to be compared be differentiated according to agreed criteria, such as a measurement scale or value relation: for example, is one form of practice more or less effective?

Secondly, there remain competing arguments as to what constitutes social work across Europe. Should only those forms that are recognised, sanctioned and institutionalised within bureaucratic systems be considered as the legitimate objects of study and comparison. Or, can social work be understood as an enterprise that can claim a more universal legitimacy in that it represents the plurality, diversity, interests and experiences of social life and thus embraces a wider range of practices, for example, in those of new social movements (Habermas, 1996). The problem here is not only that of the difference of opinions about the role and form of social work, but also the essentially different interests and forms of rationality that apply in different spheres (Habermas, 1987).

Thirdly, arising from the contested nature of its legitimate purpose, interests and sphere of activity, the heterogeneous nature of social work leads to it referring to incomensurable forms of knowledge. For example, there is disagreement as to whether social work should be approached as, or aspire to status of, either an objective or an interpretative science. If the former, its aims and methods are understood as being to achieve methodological stringency in identifying and applying general and predominately behavioural causal explanations and practical interventions in which historical-cultural factors are understood as by-products or merely contextual (Hartmann, 1995: p 10). If the latter, precedence is given to cultural meanings and historical contingencies as causal factors in their own right, and the acknowledgement of subjective and inter-subjective material and accounts and that recognise and expose the dialectics of welfare regimes and practices.

The development of comparative studies in the field of social work exposes the dilemmas, inconsistencies, divisions and contradictions within the subject matter of social work. These remain submerged below the surface of social work practice and theory and are frequently taken for granted within national contexts or single case examinations. In particular, comparative studies offer a gestalt that contrasts universal and local expressions and representations of what constitutes social work, discourses of expert knowledge with ethnographic studies and life narratives of service users and competing paradigms of received knowledge. Furthermore, comparative studies offer social work access to an analytic frame and the cultural and linguistic 'turns' that promote self-understanding, determination and representation.

Whilst there remain considerable methodological challenges to the development of comparative studies of social work, the value of such studies lies in their potential as a medium of contrast, highlighting the generative processes, transactions, interrelationships and apparent consequences that constitute social work in different countries. We argue that the current limits to the rigor, application and scientific credentials of comparative studies are outweighed by their capacity for reference to different constructions and understandings of the relationship between structure and action, identity and experience, activity and validity.

Steps in the development of a comparative science of social work

Comparative studies, in sociological, anthropological and political sciences, of the relationship between the economic and political-administrative systems and the social world in modern capitalist–democratic societies have identified the generative processes and characteristics of national welfare regimes. Such studies, (see for example, Esping-Andersen, 1990; Kiely and Richardson, 1991; Bailey, 1992; Castles, 1993; Lefebreve, 1994; Hantrais, 1995; George and Taylor-Goodby, 1996), provide a foundation upon which to examine, through comparative methods, the actual and potential role for social work within this emergent and fluid landscape.

As the capacity and credibility of nation states to ensure general social security, manage social problems and protect vulnerable and disadvantaged groups erodes, so responsibility for welfare oscillates between the duties of international institutions at a macro level, the communal interests of local and regional groupings at the mezzo level and informal commitments and obligations between individuals and families at the micro level. Increasingly, both the functional and symbolic dimensions of welfare are thrown into relief as the global and the particular emerge as the new sites for welfare practice, and meaning systems that reunite the universal and the concrete replace the narrow technological and objectifying world views of nation state welfare systems.

The organising principles of utility, uniformity, categorisation and quantification that characterise the administration of the modern welfare state are being challenged by the re-emergence of pre-modern constructions of morality grounded in religious and cultural meanings, previously discredited metaphysical and grand theories and that seek to relate the individual to the social and post-modern approaches that celebrate diversity and difference and dissent. Within this context, comparative studies offer a medium through which social work may be reconnected with its primary concern in the alleviation of poverty, alienation and oppression and the promotion of human potential for developing both individual capacities and social environments. Comparative social work studies provide examples of alternative possibilities for social organisation and movements to respond to the reality of the contingencies of dependence, loss and need that draw upon social meanings and practices and go beyond those envisaged within bureaucratic forms and determined by market forces.

Questions for Further Consideration

1. What purposes and interests may comparative studies of social work serve?
2. What are the difficulties and obstacles to be overcome in the development of a discipline of comparative social work studies?
3. What particular aspects of social work can comparative studies illuminate?
4. What forms and practices of social work would be particularly appropriate for comparative study?

Chapter Two

The Role of Social Policy in Social Work

Pauli Niemelä and Juha Hämäläinen

Introduction

Social work, as an institution, profession and form of service, is located, organised and delivered variously within different welfare regimes. The theoretical orientation and organisational arrangements are influenced by national social policies; just as the contents of social work education derive from the social and political norms, values and ideas that prevail in any given society. Thus, it is not solely the nature or frequency of occurrence of social problems that determines the form and nature of social work practice but equally the social and political interpretations of social problem causation combined with preferred models of intervention that have a key role in shaping practice.

All national welfare state regimes seek to generate social policies that both reflect a particular ideal model and also accommodate the economic, material, political, administrative and socio-cultural norms and values associated with health and well-being pertinent to that particular society. In turn, the degree of collective responsibility *for* and individual rights *to* assistance and services incorporated within different welfare regimes, arise as the embodiment of competing liberal and social ideals that are possible within the constraints and opportunities afforded by modern capitalist democracies.

In this chapter, we firstly outline the relationship of social policy to regimes of welfare; secondly, consider the welfare mix that arises within different models and forms of welfare systems; thirdly, consider the particular example of the Nordic model and finally, consider the influence of social policy from within different welfare regimes upon social work practice.

Social policy and social welfare: welfare regimes and welfare state models

Walter Lorenz (1994: pp 15–39), recognises this context and connection between social work and different national welfare regimes. He argues

(ibid: p 16) that the tasks and forms of practice of social work are influenced by the nature of the welfare system; albeit in a complex and indirect fashion. As examples, he cites the significance and importance of different meanings and associations given to key concepts such as 'citizenship' and the 'state'; the role played by religion, (particularly the Roman Catholic or Protestant churches); and the market or the state in organising and delivering services in different countries:

> ...in the handling of welfare benefits, different state traditions and different approaches to citizenship manifest themselves, with 'methodological' differences being secondary.

(Lorenz, 1994: p 21)

The idea of the 'welfare state' developed in the industrialised countries of western Europe following the end of the Second World War; although the origins of social welfare systems can be traced further back in time. The main defining feature of a welfare state is the proportion of state expenditure on social security as a proportion of the GNP (the economic term meaning the gross national product of a society—it is a measure of the level of economic performance). The main mechanisms of the welfare state system reside in:

- the provision of social and health policies manifested through social welfare legislation
- the system of national insurance
- the welfare and health service institutions and agencies

However, the existence of national social policies are not synonymous with a welfare state, for although a welfare state cannot exist without a system of highly developed social policies, welfare regimes and social policies may exist without developing into a full blown welfare state system. The key characteristics of a welfare state according to Kaufmann (1985: p 45) are:

- The provision of economic security and health and welfare services for certain categories (or all) of its citizens.

- Arrangements for a substantial redistribution of resources from the wealthier to the poor.

- The institutionalisation of civil rights, as a dimension of citizenship.

- Arrangements for promoting security for and equality among its citizens.

- An explicit collective commitment to and responsibility for the well-being of all members (citizens) of society.

Welfare state systems are funded and organised in different ways. The variation between such systems can be explained by the complex interplay of social, political, cultural and other factors. The extent of the state's function as a guarantor of well-being varies in each form of welfare state with the institutions and agencies— including social work—playing different roles in the production of social security. Three basic idealised forms or models of a developed welfare state system and associated ideology are generally recognised:

- the Nordic or Scandinavian ('social-democratic' or 'state-centred' or 'universal')

- the Anglo-American (or Anglo-Saxon) ('liberal' or 'residual')

- the Continental European ('conservative' or 'corporatist')

Corporatist regimes are considered to be heavily influenced by Catholicism and the maintenance of differentials in occupational status, in contrast to liberal regimes, which are influenced by Protestantism and the acceptance of inequality in the distribution of benefits. Social democratic regimes in the Nordic countries are associated with a higher degree of social and occupational mobility and political activity amongst the working class population and the redistribution of wealth (Deacon *et al.*, 1997: pp 42–43). Some typologies suggest that there are more than three welfare state or social service models. For example, the term 'rudimentary welfare model' is applied in connection with those countries (for instance, Portugal, Spain, Greece, Ireland and some regions of Italy) in which the legal right of the citizens for social security is minimal and in which social services are uncoordinated and organised incoherently (Lorenz, 1994: pp 26–28). Most professionally qualified social workers in these kind of countries are to be found in public employment (ibid: p 27). It has also been suggested that it is possible to assimilate the nuances within the three models into a scheme that differentiates between two essential types of regime. For example, the Nordic model has been characterised as being a 'luxury edition' of the liberal or corporatist model and that or the Continental model as a

Table 2.1: Idealised Models of Welfare State Systems			
	Anglo-American	**Continental European**	**Nordic/Scandinavian**
Ideology/Politics	Liberal	Conservative	Social-Democratic
Social policy model	Residual	Corporatist	Institutional
Social security system	Minimal, selective (only for the poorest people)	Contributory based	Universal (for all people)
Provision of welfare services	Market based	Civil society based	State based
Everyday life	Individual freedom	Achievement-orientated	Social citizenship

'discount edition' of the conservative model (Abrahamson, 1997: p 168).

Beside these basic conceptual models of welfare systems to be found in developed welfare states, others have also been proposed (Deacon *et al.*, 1997: pp 42–43). For example, the 'late female mobilisation regimes' such as in Japan, and the 'state bureaucratic regimes' of the former Soviet Union. However, here we intend to consider in detail aspects of the three basic models of developed welfare states that correspond to Titmuss' (1974) traditional classification of social policy models as marginal, that is a means-tested approach that provides minimal assistance only to those who are unable to meet their own needs; performance-based, that is the provision of selective material and other benefits based upon individual contributions to some form of insurance scheme; and universal, that is the entitlement to services on the basis of citizenship.

In the Anglo-American model, in accordance with the liberal political–economy theory, the provision of social security is primarily organised through the market and private insurance. Characteristically, in this model, those social and health services that are financed by the state are targeted to benefit the poorest members of the population, with a more limited state subsidisation of social insurance to support the social security of the majority of the population. Here, the term social security is used as synonymous with welfare—it implies protection from some forms of social misfortune. In this model, the family plays a key role as a provider of social welfare. Thus, whilst there may be attempts to integrate family care with the public welfare system of the state, much welfare is provided on a private basis. Hence, in the Anglo-American model, the role of the state is understood as primarily to provide security and welfare for citizens who are unable to support themselves rather than to extend public assistance to the population as a whole. In contrast to the other models, the state plays a residual role as a provider of social security and welfare and social workers' attention is focused almost exclusively on poor families.

In the continental European model, social benefits are determined according to people's status within the labour market. While in contrast in the Nordic model, benefits are linked to family membership; not to individuals by virtue of their citizenship. Welfare unions and associations play an important role in providing social services. From the point of view of social

care services, the continental European model is divided (Anttonen and Sipilä, 1995) into two predominant forms: the French-Belgian model, in which the nation-state has an explicit policy towards the role and support of family life and the Dutch-German subsidiary model, in which social services are organised chiefly by secular and church welfare unions in accordance with the principle of subsidiarity. This principle entails that the state financially supports the welfare organisations, which in turn have a duty and responsibility to provide the welfare services needed by the population. 'Subsidiarity' is the key to understanding the interplay between the statutory, the voluntary and the informal sector in this model (Lorenz, 1994: p 25).

In the Nordic model, which dominates in the Scandinavian countries, all citizens, regardless of financial status, have the right to receive social benefits according to general allocation criteria. The overall administration of the legislation on social security and welfare is the responsibility of the State, whereas legislation in relation to users is, to a varying degree, administered and organised by municipalities and counties. According to Sipilä (1999: p 3), the key characteristics of the Nordic model are high employment, high taxation and extensive income transfers, a strong public sector, extensive welfare policies, and intensive social integration and equality programmes in support of the social-economic structure. In the Nordic countries, social work is understood as an institutionalised element within the social service system of the welfare state. Here, social security is seen as a combination of universal, needs-related benefits for all citizens and of special, earnings-related benefits for employed persons. In the Nordic countries, equality of all citizens is emphasised and people have equal rights to social and health services as individuals rather than as members of a family or by virtue of age or gender defined group. (Esping-Andersen and Korpi, 1987; Simonen, 1995; Øyen, 1986). Generally, the Nordic model of social welfare is universal, needs-based and prevention-oriented. It aims to provide social welfare for each individual citizen according to individual needs and to prevent as well as alleviate social and health problems.

Recently, the ideals upon which the Nordic model rest have been called into question, as part of increasingly intensive political debates over the so-called 'crisis of the welfare state'. This crisis relates to both the increasing economic and political problems in meeting the financial costs of society's expectations and also challenges the legitimacy of the welfare system as a whole (Nilsson and Wadeskog, 1990). Hence, for example, neo-liberal criticism (Bergmark, 1996) has been directed at the universal, needs-based and prevention-oriented values and principles of the Nordic model.

Traditionally, socialist states are not considered to be welfare states although some of the characteristics of a welfare state are emphasised in socialist ideology and realised, at least partly, in some socialist countries. According to socialist ideology, social policy and social work are unnecessary in a fully developed socialist regime as they merely serve to compensate for the gaps and inequalities that capitalist regimes give rise to. However, it is correct to talk about a special type of welfare regime based on a socialist economic order and ideology. A key question for comparative social policy is how the socialist countries should be compared with capitalist ones in terms of social welfare development. Currently, the focus is upon how the inter-relationship between, and transition from, socialist and capitalist ideologies, influence social welfare objectives and human needs. In some socialist countries, for example China, Cuba and Mozambique, welfare in terms of social and health care and education remains undeveloped. In the former socialist countries of Europe, where the system had claimed to have effectively met the needs of citizens without need for 'paternalistic' mechanisms of welfare provisions, social work as a profession and institution is only poorly developed—if at all (Deacon *et al.*, 1997: pp 45–46).

The welfare mix

Welfare state models can be categorised by reference to the origin of provision of social security. There are three different, mutually independent, sources of social security, and these are the market, the state and private households, giving rise to three 'ideal' types of welfare mix where one form of provision is dominant. Thus, for example, the state is the key provider of social security in the Nordic model. In practice, all regimes, to a greater or lesser extent, foster a 'welfare mix', where the state, the market and households all contribute to the provision of welfare. The respective proportion and role of different providers of social security and welfare varying in accordance to particular social policy or welfare state models.

The term 'welfare mix' also relates to an increasing trend within all regimes wherein the roles and the proportional contribution of the state, market and household are changing. The welfare mix approach implies new possibilities through the emergence of: intermediary organisations, private producers (Simonen, 1995), new social movements and specialist services (Evers, 1990) and the development of new models of practice, for example, case management, for the organisation and practice of social work (Huxley, 1993).

The welfare mix can be understood as arising from the combination of each pair of ideal types of welfare providers: family-state; state-market; market-family (Niemelä, 1995), as illustrated in Figure 2.2.

The *voluntary sector*, which is made up of not-for-profit private, voluntary and charitable agencies, societies and organisations that function as welfare providers in the 'space' between the state public sector and private households.

The *privatised public sector* involves a form of organisation combining features of public (state) and private (market) services. In most instances this involves the formation of companies, such as state or municipal services operating as commercial companies (for example, State Railways, Post Office, Telecommunications, Energy, etc.) This form of organisation can act as a business that provides socially important, often technical, infrastructure services for citizens, that may be subsidised by public funds or be completely privatised.

The *commercial–co-operative sector* consists of a combination of economic (market) and customer (householder and community) interests. Here, consumers (sometimes the term 'users' is preferred) of services organise types of co-operative activities which promote their own welfare. In addition to the traditional type of co-operative activities, new social interest groups and movements have emerged, as, say, in the form of innovative co-operatives combining housing and welfare services.

Different regimes will tend to promote different combinations within the welfare mix.

Thus, the Nordic model of social policy is grounded in ideals of the collective good and public responsibility for social security and welfare for all citizens: all organised and delivered by the municipalities. In the countries associated with the continental European model, the significance of the voluntary sector and the role of non-governmental, non-profit organisations are emphasised in the provision of social services (see Chapter 8). In the liberal

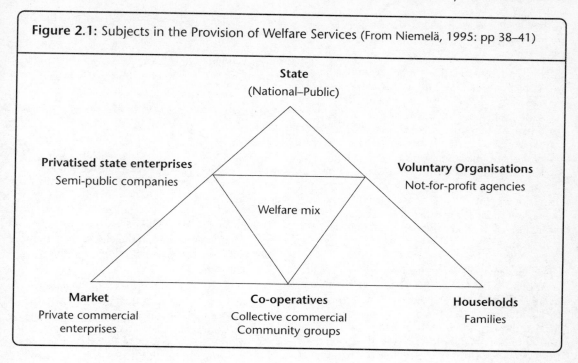

Figure 2.1: Subjects in the Provision of Welfare Services (From Niemelä, 1995: pp 38–41)

regimes, the importance of individual responsibility and the role of the free market, favours privatisation and commercialisation in the provision of services.

Thus, the particular welfare mix in any country, derived from the ideal types of welfare regimes, can be understood as arising from and located within the three dimensions of:

Figure 2.2: Dimensions of Welfare Regimes

Public	◄─────►	Private
Collective	◄─────►	Individual
Voluntary	◄─────►	Commercial

The Nordic model

In the Nordic model, the economic welfare of citizens is provided for through the independently administered, but closely related mechanisms of national insurance and social security (Hausgjerd, 1991).The current crisis of the welfare state and the neo-liberal critique of the welfare system relates to both schemes.

National insurance is a public insurance scheme to which all those who are employed automatically belong. National insurance guarantees every citizen of working age the right to draw unemployment benefit. It is administrated by state social security offices in all municipalities. The most common form of national insurance is sick pay; all employees have the right to draw sickness benefits from the first day of their illness. In the case of a chronic illness or an injury which prevents an employee from working, other rules are applied for economic assistance. In all instances, the state will guarantee the livelihood of the employee.

A substantial number of people in the Nordic countries draw disability pensions and this constitutes a considerable expense for the state and the municipalities. In the Nordic countries, services for disabled people are based on the principle of solidarity. This principle implies a collective responsibility towards the individual and the provision of necessary supports and services when unmet need arises. Economic assistance and other services are aimed at achieving as normal a life style as possible— social participation and equality for all citizens.

Social security is available to all those who are in economic difficulties but who do not qualify for national insurance. Typical cases are long-term unemployed people who become ineligible for unemployment benefit or those who are in work but whose earnings are insufficient to cover the cost of accommodation and other living costs. Such groups may receive additional economic assistance. Social security, alongside the provision of material assistance, also presumes the necessity for the maintenance of health and social inclusion and participation among the State's citizenry.

The principle of prevention in a comprehensive system of health services network is emphasised in Nordic health policy. Primary health care in municipalities is mainly provided by health centres. These are set up by either one local authority individually or jointly by authorities of neighbouring municipalities. Municipalities are also responsible for arranging home care and specialised treatment for local people. The aim is to offer a continuum of health and social services in the forms of institutionally and community based care. This requires close co-operation between social and health service agencies, particularly, for example, in the context of the reduction of hospital based psychiatric care.

The Nordic model offers a multitude of universal public services mainly provided by local municipalities. Historically, this is closely connected with the cultural, economic and political development of the Nordic societies. In fact, such an expansive universal system of municipal services, which was created in the 1960s at the time of relatively strong economic growth and political stability, derives from an earlier period. These developments are associated with the earlier Protestant separation between the 'spiritual' and 'secular' spheres of society, the relative autonomy of local government, and the cultural homogeneity on which the collective will to create welfare services for all citizens is based (Sipilä *et al.*, 1997).

The ideal of health and social services being available to the whole population is emphasised in the basic tenets of the Nordic welfare state ideology (Esping-Andersen and Korpi, 1987; Simonen, 1995; Øyen, 1986). In the Nordic system social and health services are integrated and share a common administrative and legislative basis for the co-ordination of services and the co-operation of staff. This strength of interconnectedness was severely tested during the recent national economic crisis by the need to rationalise the system of welfare services.

Solidarity as a guiding principle of social policy

Of all the guiding principles of social policy within the Nordic model of welfare, 'solidarity' or collective responsibility, is perhaps the most important. Here, collective responsibility finds expression as a sense of a) national and b) occupational affinity. These two forms of 'solidarity' are reflected in the national insurance and social security schemes adopted in the Nordic model:

- National solidarity appears in the national insurance scheme in the guise of a general, universal, basic form of insurance against the contingencies of a market economy. This approach, whilst similar to those principles enshrined in the Beveridge or Keynesian model of a welfare state, has been fully implemented in the welfare state models of the Nordic countries.

- Occupational solidarity appears as a workers' insurance aimed at ensuring a capacity to maintain a minimum standard of living and patterns of consumption during periods of adversity. This approach, which is similar to the Bismarckian model of insurance aims to minimise class conflicts and maintain social cohesion by promoting the mutual security of working people.

A third form of 'solidarity' with the disadvantaged and poor people, rests upon the recognition of a common human frailty and vulnerability and is realised in both voluntary activity and within specific social policies. Hence, social concern for vulnerable children, handicapped and sick people, takes the form of an expression of human empathy, the origins of which are found in both Christian and lay philanthropic movements.

In the notion of 'solidarity', as a guiding principle of social policy, recognition is given to both the moral and practical dimensions of social life. Collective responsibility is an expression of the possibility of a shared 'good life', which can be experienced and achieved regardless of class, occupation and which ideally is supranational and universally applicable.

However, 'solidarity' as a recognised dimension of social policy is problematic, as notions of solidarity are premised upon the assumption of empathy, benevolence and altruism towards others, particularly towards the disadvantaged and minority groups. As such they require a commitment *to* and adoption *of* a morality that does not necessarily accord with liberal capitalist societies in which individual achievement, competition and self-reliance are the primary social norms. Indeed, social policies in capitalist economies are more likely to prefer the provision of selective, minimal levels of social security, and to emphasise personal responsibility and independence; with minimal social benefits to the needy and vulnerable being only available subject to the strength of national economic conditions.

Increasingly, European societies are characterised by value pluralism, rather than general interests. Hence, the concept of solidarity is shifting in meaning in as much as it no longer arises from class or national identity but can only relate to common vulnerabilities that arise across competing versions of what constitutes the good life. Here, the project of a state welfare system becomes that of seeking to reconcile the contradictions of a society based upon a capitalist economy by avoiding both economic malfunction and social conflict.

Riihinen (Table 2.2 below) presents a comprehensive theoretical model of forms of social policy to illustrate the development of social policy in Finland (Riihinen, 1992). This model builds upon that of Titmuss (1974: pp 30–31) which identified three forms or types of social policy: the residual, the occupational performance and the universal re-distributive. To these Riihinen adds the further dimensions of 'legitimistic' and 'solidaristic' forms of social policy.

Riihinen characterises *residual* social policy as a set of public measures that promote and rely upon services drawn from either the private market or communities: services which help individuals and families who are unable to satisfy their basic material needs. Here, state services are only available for those for whom the market or community are unable or unwilling to respond. Friedman (1981) and Hayek (1990) argue that such residual forms of social welfare draw upon the same principles as those associated with the English nineteenth century poor laws (Adams and Shardlow, 2000).

The *occupational performance* model is based on the assumption that social security rests upon individuals' capacities to secure occupational income. As such, the market economy will determine how needs are satisfied. Implicit in this model is the presumption that market forces will provide the incentives, and govern levels of income through processes derived from individual effort and collective bargaining within the labour market.

The *universal re-distributive* model rests upon the concept of a comprehensive welfare state society which provides universal services, available for all citizens whose needs are not

Table 2.2: Models of Social Policy, from Residual to Institutional and from 'Legitimistic' to 'Solidaristic' (Riihinen, 1992) as Applied to Finland

		Titmuss' Models		
		Residual	*Occupational performance*	*Universal re-distributive*
		Ideal liberal	*Ideal corporatist*	*Ideal Nordic*
Riihinen's Models	**Legitimistic** *social policy*		Finland in the 1950s	Finland in the 1960s and 1990s
	Solidaristic *social policy*			Finland in the 1970s and 1980s

satisfied by the market, based upon the principles of equal rights and entitlements.

With the addition of the concept of *legitimacy*, Riihinen identifies a form of social policy, the purpose of which is to secure the social acceptance, credibility and legitimacy of the political–economic system. As such, policies that seek to ensure minimum levels of subsistence, equality and security, are essentially means rather than goals in themselves. In contrast, the concept of solidarity as applied to social policy implies that the attainment of social goals and entitlements are genuine objectives, rather than strategic political devices for ensuring social compliance.

In Table 2.2, the application of this model shows that during the 1950s Finnish social policy can be characterised as 'universal re-distributive' in which, for example, the provision of a national pension was a right of citizenship. However, the reforms introduced at the beginning of the 1960s shifted social policy towards an 'occupational performance' form of provision, with individuals becoming increasingly dependant upon occupational pensions and health insurance. Thus, Finnish social policy during the 1950s and 1960s, can be appreciated as being essentially 'legitimistic' but shifting from an universal re-distributive to an occupational performance form. During the 1970s and 1980s, in response to the political threat posed by communism in the shape of the Soviet Union, Finnish social policy shifted towards a 'solidaristic' universal re-distributive form. This shift is evident in an income policy that sought to limit differentials between personal incomes. By the mid 1990s, following the removal of the threat and the decline and eventual break up of the Soviet Union, social policy in Finland is shifting back towards an emphasis on legitimacy. Finnish social policy, since the end of the Second World War, has shifted between the *universal–re-distributive* and *occupational performance* forms, and varied along the *legitimacy* and *solidarity* dimensions.

The influence of social policy upon social work

This examination of the forms and types of welfare state models exposes the ideological principles and social conditions that give rise to the particular social policies through which they are realised, and which in turn generate the diversity in the organisation, role, forms and practice of social work in Western societies. We suggest that social work theory and practice, in different countries, can thus be understood as essentially dependent upon the particular form and type of welfare state model operationalised within that country. The functions and contribution of social work to the historical and prevailing social security and services for the protection of vulnerable citizens and mediation between the economic and political - administrative systems and the everyday, life world are thus intertwined with the developing form of welfare state in any particular country. In particular, social work plays an important political role in maintaining the legitimacy of the state through presenting and representing an appearance and embodiment of collective care and concern for the population. This is achieved through individualising or particularising conflicts, needs and the allocation of resources to selected vulnerable or problematic groups (Lorenz, 1994, pp 22–28 and 35–36). Thus, all welfare state regimes, whether they adopt a residual or universal model, or an orientation towards legitimacy or solidarity, utilise social work as a medium through which they actualise their goals in regulating and maintaining the social system. However, as the notion of the welfare state is premised upon its guarantee to secure a level of social security to all citizens, so a tension has arisen between its capacity to maintain this guarantee. This tension resides in meeting public expectations of the extent of services and level of security that the state should provide in the form of financial, material, educational, health services and so on; and the resulting burden that this imposes upon the national economy (Holmes, 1988: p 82).

Accordingly, as suggested by Sipilä (1989: p 60), social work as a profession, and a practical activity, lies within a contested territory, wherein work may be carried out at the individual, group (family) and/or at community levels. Thus, practitioners are required to have a range of knowledge and expertise that spans all these, and is applicable to work with individuals, families, groups and communities. A knowledge that derives from a host of disciplines and theories that seek to understand and explain individual and collective identity, behaviour, dynamics and the relationship between social structure and process. In short, social workers are required to be educationally equipped and practically capable of responding to the generalities and particularities, norms and rules, ambiguities and uncertainties of social life and organisation.

The extent to which social work education and practice extends across all these potential areas of concern is determined by the relative 'ambition' of the particular model of welfare state in which they are located. Thus, at one extreme, in socialist countries, where the existence of social problems may be denied (in as much as the system is presumed to produce social security and equality of itself) the need for social security and social work is not recognised. In contrast, in a free market liberal democratic system (such as in the USA) social work is either limited to state sanctioned interventions, targeted at particular problematic individuals and groups, or operates as a professional enterprise within the market.

According to Deacon (1998: p 53), neither bureaucratic collectivism nor free market liberalism adequately address social welfare needs. In European welfare state regimes, which seek to provide a level of social security at a particular point within the dimensions of the universal and the residual and orientations towards solidarity or legitimacy, a role for social work has developed that compliments and supplements social policies and other social security, insurance and income support provisions within the context of national and regional legal and administrative arrangements. Thus, in different countries the development of social work and its associated forms, methods and practices arise within a particular welfare mix.

Increasingly, since the mid 1970s, national social policies have been influenced by global economic factors and international organisations (such as the World Bank, International Monetary Fund, UN agencies, OECD, and the European Union). National policy is thus inevitably constrained and directed by trans- and supra-national agencies, actors, activities, goals and strategies and by global regulations and economic forces (Deacon *et al.*, 1997: pp 21–27).

So too, social work as an institution and profession may be influenced by an emergent global social policy. A free market global economy of social and health care opens the possibility for social workers to operate as entrepreneurs offering their services to state or private agencies and clients. In a global world:

> *...there is a place for social work activity that is more explicitly cross nationally oriented and inter-national in its form.*
>
> (Lyons, 1999: p 1)

Even at a local level, the role of social work will be influenced by inter- and supranational social political issues such as the movement of asylum seekers and migrant workers. Such developments will require social workers to have an understanding of the consequences of globalisation processes for national citizens, local communities, and displaced persons and different social welfare service systems. These are all issues which will need to be considered within already over-burdened social work education programmes (Lyons, 1999).

A global, and particularly European, social reform agenda with internationally binding regulations, conventions and political, legal and social rights is emerging (Deacon, 1998, pp 18–29). The role of social work in this context is, as yet, unclear and has not been fully debated. Such a debate may require a radical reconsideration of the knowledge base, tasks and values of social work (Lyons, 1999) and poses a challenge to existing forms of practice that remain rooted within national social policies.

Questions for Further Consideration

1. How are social needs and problems recognised, legitimised and responded to in different welfare regimes?

2. How would you explain the difference in the profiles of social work practice that have arisen within Anglo-American, Continental European and Nordic/Scandinavian welfare regimes?

3. Can you identify one dimension of globalisation that has influenced social work practice within your own country?

Chapter Three

Theory in Social Work

Peter Erath and Juha Hämäläinen

Introduction

In examining the development of social work in Europe, it is necessary to broaden our horizon of inquiry beyond that of exploring social work's relationship to the particular welfare regimes that pertain in different countries (Lorenz, 1994: pp 15–39). Differences in the development of social work in various countries are not solely determined by the nature of the welfare regime in any particular country (see Chapter 2). The development of various 'forms of social work' is also a response to how competing traditions of thought and knowledge forms, which in turn have affected the construction of theories and practice methods, have been received and adopted. The discourse of social work, its practice, the orientation of social workers, its research base and the content of training are all closely connected to theory *about*, *for* and *of* social work.

In this chapter, we first present a framework for comparative analysis of different theories in social work. Secondly, we outline the different traditions of thought that have influenced the formation of theories and practice in social work in Europe. Finally, we pose some questions intended to assist reflection upon these theories both in general terms and how they have influenced the development of social work within different countries.

The comparative analysis of different types of theory in social work

Theorising social work can be understood as a process for developing a rational argument that satisfactorily accounts for social work as a social institution and as a form of social action. Generally, these theories interpret social work from some particular point of view, by reference to its role, function and tasks, by considering its professional status and relationship to other disciplines or by specifying its knowledge and value basis. According to Payne (1997), a theory of social work is a construction arising from interpretations made by actors engaged in social

work. However, many different types of relevant theories are applied to social work. These theories have very different origins and are grounded upon often competing and contradictory principles.

Practice theories

The notion of a theory as suggested by its Greek origin (*theoria*: a system of ideas explaining something according to a set of general principles, independent of the phenomena to be explained) has led to at least two major interpretations of the term 'theory' in respect of social work.

First, there is the pragmatic position which takes as its basic assumption that theories:

> ...*provide us with models of reality and help us to understand what is possible and how we can attain it.*
>
> (Turner, 1986: p 2)

Here, people working on a practical level use theories:

> ...*to develop and refine an intellectual structure by which the complex array of facts encountered in practice can be understood, so that the nature of intervention can be deduced and the effects of such intervention predicted.*
>
> (ibid: p 4)

Payne follows a similar line, when he suggests that:

> ...*an effective theory or perspective must offer a model of explicit guidance in practice.*
>
> (Payne, 1997: p 36)

He further argues that with respect to social work:

> ...*theory is practically useful, and that its variety and confusion can be organised and understood.*
>
> (ibid: p 71)

Although he also refers to the possibility of a:

> ...*looser, post-modern view of what 'theory' is... because...most social workers use 'theory' to mean ideas that influence them as opposed to things that they do in practice.*
>
> (ibid: p 37)

His focus is upon what may be referred to as 'theory for practice'.

Knowledge theories

Second, there is another, predominantly Germanic view, that theories form part of a system of science or scholarship. Here, theories are 'scientific statements' which form a:

> *...system of inter-subjectively verifiable, methodologically obtained statements within a consistent context about a clearly defined subject.*
>
> (Dewe and Otto, 1996: p 13)

In this approach, the formation of theories arises from a process of observation of phenomena and its subsequent description and analysis that reshape these observations into a systematic construction or reconstruction.

Such competing approaches about notions of theory are themselves influenced by different interpretations of human characteristics and forms of social organisation. They can thus serve as a point of departure for either argument over the relative value of social policies and the utility (value) of different practice interventions or as meeting an 'appropriate need for entering into

questions of scientific methodology' (Dewe and Otto, 1996: p 13).

In either respect, theorising allows for the establishment of an analytical distance, a space apart from the immediacy and imperatives of action, in order to ground, reflect upon and justify our actions within an abstract model of reality. Hence, these two competing approaches allow for the term 'theory' to remain ambiguous, unless a distinction is made between different types and levels of theories. Within the field of social work, theories can be thus distinguished according to different classification schema. Below one such schema is presented.

Purpose and interest theories

Aside from the primary distinction between practice (applied) and scholarly (general) theories, theories can be further categorised according to the particular interest or purpose to which they refer:

- Theories of justification: those theories that seek to legitimate the need for social work in society.

- Construction theories: those theories that seek to explain what social work is and how it operates within society.

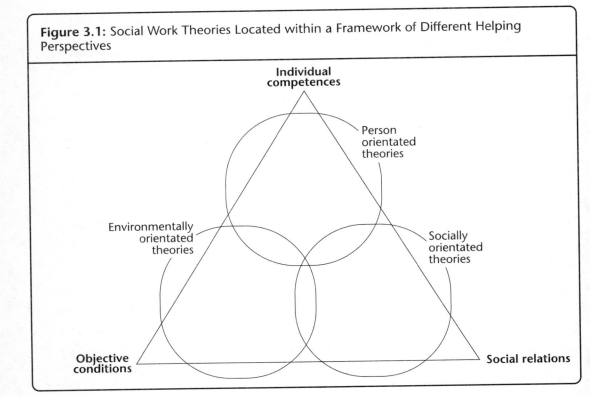

Figure 3.1: Social Work Theories Located within a Framework of Different Helping Perspectives

- Practice theories: those theories that suggest how social workers should act in order to ensure the effectiveness of their interventions.

- Reference theories: those theories derived from other disciplines that have been adopted by social work because they are useful in explaining or responding to certain phenomena.

Cause and remedy theories

Most theories of social work are concerned with practice, and especially with the question of how social work, as an institutionalised form of help for people in problematic psycho-social situations, has been and is organised. Such theories seek to address the difficult question of causality in problematic situations. However, psycho-social problem situations are characterised as arising within three separate, although related, dimensions:

- Objective conditions: where there is an evident lack of material resources.

- Subjective conditions: where there is a lack of attainment or performance due to individual deficits in awareness, capacity or competence.

- Structural and institutionalised social conditions: where groups and individuals experience disadvantage, discrimination and oppression.

Whilst both causal explanations and responses to psycho-social problems are usually understood as relating to each of these three dimensions, it is often the case that one particular dimension is emphasised in any given situation.

Orientation preference theories

The theories applied to, or developed for social work reflect and emphasise a particular orientation to one or more dimension of social work practice:

- Environmentally-orientated theories focus on the extent to which people in problem situations can be helped through the provision of concrete material aid.

- Person-orientated approaches seek to promote understanding of the causes of problem situations, mainly in terms of personal deficits that require educational, awareness raising, enabling or corrective measures.

- Socially-orientated approaches highlight social inequities and injustices and seek to promote empowerment and social change.

Whilst a focus on practice theory predominates in social work, which in turn incorporates different purposes and interests, causal explanations and remedies for psycho-social problems and related orientation preferences, to neglect the knowledge forms and sciences, to which all theory must refer back, would be a serious omission. From this wider perspective, we can identify theories *of* and *in* social work that can be distinguished in relation to a particular tradition of thought and method of inquiry.

Traditions of thought and knowledge forms

By traditions of thought and knowledge forms we are referring to the philosophical and epistemological principles and fundamental sources that provide all knowledge forms with both their rational foundations and their methods and instruments which are applied in generating new knowledge. The principle traditions of thought we will consider here are illustrated in Figure 3.2

Hermeneutics

Hermeneutics is a theory of interpretation of texts. This theory was introduced into the field of science of education by Dilthey (1888). In his view, all phenomena of life (for example that of education or schooling) can only be understood through a personal interpretation or explanation. Hermeneutic theory is grounded within the social, cultural and historical human environment. Here, in as much as humans are conceived of as essentially cultural beings, the purpose of hermeneutics is to arrive at an *understanding* of the sense and the significance of human actions and their consequences as attempts to cope with practical-moral problems. Here, social reality, including the creation of cultural objects and texts, is approached as being a construction of human behaviour, imbued with properties and values and governed by the intentions and motivations of actors, rather than by natural laws. The hermeneutic task is thus to retrieve the meaning of social reality through a process of interpretation. A person-orientated approach, as applied to social work, in which the therapeutic task is achieved by way of paying

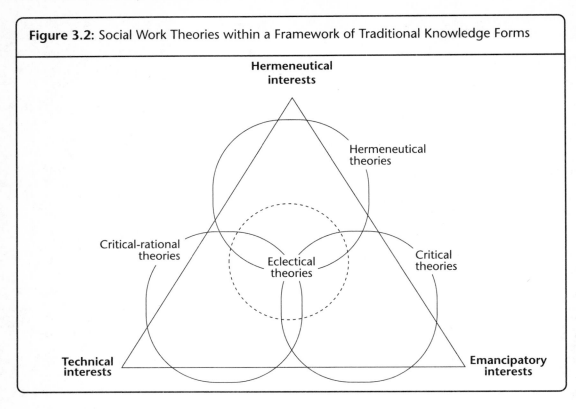

Figure 3.2: Social Work Theories within a Framework of Traditional Knowledge Forms

particular attention to another person, fits well with the hermeneutic perspective.

Hermeneutic theories of justification

From a hermeneutic point of view, there is no need for an explicit justification of social work. In as much as 'helping' is regarded as a universal form of human behaviour, albeit motivated by different social relationships and economic circumstances; and that social work as a social institution and tradition is evident and recognised, the question that arises from the hermeneutic perspective is whether social work corresponds in its form with what it purports to be. From a hermeneutic perspective, by means of an analytic understanding of the social environment and the use of the 'hermeneutic circle' (this means the ongoing process of the (re) interpretation of cultural phenomena as for example social work). Hence, this question centres upon the congruence between social work as it is represented and social work as it is experienced and perceived.

Hermeneutic construction theories

From a hermeneutic perspective, social work is assigned a primarily educational role in society. Starting with the supposition that humanity is characterised as 'culture creating and created by culture', the need for help is understood as a cultural deficit (which in terms of the hermeneutic perspective means a lack of education) that can only be compensated for by pedagogical means. Accordingly, the German social-pedagogic movement (Nohl, 1933), that developed at the start of the twentieth century, located the cause of social problems among many working class families not in their lack of economic or material resources, but rather in their 'moral and spiritual destitution' (Nohl, 1933: p 3). This kind of 'destitution' could only be rectified by measures of 'education' and 'personalisation'. Such an understanding of human beings, that is as entirely cultural creatures and shaped by cultural factors, limits the task of social work and indeed the needs, identity and circumstances of clients, to cultural determinants of both causality and remedy.

In terms of practice, social work constructed within the hermeneutic frame, of which social pedagogy serves as the prime example, consists of three stages:

1. The creation of a personal relationship, modelled on that of parents toward their child, in which the social worker has to create a 'pedagogic relationship' with the client through which love, empathy and understanding are offered to the client. Such a relationship is considered as a necessary precondition for the subsequent success of help.

2. Observation and interpretation of problematic behavioural patterns, in order to understand the 'real' problems of the client, is required in order to identify that nature of the help to be provided. Here the client's psychic and material reality is recognised and understood through what Nohl describes as an 'intuitive' process. Haupert and Kraimer (1991) refer to this as the application of qualitative and ethnographic methods; either way, 'understanding the case' and 'vicarious interpretation' become central tasks of the social worker. As it is only through gaining sufficient knowledge, by direct experience, that systematic order can be applied to a case in question.

3. Through the medium of the 'understanding relationship' the worker can educate the client to help himself or herself in the form of the client's personal development. Here, social work is always regarded as pedagogical and edifying, in as much as, the social worker provides help by enabling the client to achieve insight and self awareness, through which they are able to take responsibility for both the cause and the solution to their problems or unmet needs.

Hermeneutic practice theories

The hermeneutic construction of social work, as a form of relationship and method of interpretation, allows for a form of practice without recourse to any prescribed methodology. However, as a rule, this type of social work practice takes two basic forms:

- Individualised practice theories and those orientated towards the social environment emphasise the open and autonomous character of social work and strongly resist any methodological impositions. They stress the importance of empathy, intuition, and experience and leave the choice of concrete action to the individual social worker.

- Psychologically orientated practice theories emphasise the quasi-therapeutic character of the relationship between social worker and client, and the practice follows a counselling model.

Both forms stress spontaneity, immediacy, and the singular character of the relationship between social worker and client. Here, practice eschews the rigid adherence to a particular method but emphasises the realisation of human potential and personality development through the building of a genuine relationship.

Hermeneutic reference theories

Hermeneutic reference theories that influence pedagogical social work are primarily interpretative psychology, psycho-dynamic, humanist, gestalt and existential theories and the phenomenological and ethnographic schools of sociology and anthropology (For a full explication of the 'challenge of hermeneutics' to the social sciences see Bauman, 1978).

The relevance to social work of the hermeneutic perspective

The hermeneutic perspective highlights the importance of the process of understanding and the distinction between the social and the natural sciences. In the context of social work, this perspective emphasises the need to understand how the client experiences and understands their situation in relation to their own unique biography, prior to proposing a form of help or intervention. This orientation acknowledges the need for both an analytical approach and recognition of the emotional dimension of human experience. However, the hermeneutic approach has become subject to increasingly strong challenge on the grounds that it lacks specificity and clarity of objectives. Evaluations of this approach, which has been popular in Germany, show that although the hermeneutic approach does indeed result in the establishment of a 'good relationship' between client and social worker, these kinds of helping processes do not easily address the criteria of effectiveness, efficiency and economy now required of social work.

Hermeneutic training and research

As applied in the training of social workers, the hermeneutic perspective stresses the interconnection between the life experience of the student, a particular attitude towards understanding, and the recognition and expression of the human spirit in the development, institutions and practice forms of social work. Here, an essential task of training is to familiarise students with the tradition and 'spirit' of social work and to emphasise the importance of and relationship between individual personality and professional identity in developing a particular attitude towards clients and the helping process. From such an orientation, a relationship is revealed between historical, socio-cultural and methodological dimensions so that the purpose of social work education and research is conceptualised as being to ensure the cultural transfer of social work tradition.

The empirical-analytical sciences

The central assumption of empirical-analytical (e-a) sciences is an imposition of a clear distinction between normative and empirical statements. Accordingly, all e-a scientific statements, to be rational, must satisfy the criteria of being generally applicable, value free, verifiable and grounded in empirical evidence arrived at through systematic research. Essentially, as Merton (1973) has argued, the received view of scientific facts is that they are impersonal, empirically warranted and rigorously tested. Further, the subsequent generation of scientific knowledge presumes certain conditions that allow facts to be produced in a reliable way. These conditions, the norms of science, rest on the institutional imperatives of:

- *communality*, that requires all knowledge to be openly and freely shared
- *organised scepticism*, that all claims are assessed for their theoretical coherence and empirical adequacy
- *universalism*, that all claims are assessed by essentially the same impersonal criteria
- *disinterestedness*, that scientific status is gained through merit rather than patronage or social position

The foundation of scientific knowledge and the production of facts is through observation (empiricism) and corroboration (anyone in the same position will observe the same thing). This methodology assumes the primacy of visual experience.

Empirical-analytical theories of justification

From an e-a perspective normative statements are always of a purely philosophical nature and cannot be verified in a scientific way. Justifications for the

necessity or value of social work fall outside of an e-a purview, as these rest upon the requirement to make choices between incommensurable units of value. Rather, questions of e-a are premised upon the given (a priori) criteria of rationality as being effectiveness and efficiency. Here, issues of how social work might be organised and delivered are considered through the systematic procedures of measurement of outcomes that can be directly attributed to given actions and interventions.

Empirical-analytic construction theories

E-a theories can be characterised as grounded within natural science. In the naturalistic or 'positivist' paradigm, it is assumed that human beings are part of nature and can therefore be explained by natural science. This approach presumes the autonomy of the individual from a social and cultural context and as such rejects hermeneutic and critical theories, which are considered unable to meet the necessary criteria of objectivity, required of the natural sciences. E-a presumes a technological approach to social work, grounded in a procedure wherein the subject of intervention can and has been sufficiently objectified and stabilised within the various available classifications and categories. This technological approach to social work derives from the imperative to justify its practice within the state welfare regime i.e. within the political administrative sub system, the sphere of regulation and guidance. Here, social work is characterised by the formalised and systematic nature of work in public institutions. Of central importance is the generation of evidence of productivity and efficiency in its interventions that are aimed at prediction and control of welfare clients' needs and problems through techniques grounded in empirical-analytical methods and procedures.

In particular, measurement of the effectiveness of methods is considered especially relevant at the level of behavioural changes. Rössner (1977) identifies the task of social work as being to minimise anti- or asocial behaviours and maximise the acquisition of the socially valued behaviours. This approach argues that:

> ...*effectiveness is the lynch pin of ethical social work intervention and behavioural work has much to offer towards meeting this criterion.*
>
> (Hudson and Macdonald, 1986: p 19)

Empirical analytical practice theories

E-a practice theories often refer to the legal context or statutory duties required of social workers. The expected purpose of social workers being to arrive at institutionally sanctioned, cost effective, problem-solving interventions. These theories tend to take two forms:

Cognitive behavioural theories emphasising the scientific basis of the methods applied and deriving from learning theory (see for example, Gambrill, 1977). These interventions:

- focus on specific behaviours of concern
- utilise behavioural principles and learning theories
- present an analysis and description of problems, based on direct observation
- identify and target those factors in the environment that are considered to influence behaviour
- identify and maximise clients' assets
- involve significant others in the client's support network
- base interventions on existing research evidence
- monitor progress of behavioural change
- achieve outcomes that are valued by the client
- generalise behaviour change across a range of situations (see for example, Payne, 1997: p 115).

Task or crisis centred approaches stress the structured and progressive nature of interventions. For example, a crisis intervention approach, suggests a number of stages to be systematically followed (see for example, Roberts, 1991 in Payne, 1997: p 101):

1. Assess risk and safety of clients and others.
2. Establish rapport and appropriate communication with clients.
3. Identify major problems.
4. Deal with feelings and provide support.
5. Explore possible alternatives.
6. Formulate an action plan.
7. Provide follow-up support.

Thus, e-a practice theories seek to provide short or medium term interventions that are focused and precise, targeted at achieving specific outcomes.

Empirical-analytical reference theories

Reference theories that are applied from within the e-a paradigm derive from psychological behavioural and learning theories, (see for example, Skinner, 1953) and functional and structural sociological theories, (see for example, Durkheim, 1952). Reference is also made to e-a theory from a range of other disciplines, such as economics, management and organisational studies.

The relevance to social work of the empirical-analytic paradigm

Due to the ubiquitous public debate over the efficiency and effectiveness of social work e-a theories have been increasingly promoted and adopted. As practice is subjected to growing pressures to generate evidence of productivity and that social work interventions lead to greater prediction and control of welfare clients' needs and problems, then inevitably techniques grounded in e-a methods and procedures that allow for systematic measurement of outcomes are vigorously promoted. This has particularly been the case following changes to the welfare system with the introduction of a mixed economy of welfare, which necessitates competition between the different providers of social services, increased pressures to reduce public service spending and the generation of evidence-based-practice. Taken together, these measures have led to a situation in which social work practice has been overtly re-constructed as an instrument of social policy as opposed to a therapeutic or personal development service.

The empirical-analytic perspective in training and research

Reference to e-a theory in the training of social workers emphasises the utilisation of methods that can be quantified in respect of their efficiency and effectiveness. Particular attention is given to techniques and skills of observation, assessment and focused interventions, with less emphasis given to philosophical and ethical issues. Reference is made primarily to empirical systematic research methods and studies that evaluate the effectiveness of interventions and that will direct and legitimate future planning and practice methods. Here, the purpose of social work education and research is understood as being to construct a theoretical framework for rational action.

Critical social theory

Critical social theory is grounded in analyses and criticisms of 'modernity' and by exposing and distinguishing between the 'emancipatory-reconciling and repressive-alienating' aspects of the Enlightenment, characterised by a belief in progress and instrumental rationality. Here, through procedures of critical, dialectic argumentation, social institutions and practices are analysed and challenged, with the express purpose of promoting critical self-reflection and awareness and emancipation from oppressive social and individual conditions.

Critical theories of justification

Critical theories, or ideological critiques, have emerged from both the German tradition exemplified by the work of the Frankfurt school which exposes a dialectic through which recent forms of rationality and society are negated and critiqued, (see for example, Horkheimer and Adorno, 1973); and the French tradition of critical effective histories, which developed an historical practice, rather than any type of theory, that seeks to disrupt and problematise historical accounts of society, forms of truth and knowledge and their associated discourses, (see for example, Foucault, 1970). Both adopt a critical position towards the dysfunctional and oppressive dimensions of modern society. Foucault in particular, is critical of the regulating and normalising disciplines such as social work, and the ideologies to which they are bound, those complexes of opinions and attitudes or organised evaluative beliefs that serve to validate socially constructed 'facts'.

Critical construction theories

Social workers who adopt a critical theoretical perspective cannot be satisfied with an approach towards clients that either accepts or reduces their needs and problems to a matter of individual deficit. Rather, they are critical of individualised approaches to complex social problems that do not recognise the complex relationship between individual, social identity and behaviour that arises particularly within modern, liberal democratic, capitalist society. All in all, the 'critical perspective', not only disapproves of any society, but also any form of social work that objectifies human beings. However, the 'critical perspective' poses dilemmas for practitioners in both:

- identifying which problems do and which problems do not necessitate social work intervention

- in relation to their own position towards and within the social system

So for example:

> On the one hand, he is a dependent agent of an institution that clings to an inflexible system of classifications of problems and their solutions, on the other, he is not able to establish a coherent professional role within this institution, as his daily practice confronts him with the primary problems of the client's, which are not consistent with institutionalised classifications.
>
> (Mollenhauer, 1973: p 299)

Constructions of social work, grounded in critical theory, can be approached as grounded within the hermeneutic perspective, but developed by reference to the historical, cultural and social parameters within which social work is located and through an appreciation of how the relationships between capitalism, technology, bureaucracy and affective individualism have made problematic our understanding of how the processes of social structuring and human agency are related.

Critical practice theories

Social work practice from a critical theory perspective adopts a position from which preventative work is both possible and necessary (Giesecke, 1973). However, where problems are already apparent, the aim of social work should be to recognise the political as well as the social dimension to problems; expose contradictions and inequalities within social systems and relationships to support 'political' as well as professional actions (see for example, De Maria, 1992).

From a critical perspective social workers are expected to reflect upon their role and the institutionalised, organisational forms of social work through a process reflexivity and dialogue with the client, which are taken as the hallmarks of professional practice. Such an approach is associated with the work of Freire (1972), whose work exemplifies a universal, dialectic-critical method of education and social work:

> She or he works with, never on, people, whom she or he considers subjects, not objects or incidences, of action… [and]…to appreciate that social reality can be transformed…and can be changed by men; that it is not something untouchable, a fate or destiny that offers only one choice: accommodation.
>
> (Freire, 1985: p 40)

This form of practice seeks to expose contradictions that are revealed by working on issues defined by clients themselves. Similarly, participatory and empowerment based practices aim to not only change problematic situations, but also to generate a sense of self-control and emancipation in the client and to provide opportunities for a more developed approach to freedom from oppression through both debate and action over choice and consumption in the market place, democratic renewal in the political arena or rights and entitlements, responsibilities and duties within the law.

Critical reference theories

Reference to critical theory ranges over a wide field, including philosophical, political, linguistic and moral theorising as well as sociological, psychological and historical works. In particular, any consideration of the relationship between individual and social structures, processes, behaviour and identity has relevance to critical theory, where it seeks to expose and refute instrumentalism, positivism and reductionism. In particular, the work of Jurgen Habermas (1992) has sought to develop a reasoned critique of modernity and a theory of *communicatively structured interaction* where mutual understanding is inter-subjectively arrived at—in contrast to the *instrumental strategic actions* of administrative systems that are imposed upon the 'objects' of their interventions.

Relevance of critical theory to social work

Particularly in Germany, but also to a lesser extent in other European countries, during the 1970s, social work was strongly influenced by an increased awareness of the political dimension of its purpose, organisation and practice. Radical social work presented a challenge to traditional individualised 'case work' through its opposition and by its resistance to the system and the hegemony of capitalist ideology. Applying Marxist theory to social work practice and the adoption of a process of 'consciousness -raising' sought to redefine the subject of social work as the working class rather than the individual. However, such an orientation did not take hold amongst the majority of practitioners. Moreover, it was gradually neutralised within the education and training programmes, discredited in its application to social work practice and internalised if not erased from the professional role in favour of an integrated, systemic framework for rational interventions.

Critical theory in training and research

Training based on critical theory emphasises the need for critical reflection and analysis in respect of social structures, processes and particularly upon the nature and force of ideology. Methods of debate and social action, if possible jointly with clients, become the foci of concern. Research activity is contextualised within historical and economic conditions. In effect, recognising that social work is itself significantly affected by ideology and institutionalisation, and operates within and is allied to economic and political power structures. Thus, both research and training seek to expose the dialectics and contradictions within social work and suggest a re-orientation that promotes the development of a critical consciousness and individual and collective emancipation.

Ecological-systems theories

An ecological-systems perspective seeks to achieve a comprehensive approach to the person-in-context. This perspective is derived from general systems theory (Bertalanffy, 1950). According to general systems theory, different classes of systems, discrete sets of things which are so related that they form a unity or organic whole, can be understood through the examination of the relationships that arise within and between their micro-, mezzo- and macro-sub-systems. Here, the human environment is understood as a system of inter-related environments. The ecological-systems perspective is especially interested in the reciprocal relations and complex social connections, relationships and networks of individuals, groups and communities that arise as they developed over time and become the sites of stability and security in the social order.

Ecological-systems theories of justification

The starting point of an ecological-systems approach is that social problems and needs arise when disruptions occur within social-ecological human systems. As such, this approach accepts the existence of a normative dimension to social relationships and regulation as a necessary function of the systems. Systems theory derivations and adaptations to social work recognise a relationship between the self regulatory elements in each of the human sub-systems and that an imbalance in one sub-system, such as disease in the physiological sub-system, is likely to create disturbance in another sub-system. From this viewpoint, the purpose of social work intervention is to identify and where possible prevent, ameliorate and compensate for disturbances both within and between sub-systems.

Ecological-systems construction theories

Eco-social system theories (see for example, Germain, 1981; Wendt, 1990; Staub-Bernasconi, 1995) postulate the existence of basic units such as the family or community as sub-systems within the total human environment. These sub-systems provide order in social life. Two sets of variables affect the functioning the basic units:

1. Individual attributes, capacities and characteristics, such as personality, intelligence, that in turn represent behavioural repertoires or clusters of competence such as resilience or capacity to cope with adverse circumstances.

2. Environmental factors, such as access to resources and support networks that represent and shape the individual's or basic unit's opportunity to maximise its own internal qualities.

The role of the social worker becomes that of seeking to enable the client to address the particular circumstance of their problems more effectively and efficiently in future. This help is achieved by targeting those variables within and across the sub-systems within the total environment that either impede or may enhance current functioning.

In recognising the normative dimension to social life, ecological-systemic social work seeks to influence the effects of repressed or unfulfilled aspects of identity necessitated by the process of socialisation, the asymmetries and inequalities of relationships of exchange, disabling power structures and negated, denied or arbitrarily applied human values. (see for example, Staub-Bernasconi, 1995). Pincus and Minahan (1973) define the tasks of ecological-systemic social work as:

- helping people to use and improve their own capacities to solve problems
- building new connections between people and resource systems
- helping or modifying interaction between people and resource systems
- helping to develop and change social policy

- giving practical help
- acting as agents of social control

In general, an 'eco-systems perspective' in social work seeks:

> ...to expand the worker's understanding of the person in the situation and to provide the practitioner with a more competent armoury of interventions.
>
> (Greit and Lynch, 1983: pp 59–67)

Ecological-system practice theories

The application of ecological-systems theory has been particularly evident in the case management form of intervention. In contrast to case-work, a systems approach recognises the importance and effect of environmental influences on the situation of the client, the need to target and mobilise external variables, and mobilise formal and informal 'packages of care' and support. Pincus and Minahan (1973) and Wendt (1990) suggest the relevance of a systems approach to the following tasks:

- assessing problems
- collecting data
- making initial contacts
- negotiating contracts
- forming action systems
- maintaining and co-ordinating action systems
- influencing action systems
- terminating the change effort

Ecological-systemic reference theories

Characteristic of the ecological-systemic approach is the eclecticism of its reference theories. The search for unity, syntheses, integration, order and systematic knowledge characterise the eco-systems perspective, in which:

> Ecological ideas refer to the relationship of man to environment...systems ideas refer specifically to General Systems Theory, which has been helpful in understanding the systemic properties of social work cases.
>
> (Meyer, 1983: pp 25–31)

Aside from the application of general ecological studies, some derivative, systemic theories of counselling and therapy have been developed and applied in social work. However, it is the generality of ecological-systemic approach that allows for its application across and within all disciplines. From an eco-system perspective, at the assessment stage of intervention, theories for understanding the relationship between personality and environment are particularly relevant; following assessment, the worker may identify a suitable intervention by drawing from all available sources (see for example, Greit and Lynch, 1983: p 68).

The relevance of ecological-systemic theory to social work

An ecological-systemic perspective in social work has increasingly played a central role in the reorientation of services towards community based, multi-agency responses to complex social problems. In many European countries, attempts to provide help for individuals and families more economically have encouraged the promotion of self-help groups, family based, informal care systems and voluntary rather than state initiatives in response to problems of homelessness, unemployment and poverty.

Training and research from an ecological-systemic perspective

From an ecological-systemic perspective social work is understood as a constituent element within the social system. Emphasis is given to systems maintenance and restoration of

homeostasis in the client's situation. Students are encouraged to think in terms of networks, activate personal and environmental resources, and promote self-help groups. In the field of research, the integration of a variety of disciplines and interests through an open approach to data gathering and analysis, the use of natural observations, semi-structured interviews and ethnographic descriptions of the environment are all considered relevant to the process and procedures of inquiry.

Conclusion

In this chapter, we have proposed that theory operates at a number of levels, from different perspectives and within different traditions of thought. In particular, we have suggested that hermeneutic and critical theory represent a competing paradigm to the empirical-analytical and ecological-systems theories, in as much as the former emphasises the subjectivity of the client's experience and circumstances, whilst the latter seek to objectify the situation. Different theoretical orientations allow for the focus of intervention to be targeted at the individual, a social unit, sub-system or society in general. As such, different theories tend to emphasise either the technical, instrumental or moral, practical purpose of social work.

Questions for Further Consideration

1. To what extent are different approaches to the place and application of theory in social work acknowledged in your country?
2. Do you agree that different theories are mutually incompatible or can they be used in conjunction with each other?
3. Which theories are predominately used in your country?
4. How do national welfare policies influence the development of theoretical orientations that are considered relevant to social work practice in a particular nation state?

Chapter Four

Research in Social Work

Ivana Loučková and Adrian Adams

Introduction

In recent years, there has been a growing demand for social work to produce research evidence that justifies and validates its practice. Debate about the essential nature of social work and critiques of its relative value and efficacy as means of intervening in the lives of 'welfare recipients' is not new. However, the introduction and development of market-led approaches to the delivery of care, the expansion of multi-disciplinary teams and the adoption of the care management approach, have in concert thrown into stark relief the questions of what distinguishes social workers from other professional/occupational groups and what is their distinctive role within social welfare agencies. Accordingly, the credibility of the social work profession is increasingly being determined by its capacity to demonstrate that its interventions are effective and open to systematic evaluation.

In the UK, calls for 'evidence-based practice' and 'research-minded practice' have given rise to a number of initiatives aimed at producing such knowledge. However, it is now increasingly argued that this has also led to an over-simplification in policy making quarters of the understanding of what social work research is and what it can offer. This in turn has re-opened a debate over whether social work research employs and contributes to the full range of social scientific paradigms, theoretical constructions and research methods.

The aim of this chapter is to assist social work practitioners with the processes of understanding, selecting from and developing research strategies that are suited to generating solutions to the social problems they encounter. As such this chapter revisits many of the basic theoretical concepts, examined in Chapter Three, that inform the social sciences in general and the knowledge base of social work in particular. However, here the focus is upon the purposes and methods of research: in order to enable practitioners to decide upon the relative meaning, value and relevance of different orientations and strategies and therefore to differentiate between the ways in which research in social work can be conducted and utilised.

The problem of knowledge

The need to understand is the core motivation of the activity that is termed research. As such, research is a process of investigation through which information about the various elements that constitute phenomena are gathered. Both with regard to the relationships that are internal to the phenomenon and the relationships between the particular phenomenon and other phenomena. From this investigation, it is possible to consider the phenomenon in the context of its particular setting or environment in time and place. Moreover, in order to be able to carry out such investigations we need to understand how to identify, recognise, label and classify phenomena. Thus, developing our understanding requires the involvement of our experience and knowledge of phenomena themselves and the mental processes by which we generate theories in the context of social processes by which we attribute a shared meaning and value to what constitutes human knowledge.

Knowledge, particularly in the social sciences, is thus a dual process that arises between information and insight. Hence it refers simultaneously to both reality and experience, observation and construction and to both the external (objective) environment, its individual elements, forms, structures; the shared (inter-subjective) processes and relationships and the internal (subjective) processes that characterise the human capacity for attributing and communicating meaning through perception, categorisation, comparison and analysis.

Human knowledge and understanding of the world is essentially acquired in one of two ways. Through the direct, immediate and subjective experience of the individual, or as mediated experience, so-called received knowledge. The latter type of knowledge is arrived at through communication with others through a process of reaching an agreement as to what constitutes a fact or truth. Facts can be produced within the competing paradigms of: *realism*, within which a particular truth is known by actual observation or authentic testimony; or *relativism* whereby a fact is that which participants count as factual, i.e. something that has really occurred or is actually the case. In either case, a 'factual' description is that which is organised into a credible and objective account or report (see for example, Potter, 1996). The means and extent to which knowledge achieves the status of a fact or 'truth' is grounded in the relationship between reality, what is 'known' and reason, the method by which it is known. Knowledge can be derived from three general sources:

1. The first source is that of *a priori* method, sometimes referred to as intuition or common sense. Here reality is 'given', in as much as it appears as being in agreement with or confirmed by our unmediated experience, or arrived at directly through our senses of perception.

2. The second is indirectly derived through the *transmission of traditional knowledge*. Here that which we consider true relies upon the 'givens' of our particular cultural milieu in that reality appears as true in as much as it is in agreement with our expectations or of what has always been so. The frequent and collective repetition of 'truths' results in the strengthening of those truths to the extent that they may persist even in the face of other facts that are clearly presented and justified. Associated with this approach are authoritative claims to truth, whereby respected authoritative figures, such as religious leaders, scientists or other experts claim that something exists and such a claim constitutes a general belief or truth.

3. The third source is that of *scientific method*, a method that is reliant upon a procedure of self-correction and verification, where truth retains the status of knowledge open to being, but not yet refuted.

Additionally, a fourth source is being recognised, that of communicative reason '…the paradigm of mutual understanding between subjects capable of speech and action.'(Habermas, 1984: pp 295–296).

Here, agreement is arrived at by a process of argumentation in which both the veracity and validity of a claim is justified by reference to three sources:

1. The sincerity or authenticity of the intentions and feelings of the subjective world of the speaker.

2. The rightness or legitimacy in relation to shared values and norms of the social world.

3. The truth in relation to the objective world.

Truth then, within both the natural and human sciences, serves as an ideal rather than an achievable state of knowledge. As existing knowledge becomes at best that which remains unrefuted through subjection to strict method, relative to the historical, cultural and social parameters within which a given proposition is made. Research in its relation to knowledge is a problematic process in which we act as if that which we wish to investigate, gain knowledge about and understand has an independent existence. In spite of knowing that the process of conducting research itself influences what is being investigated. Hence, the accounts we give of the causal order of reality are both interpretations of and constituted by the accounts themselves. This gives rise to the essential problem of *method* in research and the extent to and manner in which all methods of inquiry and accounts of reality are limited, compromised and dependent.

The problem of method

The problem of method derives from the disputed nature of what constitutes social science, the *sciences sociales* or *Sosialwissenschaften* in general. This dispute relates to the extent to which the social sciences are associated with either the tradition of natural philosophy and the positivism, (for example Comte and Durkheim in France, Booth in the United Kingdom and the Chicago School of the United States) or the hermeneutic tradition of the German School. The positivist tradition applies empirical methods to social phenomena in order to generate social 'facts'. While the humanistic, hermeneutic tradition of the German School asserts that knowledge and understanding of society is more properly epitomised by Weber's concept of *Verstehen* (see Chapter 3).

The term 'social' is generally applied to those structures and processes which appear in society and which are generated by mutual relations. These occur both in the material and non-material spheres of human action, and interactions between individual subjects can be understood as referring in the broadest sense to 'society'. In general, social research can be understood as a process of epistemological behaviour at the theoretical and empirical level, with the aim of finding answers to the questions that arise in the relationship between human action and social structures. An essential aspect of social in contrast to natural science is the attribution of self-awareness and intentionality to human behaviour; that is that human behaviour, including cultural phenomena and texts, is governed by the intentions and motivations of actors, rather than by natural laws.

> *All social science is irretrievably hermeneutic in the sense that to be able to describe 'what someone is doing' in any given context means knowing what the agent or agents themselves know, and apply, in the constitution of the activities.*

> (Giddens, 1993: p 13)

In order to understand human behaviour we have to interpret its meaning. Social science is thus concerned with the theoretical questions of hermeneutics, (see Chapter 3). The complexity generated by hermeneutic philosophy has given rise to the diversity in schools of thought and approach in the social sciences. As an illustration of this diversity, Knocke and Bohrnstedt maintain that:

> *Social research is a complex activity that seeks to increase our understanding of human behaviour. Whether it is a single observer watching pedestrians in a shopping mail, or the Census Bureau analysing millions of question-naires with supercomputers, all research collects data to uncover diverse patterns of social thought and action.*

> (1991: p 3)

This complexity of researching the social world has given rise to increasingly diverse methods for generating new and validating existing data. Phenomenology postulates that the social world, unlike the natural world, is primarily constituted as an interpreted world (see for example, Douglas, 1971 and Berger and Luckman, 1967). Advocates of this view have argued that the worlds in which we live are not just there, not just objective phenomena, but are constructed by a whole range of different social arrangements and practices, wherein reality is constructed through the phenomenology, the perception and understanding, of an individual's experience.

To take another example, ethnomethodology, which has developed as a method of inquiry for documenting the practices, procedures and interactions people use to understand the world, order social life and display their conduct as coherent, and in which particular emphasis is given to *indexicality* (i.e. that the meaning of any description is dependent on its context and occasion), and *reflexivity* (i.e. that descriptions are not just representations of events but also actions in their own right) (Garfinkel, 1967). Austin (1962) has argued for the practical nature of language as a medium of action, which is *performed* in settings with particular purposes and outcomes whereby reality is constructed through talk and text.

From a different perspective, Foucault's effective histories (1980) expose the problems of the human sciences. The first problem arises from the way that a knowing subject attempts to regard itself objectively—as it would entities in the external world, what Giddens (1993) has described as the double hermeneutic of the social sciences. The second problem rests in the manner that knowledge is inextricably linked to that embedded within discourses of power:

> *Truth is a thing of this world: it is produced only by virtue of multiple forms of constraint. In addition, it induces regular effects of power. Each society has its regime of truth, its 'general politics' of truth: that is, the types of discourse which it accepts and makes function as a truth; the mechanisms and instances which enable one to distinguish true and false statements, the means by which each is sanctioned; the techniques and procedures accorded value in the acquisition of truth; the status of those who are charged with saying what counts as true.* (Foucault, 1980: p 131)

Taussig (1992), from an anthropological perspective, has condemned the division of fact from value that occurs within an empiricist theory of knowledge. He argues that the division between objectivity from subjectivity, wherein persons, experience and relations between people can be objectified, is not only false but a product of capitalist and political ideology:

> *We are then in a situation in which 'society,' inscribed and erased in thereby sacred objects, can, in this peculiarly objectified and highly concentrated form, only be seen and touched by one, presumably rather small, group of persons within 'society'.*

> (ibid: p 128)

He denounces the 'official secret', being:

> *...the epistemology of appearance and reality in which appearance is thought to shroud a concealed truth—but not the truth that there is none.*

> (ibid: pp 132–133)

Bauman in Cantell and Pedersen (1992) argues that welfare bureaucracy, the administrative site of social work, was premised upon the possibility of an empirical sociology with practical aims, which promised to resolve social conflicts, and help people or institutions to realise their aims. Particularly in its dominant American form, sociology developed out of the promise that it could help the managers of public, economic and political life. This he contrasts with the European tradition wherein sociology developed with the aim of offering an informed commentary on current experience.

More recently, some social theorists have attempted a synthesis between these divergent approaches. For example Giddens's (1993) theories of the relations between social action and social structure and Habermas's (1996) theories of the relations between the instrumental rationality of social systems and the communicative rationality of the *lifeworld*, although controversial and contentious, seek to develop a universally applicable theory that every solution and every belief is not absolute or universal, but knowledge and truth emerge and are constructed through processes of action and argumentation.

Aside from the philosophical and historical concerns that arise from within these debates, the most immediately problematic question concerns which methodology to adopt: a question that rests upon unresolved epistemological issues. How to pragmatically settle these questions and how best to obtain data and the manner in which it may subsequently be analysed are now the most important practical problems in relation to social work research.

Knowledge and method in social work research

Debates over the knowledge base and credibility of social work are well documented, (for example: Miller and Rose, 1988; Sibeon, 1989; Strom and Gingerich, 1993; Parton, 1994 and Cannan, 1994). These debates on the nature and relevance of social work practice and its knowledge base are mirrored in a similar debate over the nature and relative value of approaches to social work research (see for example: Sheldon 1983, 1984, 1986 and 1987; Raynor, 1984; Smith, 1987; Whittaker and Archer, 1990 and Sheldon and Macdonald, 1993).

Currently, these debates have been re-opened in the UK within a series of seminars organised by the National Institute of Social Work (NISW, 2000) under the title of 'Theorising Social Work Research'. Here the relationship between theory, research and practice is being re-examined by

reference to competing paradigms of knowledge construction and validity, research methodologies and contemporary interests in social inclusion, participation and identity formation. Research activity relating to social work practice can thus be approached as essentially problematic in that on the one hand it is concerned with achieving validation and legitimisation by seeking to emulate scientific methods. However, on the other hand, it is by its very nature, not an activity that fits easily within a scientific, empirical paradigm or methodology. Hence, calls for evidence or researched based social work arise in a context of competing claims amongst the whole range of research activity based on the principles and methodologies of qualitative and quantitative data collection, and experimental, ethnographic, or evaluative approaches.

Quantitative research strategy: objectivity and measurement

Quantitative research methods rest on the foundations of scientific knowledge and the production of facts through observation (empiricism) and corroboration (anyone in the same position will observe the same thing). Here scientific facts are posited as impersonal, empirically warranted and rigorously tested, and the subsequent generation of scientific knowledge, presumes certain conditions that allow facts to be produced in a reliable way, through the norms of science. The scientific approach to understanding and its subsequent impact upon research activity can be expressed as the means by which the objects of investigation are both distinguished and differentiated from each other and the process by which the investigation is conducted. Scientific practice and research thus constitutes the adoption and demonstration of a particular epistemological paradigm that both contains and refers to a systematic, coherent and plausible set of theories, laws, rules, procedures and instruments.

The origins of social research were characterised by efforts to emulate the natural sciences. Even though the object of research by sociologists, anthropologists, psychologists and social workers, was the behaviour of human subjects in various social settings, situations, groups, and systems, attempts were and continue to be made to reduce the range of influential variables or determinants, to discrete units of observation and measurement. This research ideal, modelled on the natural sciences, attempts at the systematic quantification and verification of social facts and laws and which for many in the scientific community remains the key criterion by which the quality and value of a research programme is judged, by reference to the objectivity, validity, reliability and generality of findings.

Here the maintenance of the objectivity and independence of the researcher, by the use of standardised methods and techniques and the utilisation of statistical methods of analysis, is given a high value. This form of research strategy is still applied within the social sciences in the context of the development of explicit and systematic rules of the positivist sociological methods of Durkheim (1982) and the psychological–behavioural paradigms (see for example, Skinner, 1953). The influence of the work of Skinner, whose interpretation of operant conditioning provides a means for the measurement and control of behaviours, is still evident in a wide range of research studies relevant to social work (see for example, Brown and Harris, 1978 and Loučková and Chytil, 1999a).

An implicit assumption associated with the quantitative approach is the deductive strategy: i.e. that 'facts' can be inferred by the application of a general theory or hypothesis to a particular situation. Further, that it is possible to test and confirm speculative knowledge through the answers obtained from observations, surveys, questionnaires or structured interviews.

By using quantitative approaches, it is possible to 'establish', for example: either that, children living in a stable family environment achieve better school results than children whose family environment is disturbed; or that, it is very important for family members or relatives of dying people to remain with them until the end of their lives. Here, justification of such assertions is dependent upon the scale, regularity and frequency of occurrence of particular behaviours within a stable environment.

Scientific methodology, as a complex of rules, procedures and instruments serves to verify theoretical explanation and facts, those empirically and theoretically warranted findings that are generated through scientific endeavour. Scientific knowledge gained through research proceeds in certain phases, which are logically connected. This connection is sequential in the sense that activity proceeds only on condition that a previous activity has already been completed. Scientific research is at one level established through the application of rules of procedure in four distinct phases.

Phase A is concerned with preparation, in which the researcher gathers all the available information concerning the object of examination in such a way that it determines the overall research strategy and design and the specific focus, scope and methodology of the research activity. This phase includes: the theoretical grounding of the inquiry and any speculative, anticipatory findings and hypotheses to be tested or verified; the identification of appropriate, for example quantitative or qualitative, deductive or inductive, research methods, and techniques, by which data will be generated; the concepts and categories to be used for defining and subsequently coding data prior to analysis and specifying the research environment.

Phase B consists of the concrete work of generating data on the object of examination in the field. This phase includes: direct observations and records of forms, actions and relationships within and between the object of inquiry and other phenomena within the research environment.

Phase C comprises subjecting the field data to analytic techniques appropriate to the form of and manner in which data was collected, for example statistical analysis of quantitative data or narrative or ethnographic analysis of qualitative data.

Phase D is concerned with the implications arising from the findings of the analysed data. Discussion and conclusions that may be drawn about the activity, validity and reliability of the findings can be considered by way of reference to the manner, and subsequent limitations, of the way in which the research was conducted; the extent to which it confirms or contradicts other related research findings and the epistemological grounds or level of theorising to which it relates.

Scientific understanding can be understood as knowledge which has been acquired through systematic examination and verification, expressed through empirical and theoretical constructs. As such, it must not only meet the criteria described above, but must also be accepted and legitimised as having demonstrably progressed in a methodical way, usually by scientists themselves in any given scientific field.

Although the scientific method is reliant upon adhering to this self-imposed discipline, the recognition that understanding arises through the generation and interrelationship of knowledge and meaning, leads to the problem of the epistemological grounding of scientific practice. The processes of epistemological behaviour therefore have a central position in science, in other words, its 'approach to understanding' which is apparent and inherent to its research activity. As Merton (1973) has argued, the received view of scientific facts as impersonal, empirically warranted and rigorously tested, and the subsequent generation of scientific knowledge, presumes certain conditions that allow facts to be produced in a reliable way, through the 'norms' of science.

The existence of these conditions, that all knowledge is openly and freely shared, that all claims are assessed for their theoretical coherence and empirical adequacy by essentially the same impersonal criteria and that scientific status is gained through merit rather than patronage or social position have been refuted by Kuhn (1977). In particular, the practice of 'observation' is itself a rather vague term that includes a whole range of devices for collecting information. Most problematic to the process of observation is the question of perception that challenges the notion that what is seen is necessarily determined by the object. Kuhn has demonstrated that the scientific paradigm is dependent upon a scientific community of practice, whose debate and theorising is subject to theoretical constructions of norms and values in the processes of converting observed facts into theories. Whilst this complex debate applies to the problem of all knowledge and understanding, it plays a more central role in the social rather than natural sciences.

Qualitative research strategy: subjectivity and meaning

In recent years, there has been an increased interest in qualitative research strategies and approaches, derived from the work of Dilthey (1994, 1977) and Feyerabend (1975). In such strategies, attention is given to the meaning attributed to action in accounts given by the subjects themselves. The need to identify and interpret the meaning of human action presumes that social reality is essentially constructed and reconstructed by its subjects and cannot be reduced to a priori laws or a set of determining environmental variables—as is the case in natural science. When using qualitative strategies, the aim of a research is to investigate social reality through a process of uncovering subjective

meanings. Thus, general processes relating to social practices (see for example, Bourdieu, 1997) may be inferred inductively from the reported experiences of subjects.

Such research poses pre-theoretical questions such as to how the world is perceived and interpreted by the subjects of the research. Thus, in reference to the previous examples, a qualitative approach would be used for exploring the relationship between family life and school attainment or how the world is experienced by the terminally ill, through narratives and accounts obtained from different members of one family.

Traditionally, two sources have been associated with the origins of qualitative research. The first is the early anthropological studies of European researchers into non-European cultures. In these studies, both the social practices and institutions of relatively homogeneous groups came to be understood as the effect and application of different cosmologies upon and within different societies. The second is associated with existential phenomenology. Here, attention would focus upon the purpose or project in which an actor was seeking to realise and its symbolic meaning within subjects' own accounts. Examples of qualitative research in social work are found in the work of: Anderson (1961); Becker, Blanche, Everett and Strauss (1961); Wolcott (1973); Spradley and Mann (1975); Zola (1968); and Loučková and Chytil (1999b).

A qualitative research strategy is characterised by four aspects:

1. The subjective dimension that stresses a focus upon reported experience or perception.

2. The contextualised nature of the research subject and environment.

3. Data acquisition techniques that include observation, interview, linguistic and cultural analysis (Morse, 1992).

4. Theory derived inductively or interactively, whereby the researcher moves from specific subjective observation to general concepts and thus builds theory (Strauss and Corbin, 1990).

The inductive research cycle begins, similarly to a deductive strategy, in the choice of a topic suitable for investigation. However, the process of investigation does not derive from an existing theory or hypothesis but from social practices that are evident to the researcher. This process of investigation may be located or defined by a variety of social contexts: for example, the behaviours associated with a complex of social activities within a particular social institution such as a hospital. The next step in the process is the formulation of the questions to be considered and posed to the actors within the particular context or environment. Data is then gathered in the form of records of observations, such as interviews that in turn form a basis for gathering further data. A continuous process of inquiry, analysis and refinement occurs until no new information can be obtained. In this way, a theoretical position is developed through the cycle of gathering, ordering and testing of emergent patterns and regularities within the data. A qualitative, or more properly inductive, research strategy is very demanding not only on the researcher's time, but also with respect to its methodology. A methodology that lays particular emphasis upon the ability to conduct unstructured observations and interviews; make an analysis and synthesis of textual data and delay the process of formulating hypotheses or referring to theoretical material.

To return to a previous example, but from an inductive perspective, a researcher may observe that in a hospital setting, when a family member leaves the room of a terminally ill person for a moment; perhaps to speak with staff of the hospital, to go for a walk or to take children out of the room, the terminally ill person 'takes the opportunity' to die. That a loved one died without the family or relatives being present may appear as a distressing situation for the relatives who express dismay at having missed the end of life. However, it might be inferred that for terminally ill people, in hospital settings, it is more desirable to be alone at the moment of death. Using such observations, it becomes possible to theorise about the processes involved in death and mourning within the institutional setting of the hospital.

Towards a research strategy for social work

Research in social work is affected by a wide and diverse range of factors ranging from the philosophical (questions pertaining to the nature and construction of knowledge); the phenomenological (concerning reality and experience); the empirical (concerning what can be known from experience, observation and experiment) through to the more immediate and concrete socio-political and cultural contexts

within which social problems arise. As such, the selection of suitable research methods from competing paradigms, theories and methods requires a research design that provides a structure that determines the process through which research activity is constructed and proceeds. This is of central importance if the aims and interests that motivate the research are to be coherent with the outcomes and findings.

It is perhaps no longer helpful to retain a rigid distinction or differentiation between quantitative and qualitative approaches. Increasingly, studies are combining quantitative and qualitative methods of data collection and analysis. Quantitative methods for the statistical analysis of data can be used in the inductive strategy just as qualitative methods can be applied to deductive strategies. For example, the work of the Chicago School, where the social problems associated with urban lifestyles were the objects of research, combined both empirical inquiry and Mead's theory of symbolic interaction.

What is more productive is to clarify the extent to which studies emphasise either the descriptive or interpretative elements of data and findings and the inductive or deductive methods of inference that were applied. What is of importance is that findings and conclusions are justified and arrived at by reference to supporting empirical evidence, theoretical models or constructs, and rational procedures. The systematic arrangement of categories and the division of methods into deductive or inductive is central to the tradition of modern science. A systemic approach is a pre-requisite to all knowledge forms that claim the status of a science from quantum physics, to cybernetics, semiotics to ecology (see for example: Mayring, 1993; Bateson, 1972; Lewin, 1951 and 1982; Frýba, 1995). However, social sciences differ fundamentally from the natural sciences by virtue of their subject of inquiry.

In a research strategy, where both the subjects and objects of interest are human, theory can only be systematically developed through the interaction between activity and ideas. Here, interaction is understood as a dynamic system (in contrast to a fixed system that regulates or sets the parameters of action and the range of possible actions that occurs within it) as it is the behaviour of the actors that not only reproduces but also alters the structures within which action arises. The application of systemic method in social work research requires the application of specific knowledge and skills whether in relation to quantitative-deductive or qualitative-inductive strategies and the alignment of theoretical concepts and empirical data.

Once an initial selection has been made each subsequent step is dependent upon that which proceeded it, as the research design, framework and procedures serve to both enable and restrict progress towards a conclusion. Aside from the relationships established between these theoretical, empirical and methodological dimensions, the question of the professional ethical principles that guide the practitioner and researcher are a further significant point of reference throughout the whole course of the research process. Broadly we suggest the following as a generally applicable framework:

1. The purpose and interests of research and the formulation of a particular problem for inquiry derive from individual researchers, the profession or a particular scientific discipline. General purposes and interests may then be formulated into specific aims, achieved through the adoption of particular methods. The research activity is thus increasingly regulated through adherence to the sequence or cycle associated with the adopted method(s).

2. Alongside the rigour and discipline imposed by method, the research process is equally influenced by the agency, the knowing and acting capacity of the subject. In other words, the nature of a 'social object' is approached from the researcher's particular relationship to that 'object'. For example, a 'client' is the 'social object' for a social worker, as is a 'patient' for a doctor. Similarly, the nature of an object of research in the social sphere is determined by the subject itself. For example, the nature of a problem can be specified by clients themselves, so that the research task is undertaken with regard to the opinions and attitudes, motivations, intentions, relationships and behaviour of these subjects as individuals, or social groups such as a family or community.

3. The objectivity of research that derives from the imposition of method is thus compromised by the subjectivity of individuals and inter-subjectivity of the social arena. At best, what is achieved can be better described as the suspension of preconceptions through attempts at impartiality. Both abstract and sensual experiences, everyday consciousness, imagination, dreams as well as sensory

perceptions all contribute to the context and material of the phenomenal world. As do the particular role expectations that pertain in different cultural and institutional settings and situations.

Types of research appropriate to social work

The on-going debate over what constitutes appropriate areas of inquiry and suitable methodological approaches in social work research has been polarised between those who advocate the adoption of a naturalistic, scientific approach to the generation of evidence, (for example, Thyer, 1989 and Sheldon and Macdonald, 1993) an approach that is closely associated with the biomedical discourse that presumes 'the autonomy of the individual from a social and cultural context (Lock and Gordon, 1988); and those who argue (Smith, 1987; Gray, 1995; Dominelli, 1996), that such an approach is epistemologically antithetical to social work, in as much as the proper concern of social work research is with the social and moral order. Essentially, this dispute about the most appropriate position from which to conduct social work research is between those who advocate for either *nominalism* (that universal truths are essentially a product of the attribution of categorical labels) or *realism* (that universals do in fact have an objective existence that can be fully understood in terms of their isolated parts).

Social work research can be classified and differentiated according to a range of criteria, these (see for example, de Vaus, 1994) include:

- its purposes—for example to inform, compare or improve services from the perspective of service planners, managers, practitioners or users

- its aims—these may be descriptive, diagnostic or evaluative

- its orientation—either empirical or interpretative

- its methodology—either predominately quantitative or qualitative

- its design—based upon any of the following: surveys, questionnaires, interviews, narratives, case study, single system or experimental designs

In selecting from these criteria, we suggest that two questions are of central importance in developing an appropriate design for social work research.

One: research by whom?

Social workers are engaged in a wide variety of different settings, organisations and tasks directed towards different purposes. They work with different groups and individuals in both state, independent, commercial, formal and informal settings and across legal, political, administrative and professional boundaries. As such, social workers are required to not only practice or carry out specific interventions, but also select from and evaluate the range and variety of different methods and approaches that are available. Increasingly, social workers are now called upon to evaluate and justify their practice and its outcomes against criteria of quality and effectiveness. The question then arises as to the necessity for social workers themselves to be capable of undertaking research, rather than being informed by and reliant upon the work of others, if they are to be considered competent to evaluate their own practice.

Arguments in support of social workers being research active, rather than merely research aware, range from a) the desirability to have personally experienced the research process in order to understand it, through to b) the benefits of the research process itself for improving practice by assisting in self awareness and reflexivity in general and in developing a more rigorous and systematic approach to practice. In contrast, it is argued that 'practitioner researchers' may be too enmeshed in and focused upon the immediate need or problem they are presented with to be able to identify important causal variables and relationships, including either their own actions, those of their employer, or influence from within the wider social system.

In either case, whether research is carried out by 'scientists' or 'practitioners', the research aim in the context of social work is inevitably, not to produce knowledge for its own sake, but to offer solutions to the every-day needs and problems which confront social workers. To this extent, both the social scientist and the social worker are potentially compromised, the former by their lack of reference to application, the later by their proximity to the field.

Two: research for whom?

The orientation of social work towards problem solving raises the question of what social, cultural, organisational and professional norms and values permeate and direct the research activity. The construction of a research question and the design and method of the inquiry will determine whose interests and needs the research will address and benefit.

Information from outside the immediate field, such as statistical data and related studies need to be analysed and applied to data collected within a local context. For example, the relationships that can be established between national and local rates of unemployment; or crime rates and substance misuse; or the variations in services which are offered to different age, gender and ethnic groups in different locations, all impact upon both the inferences that are drawn about the causes of and solutions to social problems.

In a multi-cultural society, reference to social norms is problematic; in as much as it is increasingly evident that a discrepancy exists between subjective experience, popular consensus and state policies; for example, an individual's right to liberty and equality of opportunity may be compromised by institutional racism and personal experience of social exclusion. Similarly, cultural diversity gives rise to contested understandings of what constitutes a social problem between generations and ethnic groupings: for example, in the recreational use of drugs and alcohol or in differing child care and rearing patterns. Thus, a social situation can be construed as either problematic or normal depending upon the extent of concern generated amongst individuals or communities. Public concern may be expressed and allayed or reinforced through the media, political, scientific and academic circles by reference to expert opinion. Accordingly, different interest groups will attach labels to different problems; for example, doctors, lawyers, social workers and the police may each, in their own way, problematise a given situation in different ways. Responses to re-occurring social problems, such as juvenile crime rates, are likely to be described, understood and 'solved' in different ways at different times.

Social research both contributes to and seeks to expose the prevailing discourses through which social problems are differently constructed. The reaction to the findings or outcomes of such research reflects the contested construction of the nature of social problems. Social research is thus always contentious, in as much as whilst the researchers themselves may seek to eliminate bias through use of valid and reliable methods, research has a social as well as a scientific obligation that may not accord with lay or existing expectations and assumptions (see for example, Giddens, 1993: pp 10–11).

Pahl, (1992) has highlighted the tensions that arise through research in social work and social welfare. She identifies two approaches that the researcher may adopt. Either 'swimming with the policy stream'—where the researcher works within the policy framework, akin to Rein's (1976) consensual approach; or 'diverting the stream'—where the researcher challenges the policy framework of the day, a contentious approach, in which the social researcher assumes the role of 'witness' to the failings of policy makers and service providers.

In practitioner social work research, the competing interests of different groups and actors may become all too apparent when research 'evidence' is made public:

> *The current emphasis on researching the views of service users sounds good when research is planned, but when the results are critical of current provision, policy makers and service managers may disown what they originally welcomed.*
>
> (Pahl, 1992: p 218)

Current approaches to social work research

From the current interest in research activity in social work, four approaches have emerged in response to the different and often competing orientations and interests in the field.

Evidence based practice: wherein it is argued that there is a need for social work practitioners to undertake research based activity as part of their professional education, practice and development. Such an approach is largely advocated by government agencies and institutions that seek to identify the relationship between possible causal processes and the application of effective forms of intervention. Further, it is associated with the modernising of the social services through the achievement of institutional change to improve standards and public confidence by raising the quality of services and improving performance through professional practice based upon evidence 'of what works' for clients.

Evaluation studies: which adopt a middle ground wherein the value of interventions are examined in terms of both their cost effectiveness in meeting specific goals and their wider capacity for individual empowerment and social change (Shaw and Lishman, 1999). In this approach, there are attempts to examine both the management and delivery of social work and social care services and the relationship between professional performance, service accountability and service user satisfaction.

Action research: which has become increasingly popular as an alternative to the perceived limits of positivism and one that is more compatible with the aims, context and values associated with social work practice. Deriving from the work of Lewin (1951) and developed in the UK by the Tavistock Institute of Human Relations during the 1940s and 1950s. Since the early 1980s, action research has experienced a revival in popularity. This mode of inquiry emphasises collaboration between participants in the research process and validates awareness raising, empowerment and utility as legitimate forms of knowledge over and above the discovery of universal laws of human behaviour. As such, this approach seeks to create a synthesis between problem definition and resolution in a range of different situations.

Practitioner research: which approaches research as a dimension of practice itself, in as much as it is argued that the basic helping cycle (Taylor and Devine, 1993) of social work requires an understanding of the process, methodology and essential skills that are necessary for research work (see for example, Heasman and Adams, 1998).

An example: social work research in the Czech Republic

In the Czech Republic, up until the 1990s, social work research comprised almost exclusively of individual case studies. This remains predominantly the situation today. Under the pre-1989 regime, general quantitative social research studies were mainly concerned with issues relating to work force management or 'labour stability and fluctuation ' in the state owned industrial enterprises. Here, the purpose of social research, within what was a socialist regime, was to contribute to the planning of the economic prosperity of the country, particularly through gathering data on what was understood as the undesirable movement of employees from one enterprise to another.

Occasionally, particular social questions, for example the nature or extent of 'anti-social' behaviour or the social position of divorced mothers, were included as a component within the broader aims of a research project. However, the situation of marginalised groups, for example: people with disabilities or members of ethnic minority groups were excluded from public awareness and not explored as part of the research process. Individual studies focusing on particular social issues were rare and when made, were usually descriptive. The aim of such research was primarily to 'map' the problems experienced by different groups in respect of income, services they received, patterns of employment and community inclusion. Since 1989, attempts have been made in all the social sciences to move beyond this narrow focus, limited orientation and restricted methodological approach to research. However, the term social research, as used by professionals and the public alike, more often than not still refers to purely quantitative statistical material.

Action research in the sense we have defined it was virtually unused in the former socialist state. The term 'action research' was understood in the Czech Republic as research which retrospectively applied the results of a particular research project to practice, rather than a process that arose during the research and which emphasised the active participation of the subjects of the researchers themselves. Although some activities of social workers in the Czech Republic might share similar aims with those of action research, that is to bring about some change in the behaviour of individuals, groups or a micro system through their conscious awareness and interaction with the social worker or researcher, they do not, at least methodologically, constitute action research.

Conclusion

The aim of this chapter has been to introduce some of the essential, if complex issues relevant to conducting research in social work. We have sought to demonstrate that knowledge and its generation is always incomplete, contestable, and subject to discourses that are themselves subject to processes of legitimisation mediated through relations of power. Inevitably, in practice, the motivation to enter into a process of inquiry and establish a clarity and focus of activity requires that all these considerations should but may not be brought to bear in every case.

We have argued that social work is a multi-paradigmatic discipline (see for example, the application of Habermas' theory to social work by Van der Laan, 1998); the interests and purpose of which are directed at the identification, explanation and correction of the social problems that can appear to various degrees and in different forms in a society. Social problems may be articulated, in a general sense, as potentially applicable to all people—problems such as social alienation and exclusion, poverty and homelessness. However there are also problems specific to particular vulnerable or dependent groups—for example children, older people or mentally ill people, or to the conditions or circumstances of specific individuals—such as being a lone parent, living on state benefits without the support of an extended family and so on.

Research activity in relation to social work arises in this context of seeking to generate responses to particular problems that arise between an individual or particular group and society. Hence, social work activity is a practical, purposeful form of intervention that draws upon the knowledge and working methods of the social-scientific disciplines, particularly of sociology and psychology and increasingly other social-scientific disciplines such as anthropology which are assuming growing importance.

In seeking to establish the relationship between research and social work, we have suggested that three essential issues arise:

- The first relates to what theoretical foundations and methodological approach should be adopted by social work researchers.

- The second concerns whether research activity should be considered as integral to the social work role, that is whether social workers themselves should be capable of and engaged in research activity or whether research studies into social work interests and problems are better conducted by social scientists.

- The third relates to the question of whose interests social work research studies and findings serve.

Questions for Further Consideration

1. Social work by definition is orientated towards the circumstances of marginalised individuals and groups. What research strategies are most applicable to generating knowledge about their particular experiences and relationships with other groups and how would you justify your choice of theory and method?

2. Older service users, in the main, express satisfaction with the nature and level of services they receive. What research strategies might be appropriate to establishing why this is the case, even in situations where their quality of life is patently poor?

3. What knowledge and skills are a prerequisite to the application of an action research programme aimed at addressing an urgent problem?

4. What characterises the tradition of social work research in your country?

Ethical Aspects of Social Work—A Common Set of Values and the Regulation of Practice: England an Example

Steven M. Shardlow

Introduction

Ethical issues have always been central to the practice of social work. The very act of doing social work implies that social workers and their clients engage with complex ethical issues because social work is concerned with fundamental human problems about how individuals should behave, be cared for, receive help or in extreme cases be removed from society. Social workers must act on behalf of the general public and the state, yet they also have to act in accordance with their own conscience. Sometimes, social workers may experience a conflict between what they personally believe to be correct and what they are required to do as part of the responsibilities of being a social worker. This type of problem is by no means restricted to social workers. These conflicts may arise because of conflicts between; the beliefs of the individual and the requirements or expectations of the employer; a disjunction between personal beliefs and professional codes of behaviour; a conflict between public expectations, private beliefs and employer expectations. Hence, it is hardly surprising that as Joseph (1989) comments, interest in social work ethics has been increasing; this growth in interest can be seen both in the growth of scholarly publications about social work ethics and within the US an increase in the level of discussion by professional social work organisations with the intention of helping to develop their members' competence with ethical issues. Certainly, there have been an increasing number of US books published on the subject, for example: Abbott (1988), Reamer (1993), Rhodes (1986); Wells with Masch (1988); and Yelaja (1993). Within Europe there has also been a similar increase in interest in social work ethics, with books published in several different countries including those by: Hämäläinen and Niemelä (1993) in Finland; Vecchiato and Villa (1995) in Italy; Banks (2001) in England; and Clark (2000) in Scotland.

The nature of values in social work

Discussion about social work ethics has, in the literature published in English, often consisted of two principal elements: an exploration of the 'values' that social workers ought to adhere or those they actually employ in practice. The word 'value' has many different meanings, and in a review of over 400 different publications, Harding (1980) identified at least 180 different meanings for the term 'values'. No doubt, if a similar more recent review were available even more might be identified! This proliferation of possible meanings of the term 'value' makes for considerable difficulties in developing a clear theoretical approach to questions of social work ethics and values, with serious consequences for social work practice. One solution to this difficulty is to adopt a working definition of 'value'. The Central Council for Education and Training in Social Work (CCETSW) is a non-governmental organisation which by statute has the responsibly for setting standards of social work education within the UK, and a working party in 1976, convened by this body made the following long lasting attempt to describe 'values' in the context of social work:

> A value determines what a person thinks he ought to do, which may or may not be the same as what he wants to do, or what is in his interest to do, or what in fact he actually does. Values in this sense give rise to general standards and ideals by which we judge our own and others conduct; they also give rise to specific obligations.
>
> Values are distinguished from personal preferences in that they have been accepted and articulated to some degree by a group…A value is used then as a socially accepted standard (at least by some group[s]) which guides the individual in the making of choices.
> A value can only be operative when the individual has knowledge of what he or she is doing, is aware of alternative courses of action and where there is a possibility of choice among these alternatives. Wherever someone acts in a certain way because he has no knowledge of other possibilities or where actions are mandatory, whether required by law, coerced by public opinion or forced by economic necessity, these actions do not spring from values. (CCETSW, 1976; pp 14–15)

Transposed into less gender specific language these statements convey a notion of 'values' which still has currency in the world of social work practice. These statements construct social work values as a set of principles that purport to command common assent among social workers and which seek to guide individual social worker's actions. Interestingly, these statements do not of themselves imply any particular content to the notion of social work values. Perhaps that is why they retain their validity for the fast moving practice of today's social work— almost twenty-five years after they were written. The content of social work values has been specified by a number of different writers as a series of listings of principles or values, these can be found in a variety of writers, many of whom are from the US, (see for example those by Biestek, 1961; Hollis, 1967; NISW, 1964; Teicher, 1967; and more recently Braye and Preston-Shoot, 1995; and CCETSW, 1991).Within the UK, CCETSW has recently specified the content of professional social work values, in terms of what a professionally qualified social worker must be able to do, as follows:

- Identify and question their own values and prejudices, and their implications for practice.

- Respect and value uniqueness and diversity, and recognise and build on strengths.

- Promote people's rights to choice, privacy, confidentiality and protection, while recognising and addressing the complexities of competing rights and demands.

- Assist people to increase control of and improve the quality of their lives, while recognising that control of behaviour will be required at times in order to protect children and adults from harm.

- Identify, analyse and take action to counter discrimination, racism, disadvantage, inequality and injustice using strategies appropriate to role and context.

- Practise in a manner that does not stigmatise or disadvantage either individuals, groups or communities.

(CCETSW, 1995: p 18)

This provides just one account of the different listings of social work values. The problem with such listings is that they tend to be mutually incompatible or the contents of one list do not correspond to the contents of another list. Other approaches to the conceptualisation of values and ethics in social work exist. For example, The Netherlands Association of Social Workers has identified three elements that comprise social work ethics. First, that the profession seeks to help individuals achieve their full potential in their social relations. Second, that there are maxims or principles that govern the practice of social work and that these can be stated as a code of ethics. Third, that both the social worker and the person-in-need have to take personal responsibility for their own affairs and to make choices (Netherlands Association of Social Workers, 1987).

Some theorists have proposed a taxonomy of values in social work rather than just a listing of ethical values for professional practice. For example, Braye and Preston-Shoot suggest that in relation to social care (where social care as a term is increasingly being used to incorporate social work and other forms of care that are neither health care or family care; the boundaries of social care in respect of these notions are not firmly marked) there are two distinct types of values, being the 'traditional values', which encourage practitioners to treat people better, and radical values which call for a renegotiation of roles and structures within society to create a more just and fair society. They propose the following categorisation of values (p 36):

Table 5.1: Braye and Preston-Shoot's Categorisation of Values

Traditional	Radical
Respect for persons	Citizenship
Paternalism and protection	Participation
Normalisation and social role valorisation	Community practice
Equality of opportunity	Equality
Anti-discriminatory practice	Anti-oppressive practice
Partnership	Empowerment, user control

A fundamental difference between those values categorised as *radical* as compared with the *traditional* is that the traditional values seek to help the individual adjust to society without seeking to change that society. Therefore, by implication, these values locate the responsibility for the individual's failure to be fully part of that society with the individual themselves. By contrast, the radical values seek to modify the society in which the individual lives and therefore gives credence to the notion that at least in part it is a societal responsibility that the individual is not able to function within society. Another means to understand social work values has been proposed by Shardlow (1998), i.e. that notions of values may be understood by reference to the domains of knowledge that are incorporated within the scope of the term social work values. Hence, Shardlow has proposed a three-point taxonomy delineating notions of values in social work; the 'restricted', the 'mid-range' and the 'extended':

- Restricted notions of values in social work are centrally concerned with professional ethics i.e. the 'rightness' or 'wrongness' of social workers' behaviours with other people (professional ethics).

- Mid-range notions include all those elements of the 'restricted notion' but also include some additional domains, such as: organisational theory; the relationship between social work and the law; the function of social work in society (political philosophy and political sociology).

- Extended definitions of values in social work include all domains of both 'restricted' and 'mid-range' notions and also: nature of social work knowledge (epistemology); an analysis of social work and social theory e.g. the construction of social work as an activity, such as post-modernism and social work; relationship between social work and religious belief systems (theology).

Hence there can be no clear and unequivocal statement of the nature and scope of social work values as the construction of social work values is part of the debate about the very nature of values in social work. We should beware of those who peddle ideas that suggest there are a single set of social work values, held and used by all social work practitioners for example CCETSW.

The function of social work

Sadly, social work is not always seen as a positive force by others. Whilst social workers themselves may see the activity of social work as a grand force that strives to challenge injustice or to put right social wrongs, as illustrated by the cartoon below. Others, such as writers of fiction or playwrights, have included characters in their works who compare the function of social work to the rather unsavoury and demeaning notion of cleaning out society's drains and postulate social workers as social sanitary workers. These notions of social work are insulting both to social workers and to the people who use social work. Within social work professional literature, there are two major strands that describe the function of social work in relation to society, these strands concern 'maintenance' and 'change'. Some, most notably Davies (1994) argue that the function of social work is to maintain existing social structures by assisting those who have difficulty in making an adjustment with wider society to fit more comfortably within that society and therefore to maximise their individual potential. Davies uses a metaphor, that social work is the oil that keeps the machinery of society functioning. His perspective is optimistic and humanist and he posits a social work that is benign. Others, often termed radical social work theorists, have argued that the current structure of society is iniquitous for various reasons, due to such as: racial oppression (Ahmad, 1990); gender role stereotyping (Dominelli, 1998); exploitative class relationships (Jones, 1983) and so on. As a consequence of these and other forms of oppression some have argued that the function of the social worker is to pursue radical change in the nature of social relations (see for example Dominelli, 1997). Fook has identified key themes found in this radical social work literature:

- A structural analysis by which personal problems can be traced to causes in the socio-economic structure: therefore the individual 'victim' of these problematic social structures should not be 'blamed' for causing them.

- An ongoing analysis of the social control functions of the social work profession and the social welfare system.

- An ongoing critique of the existing social, political and economic arrangements.

- A commitment to protecting the individual person against oppression by more powerful individuals, groups or structures.

- Goals of personal liberation and social change. (Fook, 1993: p 7)

Within these different value positions regarding the function of social work and society

there are a range of different shades of opinion as to whether social work is about maintenance or change.

Empirical knowledge about social workers ethics and values

The majority of the discussion about social work values and ethics is theoretical. There has been relatively little empirical research conducted on social work ethics and values. Little is known about how social workers respond to ethical issues in day-to-day practice (Cussom, 1992), given the size and nature of the profession, although Holland and Kilpatrick (1991) have sought to identify and categorise the nature of ethical problems that confront social workers. Empirical studies do exist in some fields such as: gender differences in the approach of male and female social workers to making ethical decisions (see Dobrin, 1989; Landau, 1997; Segal, 1992)—no conclusive evidence has emerged about whether there is a significant difference in the decision making of male and female social work

practitioners; attitudes of new recruits to social work (Gould and Harris, 1996; Pearson, 1973; Solas, 1994); social workers' responses to organisational pressures in making decision specific ethical areas such as social workers and reproductive technologies. A substantial proportion of this empirical research emanates from the US. There is a need for more European empirical research that explores the nature of social worker's ethical behaviour with clients.

Ethical practice and codes of ethics

Throughout the world, many national social work professional associations have adopted codes of ethics for social workers. Codes of ethics for social workers have been produced and published in many European Countries; see for example in Finland, France, Iceland and UK. In addition, codes of ethics have been adopted by international organisations, see for example IFSW (1988) which is available in several different languages. Banks (2001) conducted a study of different ethical codes for social workers. She found that of 15 codes of practice studied (most from Europe), the overwhelming majority contained principles that referred to: respect for the unique value of the individual; user self-determination; social justice and professional integrity. While there were considerable similarities in these respects, there were also differences between the codes with regard to the range of duties expected of social workers and the professional practice issues covered by the code of ethics. These codes of ethics usually contain a range of general and broad principles, for example the Code of the Netherlands Association of Social Workers states:

> Art. 8: The attitude to the client is based on respect of the client's personality and on the recognition of his own responsibility for the choice of action he makes.

> Art.9: The social worker offers, according to the objectives of the institution he is a part of, assistance to the client, keeping in mind the communities which the client belongs to.
>
> (Netherlands Association of Social Workers, 1987)

However, the codes tend to ignore, or fail to provide, guidance about key factors such as the acceptable boundaries between personal and professional conduct in respect of clients and social workers, for example there is often no explicit prohibition of sexual relationships between clients and social workers as might be found in codes of practice for other professional groups. The real difficulty with many codes of ethics for practitioners and clients is that they are generally non-mandatory, there is no mechanism to enforce compliance with the code and seeking redress for grievances against the code is extremely difficult. Hence, codes of practice are supposed to provide a collective statement about the principles that social workers adhere to, but in practice they are very difficult to operationalise in day-to-day practice.

The regulation of social work

The regulation of the profession of social work varies greatly across the states of Europe. In some countries the title social worker (or its equivalent) is a protected title and may only be used by those who have the requisite qualifications; certain jobs may only be taken by those with the relevant qualifications as social workers; and adherence to a social work code of ethics is a requirement for social work practitioners. France, is one nation state where these conditions apply. For example, as early as 1932 a State Diploma (subsequently modified) was introduced as the required professional qualification for all *assistants de service social* (social workers). The title *assistant de service social*, was first protected in 1951 (Ministerial Decree: 31 Mars 1951): henceforth the use of the title *assistant de service social* and social work posts in the public and private sectors were restricted to those possessing the State Diploma and who were therefore entitled to use the title of social worker. The current code of ethics dates from 1994. By comparison, in other countries the systems for regulation of social work are less well developed. In Germany, there is no binding code of ethics for *socialarbeiten* (social workers) although attempts are underway to establish a code of ethics where professional associations exist for social workers, but these are not strong organisations. In the Czech Republic in the early 1990s, Minimum Standards for social work practice were determined by the state prescribing certain elements of social work practice. Also the Society of Social Workers adopted a Code of Ethics in 1995 but it is not mandatory for social workers to practice in accordance with such a code.

Regulation of social work: England a case study

Regulation of professional practice may take many different forms, for example; the control of the number and nature of entrants to professional training; prescriptions about the desired and acceptable forms of professional behaviour; disciplinary structures to enforce desired behaviour among professionals and so on. Levels of regulation may be high or low and may use a variety of different techniques. At present, regulation of professional social work practice relies upon general employment law enforced by those who employ social workers. This entails that there are wide variations in conceptualisations of desirable practice across England as these tend to be employer determined in the light of national guidance from the government in Westminster (see below). Regulation by the profession itself is weak or non-existent as: the title 'social worker' is not a protected title; there is no required code of ethics; and there is no body able to enforce desirable practice other than employers. The situation is now changing as the profession moves toward the establishment of new structures. The development of these structures will now be explored.

A regulatory body for social work in England

The establishment of a regulatory body for social work has been a troubled and difficult process: a process that remains as yet uncompleted and may never be achieved in a pure and simple form! Early attempts to lay the groundwork for such a body were unco-ordinated and sporadic. Hence, for example, in 1907 two associations of Hospital Almoners joined forces to establish a register of licensed practitioners (Barclay, 1982) and again in 1911 when the Home Office established a register of probation officers (Malherbe, 1980). There was an unsuccessful attempt to create a General Social Work Council in 1954 (Tissier, 1990); meanwhile the Association of Psychiatric Social Workers maintained a professional register until 1970. When existing separate client-based professional organisations joined forces to create the British Association of Social Workers (BASW), the creation of a national professional organisation for social work might have been expected to lead to the development of all-embracing regulatory structures for social work practice. To the extent that this was an aim or aspiration of the early founders of BASW, then the organisation must be counted as a failure. It is not and never became a full professional organisation, hovering somewhere between a professional body and a trade union. Most importantly, it never attracted a majority of social workers into membership: no doubt to a major extent because membership was not a pre-requisite to practice as a social worker. Nonetheless, during the 1970s furious debates occurred within BASW, constructed upon paradigms about the achievement of professional status for social work, and subsequently concerning the need to establish a full professional regulatory body. BASW was instrumental in bringing together a joint steering group of associated professional interests with the intention of regulating practice. The impact of this group was insubstantial; although their arguments failed to convince the members of a major review conducted on behalf of the government. As the Barclay report set its face against anything like a regulatory body for social work, arguing that the establishment of such a council would be both premature and elitist (Barclay, 1982). Despite the apparent incompatibility of the arguments for rejecting a regulatory body, a considerable influence may well have been the concerns of the then government of Mrs Thatcher about the possible cost of such a venture. Until the mid 1980s, these initiatives to establish a professional regulatory body had been driven from within the social work establishment. They were grounded principally upon desires to improve the status of the profession. Laudable though these motives might be they did not of themselves generate the political will to achieve change. Essentially, it was not until two factors changed; a shift in public perception about the nature of social work and the need for regulation, coupled with a change of government determined to experiment with different forms of regulation in the public sector, that the development of a regulatory body for social work became possible. The first of these factors occurred from the middle of the 1980s when a series of social work disasters occurred, in particular involving: the deaths of several children (A Child in Trust, 1985); the removal of children from their families (Report of the Inquiry into Child Abuse in Cleveland, 1988); the quality of care provided for children (Utting, 1997). It was not only in respect of children but also the management of mentally-ill patients in the community and the care of elderly people (see for example Clough, 1987). All of these examples of disasters, which continue up to the present date, have undermined public confidence in the social work profession. In response the New Labour government, on election in April, 1997, swiftly moved to establish a form of regulatory body drawing upon ideas expressed in a range of papers produced in the early 1990s, most influential of these being the working group convened by the National Institute for Social Work and the publications then produced (Parker, 1990). In April, 1998, Paul Boetang, Minister of Health, announced the government's intention to create a General Social Services Council that would have the following features: individual registers, requirements for training and codes of conduct for both employers and staff. Hence, the Care Standards Act 2000 created the framework for a regulatory body to be known henceforth as the General Social Care Council for England (separate, albeit similar bodies, will be established in the other countries of the United Kingdom), and this body will have responsibility for the regulation of social work and will come into operation in October 2001. The GSCC will have powers to regulate a large number of people working in the field of social care: not just social workers. The form of regulation will consist of a series of registers for different types of staff: all will be required to agree to a (or several) code(s) of practice. The GSCC will issue codes of practice for workers and employers in social care across the broad range of social care, register suitably trained and qualified staff and will also regulate education and training for social work at initial professional and post professional levels. There will be expectations about levels of training for staff and also codes of conduct for employers. Although the final shape of the regulatory bodies is yet to be defined, it is likely that there will be a strong voice for users of social services. The arguments of those in the social work profession for an exclusive regulatory body with competence over social work have not been accepted by government. Instead a body which has a remit for the entirety of social care has been created. Will it create a separate code of ethics for social workers or will there be a code of ethics for social care professionals? The implications of this for social work will only be seen in the longer term. However, there must be concerns that the interests of social work will be subsumed under the much larger constituency of social care. Yet this regulation of social care professions through a joint body may represent the future for the social professions more widely across Europe.

Regulation: the future

In a White Paper published in August 2000 entitled *A Quality Strategy for Social Care* (Department of Health, 2000) the Department of Health outlined its strategy for improving the quality of social care in the short and medium term. Very little of this strategy relies upon the development of a code of ethics for social workers. In fact the term 'code of ethics' is not used, the term 'code of conduct' being preferred. What emerges from the document are plans, already well advanced, to create a complex and all embracing network of regulatory bodies that will seek to promote standards in social care (and therefore in social work). This complex configuration is best illustrated by Figure 5.1.

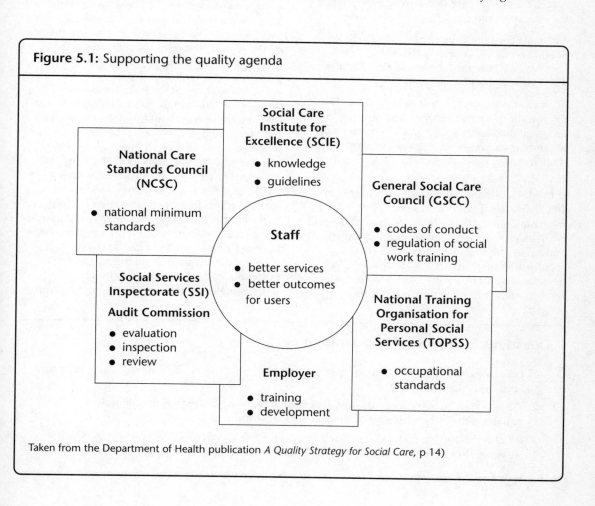

Figure 5.1: Supporting the quality agenda

Taken from the Department of Health publication *A Quality Strategy for Social Care*, p 14)

In this figure, social care staff are pictured in the middle of a whole range of new structures: social care staff with their obligation to deliver 'better services' and better 'outcomes for users'. These structures are presented as supportive but they will also be regulatory and controlling. These various bodies are:

National Care Standards Council (NCSC): this body is charged with ensuring that all 'regulated care services' in England will be provided to national minimum standards, it will set and define these standards.

Social Care Institute for Excellence (SCIE): will identify knowledge to be used in the delivery of social care and will produce guidelines on the effective delivery of social care as well as ensuring dissemination across all institutions involved in the delivery and provision of social care.

General Social Care Council (GSCC): (see above) responsible for developing and enforcing codes of conduct for social care staff as well as regulating the education and training of social workers.

National Training Organisation for Personal Social Services (TOPSS): will develop occupational standards for social care and have a role in workforce planning.

Social Services Inspectorate (SSI) and the Audit Commission: are two independent bodies, although increasingly they work in partnership to monitor and inspect the quality of work being done by social care agencies.

In addition to these five bodies, the employer still has a central function in setting and maintaining standards. How these five bodies will work together with employers and social work and social care staff to create a supportive regulatory framework remains to be seen. The agenda being set by government is to determine levels or standards of quality in service delivery and then to ensure through the range of regulatory measures and structures that these standards are maintained. This regulatory framework seems to have moved a long way from either the discussion about the nature of professional values and ethics conventionally found in the literature and the debates regarding the need to professionalise social work through the adoption of a code of ethics.

The changing nature of social work practice

It is evident from other chapters in this book that social work practice is changing rapidly as a variety of forces shape and construct new and emergent forms of practice. Notable among these trends are the forces of 'manageralism', where social work is driven by the interests of the employing organisation and where required performance indicators are set or social workers are required to ensure that their practice conforms to nationally or locally prescribed guidelines. The forces of 'globalisation' construct an agenda for social work across national boundaries, with forces such as migration, social exclusion and the power of international finance on the economic stability of countries and individuals. The changing nature of welfare provision across much of Europe has seen a reduction in the willingness of the state to provide for individuals, so that individuals are often increasingly reliant upon themselves and their families. Social work has become ever more involved in the making of financial decisions about the 'best value' to be obtained from the provision of welfare. As yet, little consideration has been given by professional associations of social workers to the meaning and significance of such changes for the development of social work values and professional ethics. These have the taste of being pickled in aspic, and are much more concerned with the nature of an individualised social work apparently untrammelled by these new and emergent forces.

Questions for Further Consideration

1. Is there a code of ethics for social work practice in your country: if so, how far do you agree with the contents of the code?
2. What is your opinion about the forms of regulation being developed in England. How do you think they might affect the practice of social work?
3. What regulatory frameworks are used for social work practice in your country. In which ways are they similar or different to those used or under development in England?

Chapter Six

The Increasing Importance of Law to Social Work Practice: UK an Example

Belinda Schwehr

Introduction

The past decade has seen something of a 'revolution' in the relationship between the law and social work practice in the United Kingdom. In the 1980s, social services judicial reviews were infrequent, but the 1990s saw a flood of legal proceedings and a corresponding increase in the influence of judicial decisions on social work practice. The coming into force of the Human Rights Act 1998 on 2nd October 2000, enabling individuals to assert their European Convention rights in UK domestic courts, means that this litigious trend is unlikely to diminish, and will be increasingly European-orientated.

This chapter explores the effect of recent legal developments in UK law on social care practice for people with disabilities (in particular as it relates to budget management and adult protection), the significance of the European Convention on Human Rights, and the **likely** impact of the Human Rights Act 1998 as an example of the impact of legal practice upon social work.

Balancing 'needs' against available resources

Section 47 of the National Health Service and Community Care Act 1990 places a duty on UK local authorities to carry out an assessment of an individual's needs for community care services where it appears to the authority that an individual for whom it may provide or arrange for the provision of community care services, may be in need of such services. The authority must then decide whether the individual's needs call for the provision of services, having regard to the results of the assessment.

In the context of domiciliary care for disabled people, this requires consideration of whether the assessed needs *necessitate* the local authority's making of the arrangements.[1]

This obligation inevitably leaves local authorities facing the perennial and difficult problem of how to meet potentially limitless need from what will always be limited resources. It begs the question how far, if at all, can a local authority's resources be taken into account in fulfilling certain of the service-related functions imposed on it by law?

A number of recent decisions have served to clarify the position. These cases have turned upon whether the functions in question are 'duties' or 'powers' and the line between these two types of functions is very often indistinct.

In the key case of *R v Gloucestershire County Council, ex parte Barry*,[2] the House of Lords[3] determined that resources **are** legally relevant to the assessment of the needs of disabled people under Section 2 of the Chronically Sick and Disabled Persons Act 1970 (CSDPA). The case established that the existence of 'needs' for services may be identified against an authority's locally agreed eligibility criteria, which have been set with regard to the authority's budgetary position, and that the *duty* to make arrangements only arises when the authority is satisfied that making the arrangements is necessary to meet the needs assessed against the budget driven criteria. On the other hand, although the criteria for 'satisfaction' of that necessity may be altered by the local authority, depending on the resources available, the law is that once the duty to make arrangements has actually arisen, a lack of resources is irrelevant to performance of the duty.

The *Gloucestershire* case has thus confirmed that eligibility criteria are a legitimate tool for rationing an authority's limited resources, a position that was by no means certain hitherto. The decision further entails that 'unmet need' of a factual human nature can now be openly acknowledged as existing, as it is unlawful to fail to meet that need only where it has also been acknowledged as constituting a need for services which the authority has agreed to provide for,

---

1. Under s2 Chronically Sick and Disabled Persons Act 1970.
2. [1997] All ER 1 and (1997) 1 CCLR 1-14
3. The United Kingdom's highest court for matters of national law

but then runs out of money. However, local authorities tempted to set eligibility criteria so high that only very few of those service users at severe risk of harm will qualify, should heed the Court's warning: the setting of criteria at an unreasonable level will be vulnerable to challenge as unlawful, by way of judicial review, as an unreasonable exercise of discretion. It is simply not open for local elected members to prioritise social services so low that other directorates get the lion's share of the budget to the detriment of the discharge of these duties.

In *R v Sefton Metropolitan Borough Council, ex parte Help the Aged*,[4] the local authority had sought to defer compliance with its duty to provide accommodation to meet the residential care needs of certain elderly persons.[5] The duty is to accommodate people who 'are in need of care and attention which is not otherwise available' to them. Whilst the local authority accepted that the claimant in this case had met its own eligibility requirements as 'a person in need of care and attention', it was seeking to rely on its lack of resources and the claimant's own remaining capital as justification for not meeting the duty placed on it by Section 21. The authority accepted that once the claimant's capital fell below a certain threshold, set by the authority itself, then the authority *would* perform its s.21 duty, *notwithstanding* a lack of resources.

The Court of Appeal, in holding that the authority had acted unlawfully, made it clear that whilst a local authority may indeed develop eligibility criteria for identifying 'need', (subject to unreasonableness) based on its own resources, when it came to an individual who has been assessed as meeting those criteria, then *unless* the authority concludes that the care so identified as needed is 'otherwise available', the authority then owes an **absolute** duty under the legislation to provide the accommodation, regardless of its own resources, (or indeed the person's, if those means are below the current capital and income thresholds found in National Assessment Regulations).

The *Gloucestershire* case was distinguished, as no duty to arrange a CSDPA service arises, even though a need is identified, until an authority decides it is 'necessary' to make arrangements to meet that need. Nevertheless, the outcome is the same: once criteria have been met, a duty arises.

The absence of any need to consider 'necessity' in residential care cases is not really significant, because it is just a reflection of the fact that those at that end of the spectrum of need who have no other means to make arrangements, will obviously 'necessitate' state intervention in any civilised society.

A recent Scottish case[6] has gone further in determining the legality of operating waiting lists for those identified as being in need of residential accommodation. The petitioner in that case was 90 years old, confused, deaf and in need of 24 hour care. He had been told by the Council that he might have a 7–8 month wait for funding, and his family had reluctantly placed him in a nursing home in the meantime.

The judge held that once it had been decided a client 'needed' the care, then it was unlawful to place someone on a waiting list **and do nothing** in the interim: somebody's budget has got to be spent on some sort of service to meet the assessed need.

Although this is a Scottish case, and therefore not binding on courts in England and Wales, the author thinks it likely that the decision will be followed by these courts. English courts have already been persuaded that a duty to meet need is triggered once 'care and attention not otherwise available' is agreed to be needed (*Sefton*), and that the duty to meet need must be discharged, regardless of a want of resources within a particular budgetary pot (*Gloucestershire* and *Sefton*).

There have also been attempts to apply the discretion-flavoured principles in the *Gloucestershire* case to the *duty* of assessment in Section 47 National Health Service and Community Care Act 1990. In the case of *R v Bristol City Council, ex parte Penfold*,[7] for example, a middle-aged single parent who suffered from relatively mild anxiety problems, wished to be able to live with her daughter and had sought re-housing through the housing authority. She had turned down offers of premises, such that the authority had discharged any relevant housing function. She then applied for a community care assessment, on the basis that she was entitled to be considered for accommodation under s.21 NAA because she was in need of care and attention (not otherwise available to her) through 'some other circumstance' than the normal range

---

4. [1997] 1 CCLR 57
5. This duty arises under s.21 National Assistance Act 1948 (NAA)
6. *MacGregor v South Lanarkshire Council* (judgement given 15th December 2000)
7. (1998) 1 CCLR 315

of situations regarded as triggering the s.21 function.[8] The authority argued that no duty to assess the claimant arose, as its policies on 'need' for s.21 care could not conceivably lead to a decision to provide such accommodation for *her*.

The Court disagreed and held that the duty was triggered by the appearance of need for any service which *could* be provided, regardless of whether it actually *was*, or was likely to be, provided, as a matter of local policy and practice (and the criteria). The right to refuse assessment would only arise in a case where no reasonable authority could possibly think that the applicant appeared to be even possibly in need of any community care service which could legally be provided under any of the relevant legislation. This impacts significantly on resourcing 'duty' (referral) systems of a level and depth sufficient to deserve even the tag of an 'assessment'. Whilst authorities have freedom to design their own assessment processes, the procedure must accord with government guidance and the law of reasonableness. A telephone assessment from an unqualified administrator might not be thought to be adequate, in the context of the *judgement* required, if such 'screening' is obliged also to constitute an 'assessment' for those turned down for services at the end of the telephone conversation.

Since 1996, the knotty task of distinguishing statutory duties from discretions (i.e. powers), has been made easier, by reference to the case law. It can be summarised as follows:

Duties: to be discharged without regard to resources

- To assess virtually everyone who is referred.[9]

- To include social and recreational needs within the assessment (even if the criteria exclude those *types* of needs, from eligibility for actual services as a necessary response to need).[10]

- To provide appropriate services for those assessed as necessitating care services arranged by the local authority.[11]

- To maintain a service package, pending re-assessment.[12]

- To find the money for mandatory disabled facilities grants.[13]

Discretions: functions that may be exercised with regard to resources

- To set eligibility criteria by reference to budget shortage (subject to unreasonableness).[14]

- To redefine a human difficulty as falling outside the definition of 'need' for a service (subject to unreasonableness).[15]

- To take the cheaper of **adequate**, alternative means of meeting need.[16]

- To re-assess a clients' needs downwards, if needs lessen *or* criteria are tightened.[17]

Faced with the wide scope for discretion in so many local authority functions, it is as if the Courts have realised that the characterisation of a function as a duty, albeit one dependent on a prior professional judgement whether someone meets discretionary criteria, is a means of fighting back on behalf of individuals.

The trend is clearly moving away from a lack of resources in any one budgetary 'pot' having relevance to the legality of failing to discharge statutory functions in community care. Those involved in this field would thus do well to become conversant in the increasingly legalistic language and principles in the caselaw, if they are to avoid making unlawful decisions based on irrelevant considerations.

---

8. This function is the basis for almost all local authority residential accommodation provision, and is geared mainly to the aged, ill or disabled (none of which Mrs Penfold appeared to be)
9. See *Bristol CC, ex parte Penfold* (1998) 1 CCLR 315
10. See *R v Haringey London Borough Council, ex parte Norton* (1997) (judgement given 15 July 1998, CO/555/97)
11. *R v Gloucestershire CC, ex parte Barry* [1997] All ER 1; South Lanarkshire
12. Ibid.
13. *R v Birmingham City Council, ex parte Taj Mohammed* [1998] 3 All ER 788
14. See the *Gloucestershire* case
15. Ibid.
16. See *R v Lancashire County Council, ex parte Ingham* [1996] 4 All ER 422
17. *R v Birmingham City Council, ex parte Killigrew* (High Court judgment, 29 June 1999) (unreported)

Adult protection functions

Another area in which the law has made great inroads is in relation to the care and welfare of mentally incapable adults. Here, European legal principles have been used to extend the UK doctrine of 'necessity' to the point where it may actually be stated that local authorities *do* have some limited adult protection powers.

Where medical treatment of a mentally incapacitated adult is required, at present the position in UK law is that no one has the authority to give consent *on behalf* of the adult. However, treatment may be given where it is necessary in the best interests of the patient and the court has power to grant a declaration that a particular treatment proposed will not be unlawful, if a doctor is concerned as to the effects of intervention.[18] The European Convention on Human Rights has long permitted interference with a person's right to respect for a private life and autonomy if it was necessary for the protection of health, and the argument as to 'necessity' is of course much stronger if the individual is incapable of reaching an informed choice as to consent or refusal of consent.

Powers of guardianship in UK law covering welfare arrangements short of medical treatment are currently to be found in the Mental Health Act 1983 (MHA), ss7–10. A guardianship application may only be made in respect of a patient on the ground that they are suffering from a limited type of mental disorder, being mental illness, severe mental impairment, psychopathic disorder or mental impairment, and their mental disorder is believed by professionals to be of the nature or degree which warrants their reception into guardianship, and it is necessary in the interests of the welfare of the patient or for the protection of other persons that they should be so received. There is no requirement that the patient consent to guardianship, but if the framework does not extend to restraint or detention, then, in practice, its efficiency would depend on at least passive acquiescence of the patient. Whether it provides a lawful basis for control of such patients has long been a moot point. The traditional approach in social work has been that it would be a trespass to the person physically to take *an unwilling person* from their home into residential care, even if guardianship had been acquired.

Until recently, it was generally thought that the only powers conferred on a guardian were the somewhat limited powers contained in Section 8 MHA. In the case of *R v Kent County Council, ex parte Marston*,[19] however, the Court suggested that Section 7 MHA confers a broad implied power on the guardian to act to promote the welfare of the patient. It was even said in *Marston* that the Section 8 express powers can override the 'perceived wishes' of the patient. It is suggested that reference to European Human Rights principles would support an interpretation which would cover physically removing an incapacitated (even if unwilling) patient without their, or their carer's, consent (for example from situations of suspected abuse) to the place where the guardian requires the patient to reside. At the very least, there is no decided case precluding the argument that Section 7 implicitly allows the guardian so to act, where to do so is in the best interests of an *incapacitated* patient.

At first sight, a qualification of the 'best interests' doctrine for statutory guardians is the fact that the Court said that the *Marston* implied duty to act for the welfare of the patient would not allow 'totalitarian' conduct by the Authority. Whether compelling someone to move into residential accommodation against their *capacitated* wishes would amount to totalitarianism might depend on whether the courts thought that European human rights principles allow interference with people's private lives for legitimate social aims, even where the person still enjoys *some* capacity, despite being seriously mentally impaired or otherwise mentally ill, so as to qualify for guardianship in the first place. But it is suggested that so long as a judgement of **incapacity** has been properly made, in a given case, it cannot be 'totalitarian' to pursue a course which has also been agreed by relevant professionals, and other consulted parties, to be in the best interests of that person. The problem remaining with the regime in UK law is that amenability to guardianship does not turn on incapacity at all, but on severe mental impairment, with its statutory connotations of 'seriously irresponsible conduct', which 'diagnosis' psychiatrists are reluctant to apply to dementia sufferers and learning disabled people.

Given the perceived inadequacies of the guardianship regime, and the apparent lack of

---

18. See for example: as in the recent 'Siamese twins' case (*Re A (a child)* The Times, 23 September 2000)

19. 9 July 1997; unreported

Parliamentary time for legislation providing for lawful authority to be awarded to a guardian covering medical, welfare and financial management (as exists in Norway) the UK courts have recently developed the remedy of declaratory relief [20] in any dispute about daily living arrangements for an incapacitated client, by extending the Court's inherent jurisdiction to declare the lawfulness of *medical* treatment in difficult life and death cases.[21]

The case of *Re S*[22] concerned a rich Norwegian on a visit to the UK who took up residence with the plaintiff, an English woman, to whom he gave power of attorney over one of his bank accounts. S suffered a severe stroke, leaving him deeply incapacitated, and the plaintiff secured his admission to a private nursing home, paying his expenses through her power of attorney. S's son arrived in the UK and, without the plaintiff's consent or knowledge, arranged to have his father discharged and flown back to Norway. The plaintiff obtained an interim injunction preventing S's removal from the UK and sought a declaration that it was in S's best interests that he remain in the UK to receive appropriate care and treatment. The Court had ultimately to decide what legal rights the plaintiff, and for that matter S's wife, had at stake to justify declaratory relief. The Court found that the only legal rights in issue were those of S. Since S was incapable of expressing how he wished to be treated, the Court had jurisdiction to make the decision in his best interests, on the evidence before it.

In the 1989 case of *Re F*,[23] the House of Lords discussed the question of how necessity justifies surgery by *medical* professionals, with one of the Law Lords, Lord Goff, suggesting that justifiable 'treatment' can extend to every part of a person's caring for another's welfare.

In the later case of *Re C*,[24] that Court treated Lord Goff's speech in *Re F* as creating a jurisdiction also governing the management of adults with limited mental capacity, including everything done by **a carer** which has to do with the preservation of life, health *or well-being, or the prevention of deterioration in physical or mental health.*

In the year 2000 case of *Re F (adult: court's jurisdiction)*,[25] the Court in determining that the perceived wishes of a mentally incapacitated adult could be overridden by the need to protect her from care which was not in her best interests, stated that, if necessary, protection could extend to a declaration justifying restraint, or even **detention**, of an incapacitated person in her best interests. Further, questions of permitting only *supervised* contact between mother and adult daughter were regarded as legitimate for the Court to decide.

If detention and restraint are part of the doctrine of necessity *outside* the regime of guardianship (see above), then it is at least arguable they are also part of the implied best interests guardianship power implicit in Section 7 MHA. Such an approach would revolutionise adult protection decision-making, in so far as practitioners could be made aware of it.

Looking at the developing case law, it appears that existing carers (whilst they undertake the caring role) can rely on 'necessity' as a doctrine which operates to make their day-to-day choices presumptively lawful, at least until challenged as 'not in the best interests' of the person for whom they are caring. It would seem that carers have a duty not merely to take reasonable steps to avoid *harm* to those incapacitated adults for whom they voluntarily care, but to avoid doing, or permitting anything to be done, which is ' not in their best interests'.

Despite the widening of the court's powers to grant declaratory relief, and the apparent flexibility that this has brought, the remedy only fits cases where singular issues, such as the best place for residence, or the desirability of contacts or certain activities or regimes, are in dispute. Guardianship would still be more appropriate for cases in which ongoing 'care and control' is perceived as necessary.

What *is* clear, is that it is essential for those involved in social work practice to be fully apprised of the law, in order to make best and appropriate use of the powers available in managing the day-to-day welfare of vulnerable adults.

The European Convention and social services

The Convention rights most relevant to adults' social services are to be found in Articles 2, 3, 5, 6, 8 and 14, as explained below. They have been

---

20. This is a remedy which is used by courts to clarify the legal rights of the parties

21. As for example in the leading case of *Airedale NHS Trust v Bland* [1993] AC 789

22. *Re S* [1995] 1 FLR 1075

23. [1989] 2 WLR 1025

24. [1993] 1 FLR 940

25. Court of Appeal judgment, 26 June 2000

surprisingly under-used in the field of social services litigation before the Strasbourg Court but once given further effect by the UK's Human Rights Act, commentators anticipate a flurry of lateral thinking, and a higher profile for arguments based on European Convention principles.

Article 2 *(right to life)*

The protection of the right to life enshrined in Article 2 imposes a broader obligation on the State than merely requiring it to refrain from intentionally taking life. Rather, the State is further required to take appropriate steps to safeguard life.[26] Could it be argued that the closure of a residential care home, for example, could lead or has led to premature mortality amongst the residents? The point was raised, though not fully considered, in the *Coughlan*[27] case in the UK. There, the Court said that Ms Coughlan's view of the loss of her accommodation as life-threatening was ' putting the reality too high' , but accepted that the enforced move would be devastating and seriously anti-therapeutic. She was a middle-aged person, however, whereas the average age of those in residential or nursing home care is over ninety.

Article 3 *(prohibition against inhuman or degrading treatment)*

Article 3 may well produce claims aimed at standards, regimes and conditions in homes and packages of services, on the basis that shared rooms, routine use of restraints such as bed-guards, over-sedation, use of complicated locks etc., could arguably amount to inhuman or degrading treatment. The European Court has allowed a surprisingly generous margin of appreciation to psychiatric professionals to conduct so-called 'therapeutic' regimes, holding, for instance, that 14 days of being manacled to a bed was not inhuman or degrading in the context of what professionals thought 'necessary'.[28] However, in *Tyrer v. United Kingdom*,[29] the European Court indicated that acts which

constitute an insult to a person's human dignity or inflict humiliation or debasement, whilst not of a scale to amount to 'inhuman' treatment, may be sufficiently serious to qualify as degrading. It is suggested that in the light of enforced Caesarean sections[30] and the alleged over-sedation of a patient to admit him 'voluntarily' to a hospital,[31] the UK courts are unlikely to give the psychiatric profession such a wide margin of appreciation.

Article 8 *(respect for home, privacy and family life)*

Article 8 not only requires Member States to refrain from interfering with an individual's right to respect, but in certain instances can be seen as imposing a positive duty to adopt measures designed to secure respect for private life.[32] The rights conferred by Article 8 are qualified by reference to the protection of health or morals, the rights or freedoms of others and the prevention of crime, among other constraining principles. In social care, the restriction provided for by article 8(2), referring to the economic well-being of the country (or the council's area, as is anticipated to be the law in the UK), will be one of the most pertinent in limiting the extent to which this article requires **positive** steps to be taken, to further or to protect others.

Residential home closures for economic reasons are bound to raise Article 8 claims. In *Coughlan*,[33] the UK Court considered whether the decision by a Health Authority to close down the home where Ms Coughlan resided, without securing alternative accommodation and after having promised her 'a home' there for life, would be in breach of Article 8, (if it had been in force in the UK). The Court adjudged that the proposed closure would be an interference with Ms Coughlan's right to respect for her home and that in this instance, such interference could not be justified under even the 'economic well-being of the country' qualification to the right in article 8(2).

Article 8 was also considered in the UK in *Re F (adult: court's jurisdiction)*.[34] In deciding that the court has the power to grant a declaration

---

26. *X v UK* (1978) 14 DR 31

27. *R v North East Devon Health Authority, ex parte Coughlan* [2000] WLR 622

28. *Hercsegfalvy v Austria* (1993) 15 EHRR 437

29. (1978) 2 EHRR 1

30. *St George's Healthcare Trust v S* [1998] 3 ALL ER 673

31. *R v Bournewood Community and Mental Health NHS Trust, ex parte L* [1998] 3 ALL ER 289

32. See *Botta v Italy* (1998) 26 EHRR 241 and *X and Y v Netherlands* (1986) 8 EHRR 235

33. Supra

34. Supra, footnote 25

requiring that a mentally incapacitated person be kept in local authority accommodation, contrary to the wishes of both her and her mother, the Court said that this approach was not inconsistent with Article 8 of the European Convention on Human Rights. A specific exception is made in Article 5 (the right to liberty) to permit the state to restrict the personal freedom of persons of unsound mind, so long as such interference is otherwise justifiable. The welfare of the patient was the overriding issue and a right to respect for family life did not allow individuals, however closely related and well-intentioned, to create situations which jeopardised others' welfare. Its purpose was to assure, within proper limits, the entitlement of individuals to the benefit of whatever was benign and positive in family life. It was potentially an **obligation** of the court and the local authority to protect the individual's welfare, given the 'positive duty' doctrine found in European Court cases on Article 8 of the Convention.

It is worth noting that joining claims under Articles 3 and 8 with Article 14 (the right to enjoy Convention rights and freedoms without unjustified discrimination) may lead to litigation about policy differences for service provision on the basis of age. Many local authorities in the UK treat those over sixty-five as for some reason entitled to a lower quality of life, through tighter eligibility criteria or lower cost guideline rates for domiciliary packages. Such age 'cut-offs' risk falling foul of the Article 14 prohibition on discrimination, if the provision of services is deemed to engage the human right of respect for private and family life, since article 14 cannot found a free-standing discrimination claim.

Article 5 *(right to liberty and security of the person)*

Article 5 has already been used in cases about the detention of individuals under UK mental health legislation. Article 5(1) of the Convention provides:

> *no one shall be deprived of his liberty save in the following cases and in accordance with a procedure prescribed by law…(e) the lawful detention of persons for the prevention of the spread of infectious diseases, of persons of unsound mind, alcoholics or drug addicts or vagrants…*

At first glance, the concept of 'unsound mind' might appear to be a rather vague 'catch-all' for almost any mental disorder, but the European Court of Human Rights was quick to lay down parameters. In *Winterwerp v. Netherlands*,[35] for example, the Court made it clear that the deprivation of liberty could not be justified simply because someone's views or behaviour deviated from the norms prevailing in a particular society. The disorder must be of a degree to justify the deprivation of liberty, whether for the individual's own safety or the safety of others.

Further, detention will only be justified for as long as the condition persists. A failure to provide a proper system of review of the detainee's condition would be a breach of Article 5(4) which provides for a speedy determination of the lawfulness of the detention. Thus as long ago as 1981, in *X v United Kingdom*,[36] the European Court of Human Rights held that the fact that a long term mentally ill patient could apply for the issue of a writ of habeas corpus[37] was not sufficient to satisfy the requirements of Article 5(4), given the limited scope of review undertaken by the court in habeas corpus proceedings.

Article 6 *(fairness in certain types of decision-making)*

Article 6 will be of central significance in social services provision if the decision as to whether a client needs a service amounts to *'a determination of a civil right'*. It would require a fair, public, reasonably speedy, independent and impartial procedure, which is singularly absent from the UK's social services assessment system. A look at the European jurisprudence shows that social security benefits, triggered by qualification under statutory *criteria*, amount to civil rights.[38] However, eligibility for social *services* in the UK is much more discretionary (see above, first section). The first-time determination of a need for a service might not engage a civil right because entitlement depends on meeting *discretionary* criteria, but the courts have held that there is a duty to *maintain* an existing careplan, pending lawful reassessment. It thus seems arguable that the continuation of services may be

---

35. (1979) 2 EHRR 387
36. (1981) 4 EHRR 188. See also *Van der Leer v Netherlands* (1990) 12 EHRR 567
37. A process which permits the court to inquire into the cause and legality of a person's detention
38. See the case of *Salesi v Italy* February 26, 1993 Series A, No. 257-E; (1998) 26 EHRR 187

seen as a civil right, requiring an Article 6 compliant procedure before any changes can be made. Whether the Courts will hold that access to the legal remedy of judicial review supplies any want of independence or impartiality at the first level of decision-making, or will hold that the absence of an independent Social Care Tribunal system is wholly incompatible with the European Convention, remains to be seen.

The virtual immunity from suit for negligence enjoyed by local authorities in the exercise of certain statutory functions may well come under attack from Article 6 challenges, following the European Court decision in *Osman v UK*.[39] The applicants were family members of a murder victim, who alleged negligence on the part of the police in the investigation. Public policy in English law gives police immunity from suit in such circumstances and therefore a domestic remedy was not available to the applicants. The European Court held that the blanket immunity applied to negligence suits against the police was a disproportionate interference with the applicants' right of access to justice. This approach was followed by the European Commission in its report on what was the *X v Bedfordshire CC* case.[40]

The Human Rights Act 1998

Since the European Convention already provides the rights and protections given 'further effect' by this important and radical piece of UK legislation, why will the introduction of the Human Rights Act 1998 make a difference?

This writer believes that the Act has the potential to bring about a radical culture change, in terms of both the *number* and *source* of complaints or claims which are made to social services authorities, and also the means for ensuring accountability of people working in the field. The driving forces behind this change are the introduction of cash sums for actions which are found to be unjustified interferences with people's human rights, and the potential for convenient local adjudication of claims about human rights, in any type of court or tribunal in front of which an authority might find itself. It will not be difficult for ordinary members of the public to allege a breach of human rights in the social services field.

Discretionary decisions (i.e. all policy-making, actions, omissions and decisions about individual entitlement) are now potentially challengeable for breach of human rights. For example, a decision that someone should be cared for in a residential setting, rather than at home, may be said to be an interference with someone's right to respect for their private, home or family life (Article 8). It may, however, be **'justified'** because of the economics of the situation or the protection of health or the rights or freedoms of others. If the reasoning process has taken account of relevant considerations, and the decision is found to be 'proportionate', then no breach will have occurred, whatever the outcome. But that does not mean that members of the public will not suggest, in good faith, that their human rights have been ignored.

Secondly, a new test for judicial scrutiny has been introduced by the Act, namely 'proportionality', for the determination of human rights issues. This test is formless enough to enable the UK's judges, if they should feel so inclined, to impose higher standards of evidence, reasoning and balance on administrators than is presently the tradition in the field of judicial review. Whereas the traditional test of 'unreasonableness' requires judges to hold off unless a public body has done something outrageous (or otherwise unlawful or unfair), such that the complainant has a high hurdle to surmount, the new test at the very least requires public officials to go further in establishing that they *had good reasons* for doing what they did and that they took human rights into consideration at the time. This new test is bound to give judges a taste for closer supervision of administrators in all but the most sensitive, specialist fields of decision making, and will increase pressure towards standardised recording of reasoning processes. As one prominent commentator has said, 'if you want to retain a margin of appreciation, you're going to have to earn it!'[41]

Thirdly, the European analysis of some of the human rights given further effect by the UK Human Rights Act has long been that acting compatibly does not merely mean refraining from unnecessary interference in people's lives: the European Court has held that some of the rights and freedoms necessarily require positive action on the part of the State to further or to

39. Case of *Osman v United Kingdom* Application No 23452/94 (1998). (1999) Crim. LR 82
40. *S and Others v United Kingdom* Application No 29392/95 (1999) (unreported)
41. Tony Child, Solicitor, Rowe and Maw's Public Law Group, London

protect people's enjoyment of those rights. This means that authorities are open to claims of breach of human rights for deciding **not** to do something (e.g. for purely budget-related reasons) when it leaves someone unsupported or protected. The annual round of budget negotiations between councillors can no longer be regarded as determinative of an authority's lawful discharge of its functions: they have to be prepared to prioritise certain discretionary functions above others, as well as ensuring that duties are properly funded.

The Act achieves its aims by requiring all courts and tribunals to take account of European jurisprudence on human rights, and there are over 50 years' worth of decisions included in that body of material. This will inevitably lengthen legal proceedings, for the first couple of years at least. Both sides have to be given the chance to argue what the European approach would be, before the UK judge can decide whether to follow European law or develop a special UK rights culture, on a case by case basis. Lawyers working for clients and social services departments have to become familiar with this body of law as well, for otherwise, correspondence about human rights will be based on moral, ethical, professional or even party political notions of what human rights *should* mean, rather on what they *do* mean, in law, for everyone.

The Act further requires everyone to read and give effect to primary and secondary legislation in such a way as is compatible with human rights, where that is at all 'possible'. This means that in a case of ambiguous UK legislation, the authority has to know enough European human rights law to act in accordance with whatever interpretation of the UK law is human rights *compliant*, rather than inconsistent.

The Act makes it unlawful for public authorities, as defined by the Act, to act inconsistently with human rights, unless one of the statutory excuses applies (i.e. where a statute or something made under statute positively demands the action or decision in question). 'Unlawful' in this sense means both *ultra vires* (outside the authority's legal powers) and *sounding in damages*, just as if a breach of human rights was a civil law wrong such as negligence,

trespass or nuisance. Public authorities are defined so as to include courts and tribunals and other entities so long as certain of their functions 'are functions of a public nature'. The question of what is a public authority will be for the courts to determine on an incremental basis, but local authorities clearly come within the definition of 'public authority'. The more difficult question is whether the private sector entities, charities and individuals which Councils now use to perform their statutory service provision functions, also count as public authorities, and hence owe a direct duty to the client, to abide by European Convention human rights principles. The likelihood is that residential home providers do not count as 'public authorities', because they act purely as independent contractors under contract with councils who have ongoing duties to their clients.[42] However, domiciliary provision under contract as an **agent** of the authority, by a voluntary body or other provider, under s30 National Assistance Act 1948, might lead to the opposite conclusion under the Human Rights Act 1998, for no good reason of policy or principle.

These questions are likely to take some years to workout, since local authorities tend to avoid litigation by means of reconsideration or compromise, rather than risk public odium and bad publicity in controversial cases. Ironically, therefore, the uncertainty about the impact of the Act in this field may well drag on for longer than is necessary. It is not merely professional enthusiasm behind this writer's plea for serious consideration as to the longer term benefits of getting points litigated and resolved sooner rather than later!

Conclusions

As this chapter demonstrates, the law and good social work practice now, more than ever, go hand in hand. Local authorities and social work professionals who make practice and policy decisions without due regard to the enormous significance of judicial review law, the ever-increasing impact of the European Convention on Human Rights, and their own 'public authority' status under the UK's Human Rights Act, not only do a disservice to their clients, but expose themselves to costly and damaging litigation.

---

42. See *R v Servite Houses, ex parte Goldsmith*, 12 May 2000 (unreported)

Questions for Further Consideration

Social work decisions and practices in the UK are increasingly being determined by reference to legal in contrast to therapeutic processes, to what extent:

1. Is this tendency apparent in other national welfare systems?

2. Are definitions of human rights, decisions about vulnerable persons' best interests and the duties of welfare agencies decided by reference to the law?

3. Are social workers educated for and experienced in working in legal contexts?

Chapter Seven

Social Work and Economic Policy: The Netherlands an Example

Geert van der Laan

Introduction

Today, two tendencies dominate the restructuring of welfare and the conditions for social work in Europe. Firstly, the withdrawal by the state of responsibility for protection against all forms of social risks and the introduction of policies aimed at promoting self-determination and personal responsibility. Here, the idea of *collective* risk and responsibility across the population has been replaced by that of the *individual* accepting personal risk and taking personal responsibility in the social sphere. Secondly, the introduction of market principles into the domain of welfare as a remedy against bureaucratic rigidity. Here, the 'self-regulating' capacity of market forces is supposed to make social care more efficient and effective.

These two tendencies are closely intertwined. As public institutions withdraw from many types of provision, a more central and guiding role is given to market forces. As the state's protection disappears, individuals have to survive as consumers in the market. Increasingly, social workers are enlisted to help in achieving this individualised and market orientated approach to welfare. For example, it is now often assumed that an important aspect of social work interventions is to enable clients to be more economically active and, where possible, to enter the labour market (Van der Laan, 2000).

In this context, social work has to re-construct its identity, to re-consider what constitutes the 'social' in social work and what is an appropriate relationship between social work and social policy. Furthermore, social work must address such fundamental questions at a time when the survival of the profession may be threatened by new social alignments in which market forces dictate which aspects of its role, form and function will continue to be legitimised. In effect, a radical re-conceptualisation and restructuring of welfare regimes in Europe presents a major challenge to the professional quality of social work. In recent years, social work seems to have responded somewhat defensively to this challenge. Social workers appear more or less confused by the fast and far-reaching changes in both the western welfare systems and those in the former communist states of Europe.

In the Netherlands, reform of the welfare state is strongly connected to the restructuring of the economy. In this chapter, relationship between social work and social policy will be analysed in the context of current economic reform. This lays bare the extent to which social work is expected to provide an economic function in society, to the extent that social workers are engaged in the task of helping clients to become economically active.

The rise of the Dutch welfare state

As De Swaan (1988: p 210) has observed, the history of Dutch social policy, in comparison to that in other countries, has been one of 'fragmentary and halting legislation'. For example, although a worker's compensation law was adopted in 1901, it took another 12 years for an invalidity law to be passed. Implementation of this 1913 sickness insurance act was delayed until 1930, and a compulsory national unemployment insurance scheme was not introduced until 1952. In contrast to the initial slow pace of development, the second half of the 20th century saw rapid growth in Dutch social welfare provision. By the 1970s, Dutch social welfare expenditure, as a percentage of gross national income, was the highest in the world. De Swaan explains that the slow start in the growth of welfare provision was due to the late arrival of industrialisation in the Netherlands, (a factor that also led to the late emergence of a labour movement).

The 1901 workmen's compensation act, (largely inspired by German legislation that had been introduced by Bismarck), was passed by the last liberal-conservative government in the Netherlands. From then, until the 1990s, the Protestant and Catholic parties occupied a pivotal position in the Dutch parliament. Both of these parties were determined to curb class conflict through ensuring the tightly knit organisation of society along confessional lines: a phenomenon that came to be known as 'pillarisation' (versuiling) (see Adams, Erath and Shardlow, 2000: Chapter 7).

Following the Second World War, the Netherlands experienced rapid industrialisation, and the religious parties began to lose their influence in politics. Yet, the rather corporatist pre-war system of consultation, between employers, employees and 'crown members' (state delegates), proved extremely effective in the creation of the welfare state. The continuous rivalry between 'confessionals' (religious parties) and social democrats helped to accelerate the legislative process. During the 1960s, two major new laws were enacted, the National Assistance Act and the Disability Insurance Act, which were to trigger an unprecedented explosion of income transfers. These laws were intended to be the crowning achievement of a great project of social security legislation. However, as a consequence of their generous provisions they were increasingly applied in the 1980s, in ways not foreseen or intended by the original legislators, as remedies for a number of difficult social problems. The disability act, for instance, was used to accommodate workers made redundant following re-organisation by commercial companies. Such conditions exposed the negative features of the Dutch culture of consultation as these disingenuous methods had received the approval of both employees and employers. Together with the crown members, they had a decisive voice in the supervisory bodies.

The subsequent crisis of the Dutch welfare state in the 1980s, and the harsh restructuring measures implemented in the 1990s, can thus be understood in the light of these earlier events.

Social work and social policy

During the past century, the relationship between social work and social policy in the Netherlands has not been exactly harmonious. In practice, social work has focused mainly on care and assistance to individuals and families at the micro-level, while social policy has concentrated on the macro-level. Yet, the core component of social work, the classic social casework approach, could also be interpreted simply as social policy in the form of individualised, 'tailor-made to suit the individual' assistance. In this sense, social workers have followed the requirements of social policy, such as income policy, housing policy and family policy. In so doing, they gave expression to the societal element in social work, by helping individual people to function in society.

Although, not everyone is fully agreed on such a conceptualisation of social work—as the individualisation of social policy: as many social workers approach social issues largely in terms of the need to change social structures. Nonetheless, the role of social work in strengthening the individual capacities of its clients has returned as the key professional concern in recent years.

Three developments have given a new impulse to the relations between casework and social policy in the Netherlands:

- The first is the current trend to bring social policy closer to the people, for example, as in the creation of 'local social policy'. This is already a significant step towards a customer-orientated form of provision.

- Second, there is the renewed tendency to individualise social welfare provision. The individual assessment of referrals and the idea of tailor-made provision as a guiding principle in policy implementation have led to a greater focus on the micro-level in social work practice. This has seriously jeopardised the quality of the work of social workers in their direct contacts with clients.

- Thirdly, the practice of individual assessment has tended to erode traditional forms of organised solidarity. Individual duties have been set against collective rights. Stiff demands are made on the responsibility of individuals to secure their own resources in society, but responsibility that is more individual also entails that more risks are borne by individuals. Many of the more vulnerable members of society have insufficient resources to prepare adequately for these risks. Hence, from time to time they have to fall back on social workers and other providers of welfare. The challenge for social work is how to meet these needs without reverting to the paternalistic practices of former times.

The social and the psychological

A concern with the personal side of social problems need not be exclusively paternalistic in nature. Berteke Waaldijk in her book on the history of social work in the Netherlands and the United States (Waaldijk, 1996: p 79) refers to developments in US social work in the early 20th century. She cites many historians who have linked pre-First World War social work in the United States to movements for social and political reform: movements in which social workers were involved quite intensively in the shaping of social policy. In the years after the First World War, however, 'method-based work' with individual cases rapidly gained ground, with social casework proclaimed as the essence of the profession.

Therefore, an antithesis between individual social work and ideological positions came to dominate the historiography of social work in the United States. Opinions about what contribution social work was making to social policy varied, depending on the political and social forces dominant at the time. Although some observers condemned the gradual 'psychologisation' of social work, others welcomed the introduction of psychoanalysis as it was claimed that it would offer social work a scientific legitimacy. In the early twentieth century, a scientific approach was seen as essential to developing a professional self-awareness that could resist being dominated by social policy imperatives (ibid: p 283). In the Netherlands, by contrast, social reform and the creation of the welfare state have been treated as part of economic and political history rather than social work history.

According to Waaldijk, this was because in Dutch history one does not encounter female community educators articulating progressive ideas about social welfare until far later than in the US. Here in the Netherlands, social policy was men's business, and social work became the business of women. Later debates on social reform were dominated by communists and social democrats, but in those circles, there was no great interest in social work. Other contemporary observers even argued that casework might not even be needed at all, since the level of Dutch social welfare far surpassed that in the US. Waaldijk tersely summarises the difference as follows:

> Whereas in the United States the need for psychology was not questioned, in the Netherlands the need for social welfare was beyond discussion.
>
> (Waaldijk, 1996: p 291)

Following the Second World War, social work did figure more prominently in the Dutch political discourse on national reconstruction. One indication of this was the (albeit temporary) existence of a national government ministry of social work. Dutch historians have nonetheless devoted more attention to the disciplinary aspects of social work than to its role in social policy. In their view, Waaldijk concludes, social workers had no more than a walk-on role in the development of the social welfare system, but

they did play a leading role when it came to disciplining the people!

The debate about individualisation versus collectivisation is certainly linked in many ways to the issue of paternalism and discipline. In a collective approach to social problems, the rights and duties of individual citizens are necessarily formulated in very general terms. This approach relieved the officials who carry out social policy of the need to make drastic individual assessments. In this sense, the introduction of social welfare measures was, especially in the post-World War Two era, a good way of relegating all sorts of paternalistic practices to the history books. Now, since the 1980s, the collectivist expressions of social solidarity have come under pressure, and social policy is subject to renewed individualising tendencies, disciplinary practices are again becoming commonplace. For example, under the policy of 'activation', social workers are expected to apply pressure and coercion to get social benefit claimants back to work.

The rationality of policy and its implementation

Van der Veen (1990) has argued that the rationality of a policy cannot simply be translated into the rationality of its implementation. Implementing policies or legislation entails a social process, guided only in part by rules and laws. In Van der Veen's analysis, the social order is a social construction which is continuously being produced and reproduced in the social action of human beings. To understand adequately the workings and the consequences of policy, one has to focus primarily on how policy is implemented through the day-to-day contacts between clients and public officials or professionals. In reality, policy takes shape within these contacts and in the decisions reached therein. The process of implementing policy can be characterised more as a social process than as a rational process of logical application of principles.

The rules that develop out of a policy are context-specific. That is, the real meaning of these specific rules is contingent on the situations wherein they are applied: by definition, such rules are unspecified and ambiguous to a certain extent. In some cases, the regulations can only be concretely elaborated by people in the lower echelons, since they have the requisite professional or technical knowledge. This places social workers in the role of intermediary between the management of the implementing organisation and the clients who are undergoing assessment. Given the professional activity involved in filling in this discretionary space, it is very difficult for management to exercise control over the outcome.

According to Van der Veen, bureaucracies strive to achieve a rational organisational order governed by formal rationality and guided by rules. Decisions are based on generalised rules applied by officials to individual cases. It is simply a question of logical application. Formal rationality assumes unambiguous rules, knowledge of the individual factors relevant to the decision, unambiguous organisational objectives and insight into the potential consequences of the decision for individual cases. In theory, a bureaucratic model of government policy implementation holds no place for a discretionary space for public officials. After all, officials are not supposed to make policy decisions (Van der Veen, 1990: p 139). However, since no two situations are alike, he questions whether the discretionary space can ever effectively be eliminated. Strict application of regulations will always generate problems, however differentiated the regulations may be. This is because the reasoning applied by the people implementing the policy is not rule-based, but case-based (Van der Laan, 1996 and 1999).

Social casework is the historical outcome of this case-based rationality. A case-based line of reasoning begins with the uniqueness of each case and then generalises by recognising common patterns. This makes it theoretically possible to base generalised policy on case-based reasoning. Because of their 'antenna function' vis-à-vis social problems, social workers can 'talk back' to policy, thus guiding or correcting policy from the bottom up. Unfortunately, there are few known examples of this, but a project in The Hague comes close to exemplifying this process (Van der Laan, 2000). The problem remains how to avoid various paternalistic practices during the process of individualisation. For this, too, we can find lessons in the history of social casework.

Social work as a basic discipline of social policy

Roebroek (1999) regards social work from a historical point of view as a basic discipline of social policy. He untangles the concept of social policy into three main strands:

- Regulating labour relations and the labour market (for short, labour).
- Guaranteeing security of livelihood (income).
- Structuring the necessary conditions for social life and the life contexts of the members of society (care, social participation, emancipation, health and environment).

These three components of social policy interrelate in specific ways, but the nature of these relationships and the tensions between them are constantly changing. Not only the relationships between the components are subject to change, but also the specificity and the forms of the components themselves.

The historical starting point of a welfare state can be defined as the moment at which the nation state first undertakes activities and interventions in the areas of social security, labour market policy, education, health care, public housing, social work, emancipation and environmental policy. In the Netherlands, this was the period between 1870 and 1900. Although the welfare state then accounted for no more than a tiny proportion of the activities and interventions of the state (and an equally marginal part of its expenditures), it was a beginning.

In this strictly analytical sense, Roebroek argues, social work was part of social policy, and it was later part of the welfare state too. Its more precise position was as a component structuring the necessary conditions for social life and the life contexts of the members of society. In a historical sense, social work had actually been part of social policy since the first forms of social policy became visible in the medieval 'hospitalitas'. This means that social work historically acquired its form and content from two sources: the social and political activities of classes, groups of citizens and individual citizens at local, regional and later national levels; and its specific relationships to labour and income, the other two components of social policy.

Roebroek believes that social work can now prepare itself for a return to its position as a basic discipline of social policy. This would mean involving itself not just with the lowest rungs of society, but with problems at the heart of the working world, where new forms of occupational illness and new participation problems have underlined the need for reflection on the content and form of social policy. This would include working conditions, security, health, training, child-rearing and care, in short, employability.

Individualisation and collectivisation

The tension between individualisation and collectivisation and the segregation of material from non-material problems have been issues since the very inception of social security legislation. An analysis by Schell (1995) of the history of the Dutch National Assistance Act has shown that conflicting tendencies have always been present. When, during the post-war expansion of social security, 'the needy' became redefined as fully fledged members of society, this transformed them from objects of care to holders of rights. In the material realm, the role of private and church initiative was gradually curtailed. As Schell has observed of general social work in that period:

> *Employees in those circles set out in search of new work, and they found it mainly in non-material assistance. This helped to crystallise the differentiation between material and non-material assistance.*
>
> (Schell, 1995: p 12)

It was not until the mid-1960s that these modified ideas and practices in the struggle against poverty gained legal status with the adoption of the National Assistance Act. This provided for material assistance only. Non-material aid remained outside the scope of the legislation. The responsible ministers asserted that the former poor relief practices, which allowed social work a good deal of leeway to link non-material problems with material ones, were founded on incorrect assumptions. Sociologists had argued convincingly that individuals and their personal environments were normally not to blame for poverty. Furthermore, people who needed social work often needed other types of services too, such as health care, sheltered employment and socio-cultural activities. So why should financial support be linked to social work?

No one wished to deny the connection between material and non-material problems, and the social services were to give 'personal attention to the individual in question'. This did have some consequences for the job descriptions of in-house social workers within the social services. However, as can be seen below, social services departments increasingly took on the character of 'benefit factories'.

Over the years, appeals for nation-wide standardisation of national assistance norms regularly alternated with calls for a more individualised approach—in other words, customised provision at municipal levels. The essential issue being whether entitlement to national assistance was a collective right of citizens with no source of income, or alternatively should every case be assessed on its own merits? This debate re-emerged in the 1990s. For example, in his book on the 'heart of the welfare state', Kees Schuyt (1991) argued that a system of administrative solidarity has grown up in the Netherlands:

> *The fundamental principle of solidarity, the moral basis of the welfare state, has become narrowed down to an administrative norm, impersonally applied by professional service providers in an array of bureau's and agencies, which are highly autonomised and fragmented amongst themselves.*
>
> (Kees Schuyt, 1991: p 10)

According to Schuyt a distinctive characteristic of the present welfare state is its:

> *...inability to localise the neediest and most vulnerable members of society, except as administrative categories of anonymous persons.*
>
> (Kees Schuyt, 1991: p 11)

The peak of this trend was reached in the 1980s, when, in the early 1980s, the social services departments came under extreme pressure due to a tremendous growth in the numbers of benefit claimants. The prevailing economic recession, the government spending cuts and the implementation of the long overdue restructuring of trade and industry had brought about mass redundancies and given rise to new forms of poverty.

Many social services departments did hive off their last remnants of non-material assistance to general social work or mental health care agencies, and retreated into their core activity of granting benefits. They were transformed into 'benefit factories'. This characterisation of a social service agency as a production line is derived from the 'conveyor-belt' style of work that was increasingly performed by such agencies. Strong appeals were made in the mid-1980s for the introduction of market principles into the social sector, and business administration terminology came into vogue. In 1986, for example, the social services department in the town of Groningen announced that non-material assistance would be dropped from its service package. The change in policy was couched in terms such as 'control over the production process', 'effective management', 'efficient organisational structure' and 'flexible personnel policies'. The new policies were necessary because the massive influx of clients had 'resulted in an untenable situation', in which, as one employee put it, 'some of us got depressed and others aggressive'.

The inflow of clients also altered the attitudes of the in-house social workers towards the relationship between material and non-material assistance. As one social worker commented in the magazine *Welzijnsweekblad* (7th February, 1986):

> *Eight years ago I stood nearer to the group that claim you can't separate material and non-material help.*

However, he is now convinced that the burgeoning clientele necessitates a different approach:

> *We've got to make the throngs of people who pour into the building daily more manageable.*

Although, he still doesn't regard this as a radical about-turn:

> *No, I've not lost faith. It's just that my antennae now point in a different direction. I think material aid is of equal value to non-material aid. By scrapping the non-material help we can improve the quality of the material help. We want to deliver a better product.*

Since then, the new realism, in this particular department, has borne fruit. Press reports mentioned that the Groningen social services department was amongst the best in the country. A study of 21 Dutch social services departments carried out by the Consumers' Association found that the one in Groningen particularly excelled in 'the provision of information to clients'. One might summarise the policies of such departments as follows: the transition from *discontented clients* to *satisfied consumers*. It has always been the ambition of the municipal social services departments to work at the intersection of social work and social security policy, but social security policy in the 1980s forced the social work function out of the picture.

Renewed individualisation

By the end of the 1980s, the government acknowledged that the balance had tipped too far in the direction of national standardisation. It gravitated towards the view that the principle of individualised provision, one of the essential premises of the National Assistance Act, had fallen into neglect. Also, the function of benefit was not to be confined to filling gaps in subsistence costs, but it was meant to reopen the perspectives of claimants to eventually support themselves i.e. to become economically active.

This was part of government policy to stimulate recipients to seek gainful employment. This new policy was triggered by the noticeable, it unintended consequences of the Dutch welfare state.

The adoption of the new National Assistance Act in 1995 marked a shift in policy towards a more individual approach to social security. One expression of this is the new requirement that single mothers with children over the age of five should seek paid employment. The various obstacles to this, such as possible psycho-social problems, are intended to be removed with the aid of social work counselling. Here the declared function of social work intervention is to help make the recipient of help become economically active. The new policy attempts to turn the safety net of the welfare state, which had been used too much as a 'hammock', into a 'trampoline' (see Adams, Erath and Shardlow, 2000: Chapter 7). This shift implied that the in-house social workers in the municipal social services, who still remained, were to be approached again on the basis of their particular and specific role and function in respect of particular groups of clients, and that social workers elsewhere (i.e. general social workers) were to be increasingly drawn into the attempts to reintegrate benefit recipients into society, mainly through paid employment.

Encouraging the social participation of clients has, of course, been one of the objectives of social workers from the earliest days of the profession, so it was only proper that they should be approached in terms of the task of economic re-integration. Unfortunately, showing people the way to achieve paid employment has become a very difficult task since the economic restructuring programmes of the 1980s. When compared to neighbouring countries, the Netherlands boasts high labour productivity, but also a low rate of labour participation. Briefly stated, the small part of the population that works, works very hard and efficiently, while the other part of the population is relegated to the sidelines because no lesser-skilled jobs are available or because they cannot keep up with the high pace of production. Work has become a 'high achievement activity'. The heavy demands of work make people more vulnerable to injuries, or consigns them to the 'unproductive bench' because of poor performance. The authorities therefore initiated a policy designed to boost the rate of labour participation and to rescue benefit recipients out of their passivity and social isolation.

Under the influence of all these developments, social work is now being called on more and more to fulfil societally defined tasks, such as mediating in labour market re-entry, arranging housing and helping to curb the 'nuisance' of so-called 'deviant people'. This means that the therapeutic skills of social workers have to be applied in new ways. They can no longer just give therapy in their consulting rooms to well-motivated clients. They have to be more assertive, reaching out and working with unmotivated clients to meet the economic imperatives of social policy. Therapeutic skills will now have to be put to use 'around the kitchen table', for instance while giving budget guidance, using household account books with people with debt problems.

Many policy documents pose a challenge for social workers, that of 'activating benefit claimants into social participation'. However, there are many snags in *practice* to the achievement of this goal. For example, benefit recipients may not only have psychological or interpersonal problems, but also many will have debt problems too. A large proportion of clients who are theoretically eligible for special employment projects have been found to be facing such serious financial problems that the resolution of these problems have to take priority over and above work experience projects. In the following sections, a more detailed overview of the economic reforms and the implications for social work in Holland is presented.

The Dutch welfare state: from Dutch disease to Dutch comfort

In 1986, the Swedish sociologist Therborn dubbed the Netherlands as perhaps the most spectacular employment failure in the advanced capitalist world. In 1984, unemployment had reached a record number of 800,000, nearly 14 per cent of the labour force. An almost equal number of workers had been eased out of the labour market through disability benefits and early retirement. The Netherlands was a prime example of Esping-Andersen's pathology of welfare without work, which is typical for continental European welfare states. The expression 'Dutch disease' made its appearance in economic textbooks as an example of expensive and unsustainable public welfare politics. The then Prime Minister Lubbers proclaimed in the 1980s that the Netherlands had become a 'sick country' (Visser and Hemerijck, 1997). Ten years later, Dutch policies again draw

international attention. Jean-Claude Trichet, president of the French Central Bank, makes mention of a 'Dutch miracle' of fiscal rectitude, welfare and labour market reform, social consensus and job growth (Visser and Hemerijck, 1997).

In the same text, Visser and Hemerijck used Trichet's statement as an inspiration for the title of their book, *The Dutch Miracle: Job Growth, Welfare Reform and Corporatism in the Netherlands*. In this book, they describe how in an attempt to trim the sails to the prevailing economic wind, the policy of wage moderation was developed. Above all, this was an adjustment to changing conditions in the world markets, which was necessary because the Dutch economy had developed into a service economy with productivity rates per person consistently below those in manufacturing. This policy resulted in strong job growth, the recovery of profitable firms and, last but not least, strong union membership growth after a decade of decline. In addition, a redistribution of work through a general reduction of labour time (i.e. the average time spent in work by a person during the week) has played a small role. More important has been the extraordinary growth of part-time employment and flexibility. Eventually, Dutch trade unions have come to support these changes.

The 1981–1983 recession

The policy changes started in the beginning of the 1980s. The 1981–1983 recession in Holland was exceptionally severe, characterised by:

- National income declined during eight consecutive quarters.

- The net investment rate, which had decreased from 7 per cent in the decade before the first oil crisis (1973) to 4.6 per cent in the second half of the 1970s, slumped to a mere 2 per cent.

- One of every 25 firms in manufacturing went bankrupt.

- Between 1981 and 1983, 300,000 jobs were shed, mostly in industry and nearly all full-time.

- Unemployment soared at a rate of 10,000 per month, to a record of 800,000 in 1984 and seemed unstoppable.

- By 1989, the number of people receiving disability benefits threatened to reach the staggering figure of one million, i.e. one-sixth of the employed labour force.

- The trade unions lost 17 per cent of their members and of the remaining membership nearly one-quarter was out of work, on social benefits or in retirement.
- The average disposable income of employed workers fell in three consecutive years (1981–1983) by nearly 10 per cent. Social benefits fell even more.

The Netherlands shared the structural problems of most continental welfare models, these may be summarised as follows:

- the adjustment to the changing conditions of international competition
- the challenges of industrial change
- a vicious circle of high productivity growth and job decline
- an ageing population and longer life expectancy
- rising health costs and health risks
- changing family patterns
- individualisation of life styles
- strong bias towards protection of steady employment
- a presumption of male breadwinners and subsidised labour exclusion

Policy makers were faced with the following vicious circle: the social security budget of the Netherlands was already proportionally the highest in the world. If social security expenditure rises rapidly and is financed out of earnings-related contributions or taxation, then the difference between gross and net pay significantly increases. This adds to labour costs, threatens the price competitiveness of firms and undermines the support of unions and workers for wage moderation. This type of mechanism is hard to change. How could the politics of welfare reform in the Netherlands be successful?

Visser and Hemerijck (1997) argue that in advanced welfare states the politics of economic and industrial adjustment, social protection, and labour market management appear as three institutionally separated policy domains:

- *Industrial rights* are connected with industrial relations. Industrial rights are established through labour law, collective bargaining and employee participation.
- *Social rights* are politically disengaged from the labour market. Social rights serve to protect the non-working population: older people and people with disabilities, and address the right of participation and integration into society. Social rights are institutionalised in social security entitlements and public assistance.
- *The right to work* addresses the right of participation and integration into society by paid labour. The right to work may be anchored in a public commitment to uphold full employment that is underpinned by an active labour market policy. In a capitalist economy, this right is crucially dependent upon the voluntary co-operation of autonomous employing firms. These three separate domains are located in different places in the academic division of labour: industrial relations, social policy studies and labour market economics.

From this analysis Visser and Hemerijck developed the hypothesis that the corporatist format of the Dutch economy facilitated a problem solving style of policy making, i.e. that policies which recognised the interests of different groups inform and assist with implementing centrally agreed policies. A model in which, when learning is blocked and when corporatism stifles reform in one policy domain, allows for organised support for fundamental change in another domain. They also argue that there are obvious limits to disengaging the policy domain of social rights from that of economic adjustment and labour market efficiency. They try to bridge the gap which divides the study of industrial relations and welfare state development, and show how the problems and solutions in the three policy domains, wage formation, social policy and labour market policy, are related. The three policy shifts at these domains, although embedded in different institutional surroundings and involving different actors, are interrelated and could not succeed on their own.

Wage moderation

The return to wage moderation took place in the early 1980s and was above all an adjustment to changing conditions in the world markets. This was important because, as stated above, the Dutch economy had turned into a service economy. Wage moderation entailed two political exchanges:

1. Between workers and employers: wage moderation was traded against a modest reduction in annual and weekly working hours.

2. Between workers and employers on the one side and the government on the other: wage restraint was compensated for by lower taxes and social benefits. This helped to maintain spending power and boosted domestic demand, especially in services.

Visser and Hemerijck conclude that this sharp shift in policies occurred within the existing institutional framework of industrial relations. The most important factor being the return of the trade unions to the consensual policy style of the post-war years.

Reform of social security

In the early 1990s there was a major overhaul of social security. This was prepared for by a freezing of the benefits in 1983 and an overhaul of the unemployment insurance in 1987. Major reforms took place in the early 1990s with the tightening of the two main exit routes from the labour market: disability insurance and sickness leave. These routes were a major factor in the low labour market participation rates.

The restructured Social Assistance Act came into force in 1996. Government's intention was to create a stronger link between benefit payment and efforts by the recipient to find suitable work. Thought is now being given to how the financial interests of local authorities can be increased when the amount of assistance is reduced.

The Continued Payment of Salary (during sickness) Act came into force in 1996, largely replacing the Sickness Benefit Act. Since it came into effect, employers have been solely responsible for paying the financial burden of sick leave in their own firms, and therefore are supposed to have a personal stake in reducing such burdens.

In 1997, Parliament passed the Disability Insurance Act. The effect should be that a comprehensive system of contribution differentiation and voluntary own-risk periods is introduced and the disability insurance contributions will in future be purely an employer's contribution.

In 1995, the Unemployment Act further tightened the eligibility criteria. The new law is also geared more directly towards getting people into work. In order to combat abuse and fraud, 1996 saw the coming into force of the Social Security Benefits (fines and recovery) Act.

Labour market policies

From the mid-1990s, the adoption of an active labour market policy gained political currency. Wage (cost) policy was introduced: creating jobs by making labour cheaper. Government policy was concerned with wage cost moderation. Given the concentration of unemployment and non-activity among the low skilled, these measures were designed to reduce the wage cost of jobs at a level at or just above the minimum wage. Hence, the aim was to reduce the gap between the lowest wage categories and the statutory minimum wage. A second policy was to make the job market more flexible in terms of employment contracts and working hours. Government policy was intended to achieve a fair balance between flexibility and security/social protection. Both employers and employees, who increasingly wish to combine paid work with other activities such as caring and education, need more flexibility in terms of working patterns and the duration of the working day.

In the collective sector, some 40,000 extra jobs per year were planned to be created in 1998 and in subsequent years for the long-term benefit-receiving unemployed. These job creation measures are financed in part by money that the persons concerned would otherwise have received in the form of unemployment benefit. The policy is to get people who have 'grown away' from participation in the labour market, back into work eventually: initially via socially useful tasks and regular, unpaid voluntary work.

Because young, poorly qualified people continue to have a weak position in the labour market, it is important to have a special policy for this particular target group. Participation of young people under the Youth Work Guarantee Act increased up to some 250,00 people.

Economic policy was aligned with budgetary policy (with the aim of reducing the budget deficit and the level of debt) to achieve a structural easing of burdens, for the population as well as for business. Later the government tried to make the taxation system more employment-friendly. In addition to a general burden-lowering exercise, employers' contributions at the lower end of the labour market were subject to targeted reduction, by giving employers the right to a reduction in employees' tax and social security contributions.

In 1997, almost a third of employers' contributions at minimum wage level were removed. The aim was to eliminate employers' contributions at minimum wage level. The economic structural policy was concerned with strengthening the market forces and reducing restrictive rules and regulations, with a view to unleashing the economy's inherent dynamism and competitiveness. This was the thinking behind the new legislation on competition, business establishment and shop opening times.

In the mid 1990s additional measures were taken, such as the introduction of the Working Time Act, to improve opportunities for tailoring working hours to the needs of employers and employees, and the introduction of the Law on non-discrimination in respect of working time. Part-time workers are given parity with full-time employees. Existing leave arrangements have been extended and strengthened. The intention is to make way for annual leave and career breaks. In 1997, two bills were passed, one concerning flexibility and security, the other concerning the provision of manpower by contract agencies. The bills incorporate new rules for fixed term contracts, contract labour and the law on dismissal. In 1998, the Job-seekers employment Bill was introduced.

The starting point for activating the entire social insurance system was the improved co-operation between benefit agencies and the public employment service. Unemployed people should deal with a one-stop shop for both benefit and job replacement. The scheme is intended to incorporate both incentives and penalties. In connection with that a performance-related contribution for the public employment service was introduced, concentrating on finding ways back to work, principally for job-seekers already some way removed from the job market. The new Employment Service Act came into force in 1997. The aim here was to achieve a statutory obligation to co-operate between the employment service and the social security agencies.

Recovery

In 1997 the Dutch ministry of Social Affairs gave an overview of the implementation of the annual programme: Employment in The Netherlands (SZW, 1997). In the Netherlands, the growth in per capita GDP between 1973 and 1988 had lagged behind the rest of the EU. Since 1988, growth has been faster than in the rest of the EU. In 1995, real per capita GDP was 6 per cent above the EU average. Over the past ten years, employment in the Netherlands has grown at an average annual rate of 1.8 per cent. This strong growth is expected to continue over the coming years. This employment growth has resulted in a gradual increase over the recent years in the employment participation rate. In 1985, 56 per cent of the potential working population was actually in work, compared with 66 per cent, 10 years later.

In the year 2000, the Netherlands is confronted with a situation of almost full employment. The major remaining problem is the high rate of disability. The significant increase in the net employment rate in the Netherlands is associated with major elements of part-time working. Something like a third of all Dutch employees are now employed part-time. There is also an increase in the economically active population, which grew over the past ten years by an average of 1.6 per cent, compared with 0.4 per cent in the EU as a whole. This is very largely accounted for by the increased rate of employment among women. Therefore, employment is growing more strongly than the active population. Since 1995, the economically non-active/active ratio is declining in the Netherlands.

Not all that glitters is gold

The 'Dutch miracle' is however only a second-best solution. The reforms have brought new opportunities but also new inequalities. Social workers have to face both realities. Important to note is that there still is an element of concealed unemployment in the disability arrangements. Another major problem is that the psychological causes of disability (i.e. stress related 'burn-out') are growing. Sick leave and incapacity for work are still twice as high as in other countries. The fall in unemployment has had a much less marked effect on the fall of the number of benefit recipients. The extent of non-activity is still high, particularly among the unskilled and semi-skilled. Unemployment is twice as prevalent amongst the lower skilled. Half (49%) of all unemployed people have been without work for more than a year. Consequently, the proportion of long-term unemployed people is still higher than in countries like France (40%), Germany (48%) and the United Kingdom (40%) and considerably higher than in the USA (10%) and Japan (20%).

Most of these long term unemployed are people who are unable to keep up the pace required in the producing sectors of our society: work has become a top-class sport. That means that a huge group of citizens are isolated from society for the rest of their lives. As Sygmunt Bauman argued in 1999, in his lecture celebrating the foundation of the first school of social work in Amsterdam in 1899, social work still is faced with an underclass:

> *Let us be clear about it: people traditionally called 'unemployed' are no more the 'reserve army of labour', just like the adult Dutch or Englishman are no more the army reservist about to rejoin the troops in case of military need. We are fooling ourselves if we expect industry to recall the people it made redundant. Such an eventuality would go against the grain of everything relevant to the present day economic prosperity: the principles of flexibility, competitiveness and productivity measured by falling labour costs. And let us face the truth: that even if the new rules of the market game promise a rise in the total wealth of the nation, they also inevitably, make virtually inescapable the widening gap between those in the game and the rest who are left out.*
>
> (Bauman, 2000: p 6)

Bauman states that the poor are not only devalued as producers but also as consumers. They are being re-classified as an 'underclass':

> *…no more a temporary abnormality waiting to be rectified and brought back in line, but a class outside the classes, a category cast permanently off-limits of the 'social system', a category without which the rest of us would be better off and more comfortable than we are now.*
>
> (Bauman, 2000: p 7)

From this perspective, Bauman argues, the principal objective of the welfare state, keeping the local poor in a decent human condition, is utterly devoid of 'economic sense'. The welfare state is on the defensive. It must apologise and continually argue its raison d'être. In so doing, it can hardly use the most popular language of our times, that of interest and profitability. However, no rational arguments can be raised in favour of the continuing existence of the welfare state. The care of the well-being of the 'reserve army of labour' could formerly be presented as a rational step to take, indeed as the only rational choice. However, within the current climate, maintaining the 'underclass' defies all rationality and serves no visible purpose.

One measures the carrying capacity of a bridge by the strength of its weakest pillar. In the view of Bauman, the human quality of a society ought to be measured by the quality of life of its weakest members. Since the essence of all morality is the responsibility which people take for the welfare of others, this also serves as the measure of a society's ethical standards.

The example of the Netherlands suggests that, with the demise of the post war welfare state project, the relationship between national economic and social welfare policies has been brought into a closer alignment. Accordingly, the function of social work, as the concrete implementation of welfare policy, has been re-shaped towards two key tasks:

- Firstly, to contribute to the reactivation and return of welfare benefit claimants to the labour market.

- Secondly, to minimise the social nuisance and cost of the economically redundant 'underclass'.

All forms of social work interventions are now aimed at addressing one or other of these two tasks.

Questions for Further Consideration

1. To what extent does your country appear to be following the same alignment of economic and social policy as the Netherlands?

2. Are social workers in your country increasingly divided into separate roles and projects that are aimed exclusively at either activating the economically viable, or placating the economically redundant?

3. What possibilities can be identified for achieving social inclusion and participation for those who cannot secure a livelihood within the labour market?

4. What opportunities remain for the socially 'disaffected' in a society in which 'work has become a top-class sport' for which there are an increasing number of spectators rather than players; and where social value is measured by economic participation and success?

Chapter Eight

Social Work and the Third Sector: The Example of the German Welfare State

Wolfgang Klug

Introduction

Welfare services are in general provided by three different sectors: The state, the market (commercial enterprises), and charities (not-for-profit or self-help organisations) (see Figure 8.1).

Within any society, the emphasis given to each of these sectors arises from the political consensus about the extent to which each sector should provide help in respect of different forms and cases of welfare. Traditionally, it has been assumed that social policies of political parties and governments in Western Europe can be characterised as: *conservative* or Christian-Democrat, which emphasise the role of the family and community networks (and to a lesser extent more recent forms of self-help movements); *socialist* which emphasise the collective and stress the regulatory role of the state, and *liberal* which emphasise individual rights and responsibilities and rely primarily on market forces (see Chapter 2).

However, these one-dimensional constructions are becoming increasingly irrelevant under the impact of global factors and with the growing recognition and appreciation of the complexity of the inter-relationship between the state, the economy and social forces in determining arrangements for social welfare and social security in any state. Consequently, 'conservatives' whilst still favouring the promotion of self-help under the rubric of subsidiarity, are increasingly challenged by the democratic and economic demands made by 'new social movements'. 'New Labour', in spite of the vestiges of a socialist history, increasingly embraces market forces and seeks to delimit the role of the state which 'neo-liberals' are increasingly inclined to accept as the role played by the state (Evers, 1991: p 221).

As the traditional ideological orientations and boundaries between political groups become blurred, debates over the 'welfare-mix' (see Chapter 1) and the relative importance of and interconnection between the various sectors become increasingly contentious. So too has the implicit alliance between the imperatives of market forces and state regulation emerged more clearly in the form of public service management in conjunction with co-ordination, deregulation and privatisation of direct service provision (Heinze, Olk and Hibert, 1988: p 228).

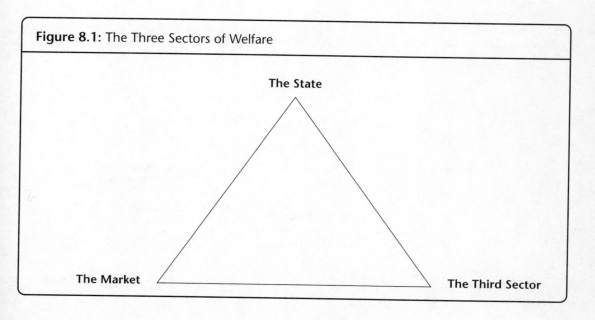

Figure 8.1: The Three Sectors of Welfare

The State

The Market

The Third Sector

Across Europe, the primary political associations and the three key sectors in the welfare complex they have tended to privilege, are undergoing profound changes in response to global economic, political and social forces and emergent market-oriented forces forms beyond the immediate control of the state. Here, I will consider the role of the third sector, that is, not-for profit organisations and their changing role within the German welfare system.

The German model: between individual responsibility and state welfare

In Germany, charitable organisations have played a key role in the implementation of post war social policies by providing a middle way between a completely de-regulated system and a state monopoly system. The German corporatist model of welfare provision, coupled with the application of the so-called 'principle of subsidiarity', has thus enabled the development of a welfare system that avoids both a state-interventionist and a completely market orientated organisation of social work. Consequently, in Germany, there has been an enormous growth of state funded charitable organisations. However, one side effect, apart from achieving stability in the welfare system, has been the creation of cartels of social care. Criticisms of the inefficiency of these cartels have led to a reorientation towards a more market led approach. Increasingly in Germany, as in other

European states, an emergent priority in the arrangement of welfare services is to achieve as efficient a mix as possible between free-market, welfare state and privately organised forms of help. It seems doubtful whether the German system will be able to sustain its traditional approach in the future as both market forces and increased state regulation impact upon reconstituted forms of welfare organisation and provision.

German welfare institutions see themselves as 'intermediate authorities': i.e. they understand their function as being to mediate between the state and the citizens. Moreover, their accepted role is to negotiate citizens' interests with regard to the state and assume a location somewhere between the market and the state, operating neither within the market sector, nor as an agent of the state, as illustrated by Figure 8.2 below.

The emergence of the German welfare system

The 'dual' system of co-operation between public and private welfare and local administration and nation-wide non-governmental organisations, a system which is so characteristic of Germany, has its roots in the way social work was organised following World War One during the period of the so-called Weimar Republic (1918–1933). In the Weimar Constitution of 1919, the state took on the responsibility to safeguard an increasingly well-defined standard of social policy (art. 119; 122; 161;

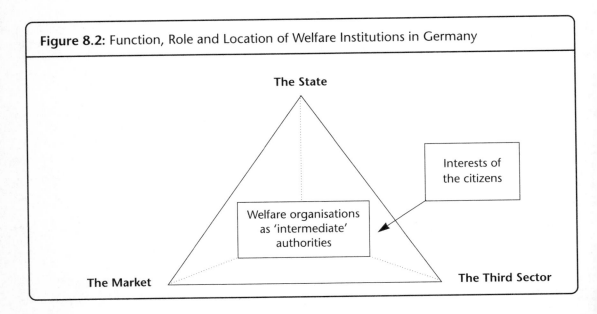

Figure 8.2: Function, Role and Location of Welfare Institutions in Germany

The State

Interests of the citizens

Welfare organisations as 'intermediate' authorities

The Market

The Third Sector

163). To co-ordinate and fulfil these governmental aims, an independent Ministry of Labour (*Reichsarbeitsministerium*, or *RAM* for short) was founded, exemplifying a greater emphasis on social concerns. Gradually, this Ministry expanded its remit. As it took charge of an increasing number of policy areas, a centralised administration was established that imposed standardised criteria for the provision of services (Didicher, 1987: p 227). As Didicher comments:

> How else was the scope of decision making to be made possible and monitored in a co-ordinated way, how could services and their quality be compared and measured, regardless of regional differences and of differences arising from membership of different groups, unless secured by a legislative competency which would be centralised and on a legal basis.

(ibid: p 238)

Matters that had previously been regulated independently by the regions (*Landkreise*) became the responsibility of the state as a whole. To this extent, *RAM* institutionalised the previously fragmented financial and organisational arrangements of services and its effect was to establish a central bureaucracy for the administration of welfare:

> What came about is, in fact, what we have since become accustomed to refer to as a form of 'social justice' and 'sensitivity for social concerns'. For the first time social services were increasingly put under state control, and their status, continuity and permanence, was partially secured in respect of the provision and standards of services by law.

(ibid: p 231)

and

> As it was intended to regulate rights and services, and especially the control of their potential utilisation, in a more detailed, specialised and legally secure way, regulations concerning responsibilities were bound to lead to a maze of regulations, which could not at all function without bureaucratic division of labour, respective organisation of labour, and competencies.

(ibid: p 242)

Some of the consequences of World War One, such as the misery of the mass of war-disabled soldiers, widows, orphans and refugees, gave rise to the realisation by both government agencies and private organisations that the needs of these groups could not be addressed adequately solely by voluntary assistance. Therefore, it would be necessary to develop a systematically organised welfare service employing professional social workers. In particular, the Social Schools for Women (*Soziale*

Frauenschulen), which had been founded at the beginning of the twentieth century, facilitated the subsequent process of professionalisation of welfare services. This professionalisation was achieved by establishing work related 'criteria of achievement' or 'job descriptions' for social work practice. Hence, social work practice was defined with increasing frequency as a methodically planned and professionally executed system of assistance, in place of the unregulated work of voluntary helpers.

Faced with this potential loss of their importance and an increasing governmental influence through the centralisation of welfare, independent welfare organisations sought to re-establish their political influence within the newly developing welfare system. As early as January 1923 the welfare organisations wrote to *RAM*, that they were concerned about their own survival. In order to lobby for their interests, exert more pressure on the *RAM*, establish common objectives, and develop strategic plans, the independent welfare organisations united in 1924 as the 'German League of Independent Welfare Organisations' (*Deutsche Liga der Freien Wohlfahrtspflege*). An internal memorandum of the German Caritas association makes the strategic and power-specific orientation evident. It describes openly its target:

> ...so that the 'groups marching separately' can co-operate efficiently and eventually achieve their task together.

(From Deutsche Liga der Freien Wohlfahrtspflege memorandum 1921, cited in Didicher, 1987: p 363)

The preamble of the league states explicitly that its aim was to secure both the co-operation of public and independent welfare organisations and the independence of non-governmental organisations (cited in Sachße and Tennstedt, 1988: p 166). It was the intention of the organisations to monopolise all social services in co-operation with the public agencies. This intention was also reflected by government in a letter from *RAM* in 1923 that stated these intentions were:

> ...on the one hand, to inform the organisations about measures and intentions of the ministry...and discuss their implementation...on the other hand, however, to make known the views and wishes to the ministry, as well as to discuss general questions of welfare and to find conjoint ways of fighting misery.

(Didicher, 1987: p 374)

The practical effects of this co-operation were the distribution of public finances through the welfare organisations - with membership of one of the organisations as a precondition for receipt of government financial support. Art. 8 of the 'Third Decree on the Implementation of the Law on the Redemption of Public Loans of 4th December 1926' eventually recognised and defined the social function and legal position of independent welfare organisations. This legal status has remained unchanged, in essence, since that date. The idea that social work was a professional discipline that could be taught survived the twelve years of the Nazi regime.

The present status of public and independent welfare

The law on regulations for a 'social state' in Article 20 of the basic Constitutional Law is fundamental for the status of welfare organisations in the Federal Republic of Germany.

Consequently, Art. 17 sect. 3 of the first volume on social legislation (*Sozialgesetzbuch* [*SGB*] I) states:

> *In co-operation with charitable and independent foundations and organisations it is the aim of the service providers that their activities and those of the foundations and organisations named above are combined and effective in the interest of the service recipient. In this, they have to respect their independence regarding both aims and implementation of their tasks. The control of the adequate use of financial means is not affected by this.*
>
> (Art. 17, sect. 3 , SGB I)

The practical implementation of the 'principle of subsidiarity' which is the basis for the co-operation between independent welfare organisations and public service providers can be illustrated with the example of the process of granting welfare benefits (Schulte, 1990: p 47). As a rule the service providers, governmental agencies, associations, and administrative departments (as named in Art. 18 to 29 SGB I) are responsible for granting welfare benefits:

> *These matters are within the responsibility of counties and cities, of the nation-wide welfare providers, and for special tasks of the public health departments. They co-operate with the independent welfare organisations.*
>
> (Art. 28, sect. 4, SGB I)

Here we find the distinction between welfare providers under public law (i.e. governmental agencies, associations etc.) and independent welfare providers, (i.e. 'independent welfare organisations'). Providers under public law have to ensure that services are rendered but they are

able to delegate service delivery to independent providers and thus buy services from welfare organisations for people entitled to welfare benefits. If an independent welfare organisation is able to provide the service in question, public providers are not to take measures of their own: as there is the fundamental principle of a preference for independent provision of services enshrined within the law (Art. 10 sect. 4; 8 sect. 2 of the Federal Welfare Law [*Bundessozialhilfegesetz*, BSHG]). Moreover, legislation assigns a basic duty of support to the public provider with regard to the independent welfare organisations (Art. 10 sect. 3 BSHG).

This legislative basis ensures the preferential position of independent welfare organisations in comparison with other providers of social services, and it gives German welfare organisations a uniquely strong position in Europe. The possibilities for the welfare organisation to influence the planning of social measures are also regulated by law. In this respect, social legislation makes the special position of welfare organisations evident. For instance, with regard to local projects of child and youth help (such as building of kindergartens, establishment of youth centres) independent organisations' participation is to be assured in all phases of planning' (Art. 80 sect. 3 Child and Youth Help Law [*Kinder-und Jugendhilfe-Gesetz*, KJHG]). For this purpose, public providers are to establish working groups that include welfare organisations as well (Art. 78 KJHG).

Critiques of the German welfare system

Critiques of corporatism first emerged in the late 1970s and centred upon the proximity of welfare organisations to the state. These organisations appeared to be operating as semi-state organisations in as much as they were perceived as being under the direction of and controlled by the state's 'golden rein'. Hence, they were seen to be completely dependent on the state's financial support and as such were not operating autonomously:

> *The welfare organisations' interest in a lasting co-operation within governmental policies results mainly from the fact that by means of their incorporation their capacity to act is safeguarded in both the legal and the financial respects in the long run.*
>
> (Heinze and Olk, 1981: p 107)

As such, the welfare organisations did not, in reality, follow the rationale of a corporatist model but rather primarily served the interests of the State and those of the organisations themselves. The organisations were reluctant to endanger their good relations with government thus creating a service monopoly, which in fact hampered developments within society and no longer represented citizen's interests as illustrated in Figure 8.3.

As a result of these criticisms and in line with the changes that were occurring in the political-economies of other nation states throughout Europe the role of welfare organisations in Germany also changed. Under the conditions of emergent liberalised welfare markets, these organisations were forced to re-orient themselves towards market principles and sever their traditional links with the state (Klug, 1997: p 221).

These dramatic changes in the German welfare regime are thus closely related to the wider socio-political changes occurring throughout society. In particular, Anglo-Saxon theories of liberalism continue to exert their influence on the formulation of key axioms of social policy. These developments are taking place at a time of both crisis over public finances more generally and of discussions about the efficiency of the social services and their organisation in particular. The relationship between the state and welfare organisations that had remained stable over many years has been 'exposed' as being monopolistic and cartel-like. A criticism that is increasingly voiced by both audit departments and the media, and has led to inroads into the monopoly of social services by welfare organisations (Meyer, 1997: pp 6–7).

Whereas welfare organisations were, only a few years ago, able to talk about 'partnership' they have now been forced to recognise that this partnership is ending. The conditions of this relationship changed fundamentally in the early 1990s through the sanctioning of private-commercial service providers with whom the welfare organisations were forced to compete. A result of this shift was that political figures claimed that their former 'partners' were demanding too a high price for their services. Competition with the private-commercial sector has also entailed increased pressure for the demonstration of effectiveness and efficiency and the legitimisation of social work services. A recent instance of this phenomenon occurred during discussions about private nursing insurance, when leading politicians openly opposed the financial calculations of certain welfare organisations.

These changed conditions have also affected the relationship between welfare organisations and local administrative agencies. Manderscheid (1995: p 239) has identified three strategies of local administration that are consequences of the new relationship between these agencies and welfare organisations:

- lowering standards

- introduction of competition

- substitution of professional work by volunteers

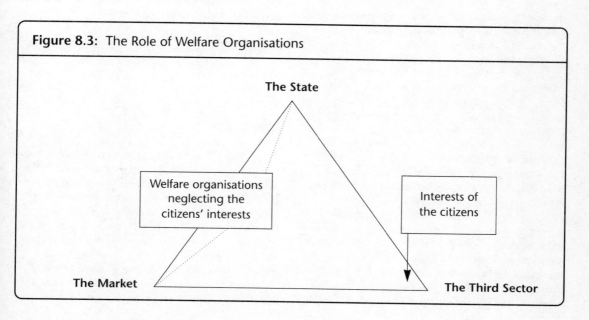

Figure 8.3: The Role of Welfare Organisations

The State

Welfare organisations neglecting the citizens' interests

Interests of the citizens

The Market

The Third Sector

The result of cuts in funding has been twofold: bankruptcy for some smaller service providers; whilst larger agencies often enough struggle with the consequences of a burgeoning bureaucratic apparatus developed in response to municipal accounting measures and procedures. This new relationship between local authorities and welfare organisations which has been referred to as the 'New Directive Model' (*'Neue Steuerungsmodelle'*, NSM) is characterised by the introduction of new arrangements for contract management, output-orientated objectives, budgeting, and decentralised responsibility for resources. What lies behind NSM are: the imposition of efficiency measures; a redefinition of the tasks of municipal administration; and the development of a debate on the whole question of appropriate models of public administration. However, this debate is occurring within a context of a lack of capacity and experience amongst managers of the traditional service providers about how to operate in a competitive market orientated environment. Hence, these services are still operating with a deficit of alternative models; clear decision-making structures, regulatory standards and control mechanisms, public relations, fund raising and marketing capacities and personnel and workforce planning strategies and operations.

The future of social work in the new welfare complex

Despite all the criticisms of the corporatist German welfare system, it has ensured a limited guarantee of social provision for disadvantaged members of society, something that cannot be claimed for liberal, market orientated social policies such as those of the United States. In particular, the principle of subsidiarity, which forms a constitutive element for the German model, has had the effect of supporting the development of many grass roots initiatives and 'new social movements'. Consequently, in Germany a broadly based movement for self-help has emerged, this is considered to be an indispensable dimension of contemporary social services and which could not have been achieved—to the same extent—by a purely state determined model of social work. However, the over-dependence of the Third Sector upon the state has weakened the Third Sector's capacity to represent the interests of citizens and develop measures and practices that ensure maximum effectiveness and efficiency in the organisation and delivery of services.

In seeking to re-align itself in relation to both the state and the market in the new welfare complex, a recognition of the strengths and weaknesses of the Third Sector arise because of its proximity to state and market. The weakness of the state sector lies in its tendency to reduce matters of welfare to legal and bureaucratic issues and ignore the needs of politically uninfluential, marginalised and minority groups. The strength of the state rests in its ability to guarantee social and territorial rights and equality of access to necessary levels of social security and material provisions. The weaknesses of commercial providers and the market sector in general lie in the incapacity to cater for generalised 'needs', as the market responds only to the demands of those 'customers' who are able to secure the finance to pay for services. On the other hand, the strengths of the market lie in its capacity to deliver mass, cost-effective welfare commodities and services, in response to customer demand.

In contrast to these strengths and weaknesses, the strengths of the Third Sector lie in its capacity to promote the development of informal and self-help groups and initiatives and its:

> *...receptivity to emotional and communicative needs that are beyond any norms, in the cultivation of trust and forms of security that cannot be created by money or law.*
>
> (Evers, 1991: p 228)

However, the Third Sector's weaknesses are exposed if it seeks to institutionalise individual and social rights as its:

> *...ties and responsibilities with regard to the community reach their limitations all too soon if they are based on indispensable claims for personal autonomy and individual independence.*
>
> (ibid: p 228)

Conclusion

In Germany the traditional welfare organisations are situated between the three dimensions of the state, the market and the third sector that collectively form the welfare complex. As such, they are subject to the rules of the market as competitors of commercial providers, they are 'partners' of the welfare state in providing basic social services and they are part of the Third Sector in that they provide an umbrella for and represent and support the initiatives of social and community groups and interests. Hence, traditional welfare organisations retain a capacity to act as intermediaries in that they provide and legitimise the connections between these three dimensions. For example, in the case of nursing services: where welfare organisations operate as service provider and initiator and mediator for self-help groups, they serve to integrate, complement and connect the relations between different helping authorities, the interests of community, solidarity, collectivism and government.

In a society that is increasingly characterised by heterogeneity, plurality of competing interests and demands it may be conceptually simpler for both consumers, administrators and providers in the welfare complex services if they were organised and co-ordinated under one roof.

However, such a scenario would no doubt generate an identity crisis for social work practitioners working in such an organisation, if they were required to represent rather than mediate between the three dimensions of welfare (Klug, 1997). The future of welfare in Germany and indeed across Europe depends upon conditions that arise from a wider context than purely national considerations. These conditions will be determined by whether and in what form a European social policy develops; in particular the capacity and political will of government to finance social security systems; the role, function and scope of social work within emergent welfare regimes and the legislative base for establishing entitlements to welfare services.

Questions for Further Consideration

1. How might the role, function and interests of the three sectors within the welfare systems be best described?

2. To what extent do the forms of organisation and the current problems within the German welfare complex differ or mirror those in other European Countries?

3. What possibilities are there for professional social work practitioners with not-for-profit welfare organisations in emergent forms of welfare in Europe?

Chapter Nine

Social Alarm and Public Reassurance: The Italian Example

Rino Fasol and Franco Fraccaroli

Introduction

Anxiety about crime and the demand for 'law and order' are phenomena of increasing importance in most Western countries. A survey by Mayhew and van Dijk (1997: pp 50–52) reports that 53 per cent of French citizens believe that it is 'likely' or 'very likely' that they will be burgled over the coming year; England and Wales rank second (41 per cent), while the lowest percentage is recorded in Finland (11 per cent). The overall average in the eleven industrialised countries surveyed is around 27 per cent. The same survey also shows that, on average, one in every five citizens (22 per cent) is concerned about being out alone after dark, with a maximum of 32 per cent in England and Wales and a minimum of 11 per cent in Sweden.

In Italy, mounting social alarm and a preoccupation with personal safety are phenomena that were closely associated in the 1990s with concerns about so-called *microcriminalità* or street crime. According to the interviewees of the Censis survey on the fears of the Italians, the main problem in their neighbourhood is street crime, which was cited by 37.1 per cent of the sample. It was more important than unemployment (36.4 per cent), urban traffic (27.3 per cent), drugs (24.8 per cent), non-EU immigration (21.9 per cent) and the shortage of social and health services (21.4 per cent). Comparison with the data collected by a similar Censis survey conducted in 1997 shows that, among the problems regarded as most serious by Italians, petty crime had increased significantly, rising from its fourth place of three years ago (24.8 per cent) to its current first place with 37.1 per cent. Undoubtedly the most significant finding is that the demand for law and order is expressed, albeit with differing degrees of intensity, by the whole of society and across all age groups, educational levels, income levels, geographical area and size of commune of residence (Censis, 2000: p 1).

It is well known that the actual amount of crime and the fear of crime in a community are not necessarily correlated. We know, however, that if a community is convinced that it is unprotected against crime, this will have consequences:

> *The psychological consequences include decreased neighbourhood satisfaction, an increased desire to relocate, increasing fear, and a weaker attachment to place and sense of community. The social psychological consequences include decreased willingness to intervene in events on the street, more mistrust between neighbours, and less co-operation.*
>
> (Taylor, 1995: p 29)

There are then economic consequences and ecological implications, and in addition behavioural consequences. For example, 53 per cent of the homes of those interviewed as part of a survey conducted by Mayhew and van Dijk (1997: p 54) had at least one security measure (such as a burglar alarm, special door locks, or grilles on doors or windows). The maximum being in England and Wales (76 per cent) and the minimum being in Finland (31 per cent). Although, as we have seen, no social group is entirely excluded from this type of anxiety:

> *Fear of crime is a multiplicative function of both perceived risk and the perceived seriousness of the offence… Women, older persons, racial and ethnic minorities, and urban residents are more fearful of crime than are members of other groups.*
>
> (Miethe, 1995: pp 18–19)

> *Social alarm grows and spreads when the community as a whole feels that the values which underpin social co-living are being threatened. What matters is as much the nature and seriousness of the problem as any uncertainty or lack of agreement on the solutions to adopt to cope with it.*
>
> (Fedele, 1993: p 71)

These not entirely 'rational' mechanisms also operate at the level of public policies hence:

> *…crime control policy is driven less by street crime than by a variety of other anxieties and insecurities that transcend street crime but are effectively related to it.*
>
> (Scheingold, 1995: p 157)

A sense of social alarm is therefore tied to the emotional perceptions of the existing balance among forces such as social deviance, social control and repression:

Put briefly, one may say that deviance indicates both what has evaded the processes of 'primary' social control and what 'secondary' social control should contain, re-orientate or repress.

(Pitch, 1988: p 28)

Without elaborating the position that 'definitions' occupy in the debate on deviance and social control, we would emphasise the importance of the:

...problem of the definition, the constitution of deviance as a property attributed to behaviours and individuals during interaction (dimension of definition), and there-fore of the problem of the distribution of definition, of study of those in society who possess the power of defi-nition: that is, study of the agencies of social control (dimension of power).

(Baratta, 1982: p 87)

We would emphasise the conventional, socially constructed, dimension of deviance, where the interaction among individuals and among social groups is crucial:

If deviance is a property intrinsic not to behaviour but to the interaction between the person who commits the act and the others that respond to it, the deviant is deemed to be in breach of the norms of at least one sector of society.

(Cesareo, 1987: p 148)

Control is also performed in the interaction among individuals, in the process that 'fixes' meanings and makes communication possible (Mead, 1938), which marks out the boundaries between normality and deviance, between the lawful and the unlawful.

At the societal level, control is the mechanism that should protect the social order against the dangers represented by deviance, operating both as 'reactive social control', that is, social control which censures and inhibits behaviour, and as the 'active social control' which produces rather than prohibits behaviour (Melossi, 1990: p 5).

With its twofold function and nature, social control can be viewed as a primary function from a functional sociological perspective. We are not thinking here of those authors of Marxist inspiration who have argued that advanced capitalist societies require an infrastructure of welfare policies to help to maintain order, buy off working-class protest and secure a workforce with acceptable standards of health and education (Hill, 1980: p 3; Hill and Bramley, 1986: pp 32–33). On this view, social policy is considered a tool of social control and social workers as agents of social control (Higgins, 1980).

We instead consider social control not only as repression or intervention to change *dissent*, but also as the production of *consent* and therefore as motivating action. This view of social control refers to an area of processes and institutions which:

...assumed and expertly intervene in aspects defined as problematic, supporting or replacing the agencies of primary socialisation.

(Pitch, 1989: p 19)

The fact remains that the agents of social control, including those that operate in the welfare system, have not only the power to define what is to be considered deviant but also the power to decide what type of reaction to activate in response to every form of behaviour deemed deviant (Hess, 1983).

The majority of social workers seem to regard the function of social control assigned to social welfare as inappropriate to it. As Cowger and Atherton (1974) point out:

...part of the problem lies in the term social control, which to many has become equated with the arbitrary exercise of power by an elitist group...Because of their orientation to humanistic values, social workers may view social control as antithetical to social work practice although they must concede that social control is a necessary and important element of any culture...Social workers do not like to entertain the idea of social demands on behaviour. Nor do they like to think that their work is part of a process to produce social competence for the good of the society. Nevertheless, whenever a social worker, parent, educator, physician, anyone, engages in an activity to modify or set boundaries on human conduct according to valued norms, that person is engaging in social control.

(ibid: pp 456–457)

It is within this theoretical frame of reference that we now conduct our discussion of the relationship between social alarm and social work. We examine the link between deviance, social work and alarm in the community, asking in particular whether there is (or there should be) a connection between social work on deviance and the level of concern expressed by the community. We do not look for causal nexus between the efficacy of social work and the reduction of social alarm. Instead, given that the fear of crime and alarm at various forms of deviance can be taken as indicators of distress in a community, we enquire whether it is possible (or necessary) to include them in the elements considered when the quality of social work is assessed.

Our discussion is based on the results of a survey concerning the role of workers in the social and health services as providers of discipline and social reassurance. The survey was carried out for the regional administration of Emilia Romagna as part of the 'Safe Cities' project (for a summary, see the report by Lagrange, Peretti, Pottier, Robert and Zauberman, 2000).

The focus of the analysis was the way in which social workers view the conflict between care and control and how they consider the relationship between their activity and the level of alarm in a community with regard to the problems addressed by social work. According to how social workers conceive the problems that they deal with, the aims of their work, and their images of problems and social work in the community, they assume different attitudes towards social alarm and more or less coherent forms of coping. Of central importance, is the opinion of social workers concerning the relation between the functions of care and control, their professional and ideological mode of explaining deviance and interpreting their role in the welfare system.

In what follows we shall propose various conceptions of the form that action to foster social reassurance and reduce social alarm should take. This is not a typology in the proper sense of the term, but rather a summary of the points of view that emerged during the survey. These are arranged within a more general framework of analysis on the topics previously considered.

Reassurance as a sub-product of social work

According to this point of view, the community should be reassured by the fact that services exist which concern themselves with social problems (such as juvenile delinquency or drug addiction). The community 'knows' that someone has taken charge of these and other causes of social alarm, and even if the means and methods used are not necessarily known, this suffices for public concern to subside. Care work, taking on the problems of marginal social groups or others 'at risk', seeking to alleviate suffering and hardship 'by mandate', should therefore enhance the integration and well-being not only of those directly concerned but also, indirectly, of society as a whole.

This is undoubtedly a 'reasonable' perception of social work (one might say that it is a simplified and 'ingenuous' view of Parsons (1951) model of the structure and workings of the social system): knowing that there are those who

take responsibility for persons in difficulties is certainly more reassuring than seeing them left to fend for themselves. One may reasonably expect that the provision of help in situations of social deviance is valued by the members of a community not only because it retrieves and reintegrates forms of deviance, but also because it may prevent 'contagion' within the community, as well as defence against the threat that deviant individuals represent.

The 'visibility' of services is the first aspect to consider when verifying the extent to which the 'reasonable' expectations of practitioners are effectively matched by the community's actual perception of their work. In fact, the general public is not always correctly informed about social services, their work and their objectives.

However, it is above all regarding the efficiency of services that substantial differences may emerge between the public and practitioners. For the practitioners, there is a danger that they will persuade themselves that they can perform a service for the community 'simply' by doing their jobs. Taking care of the socially excluded, dealing with deviance, taking responsibility for those who have rejected (or have been rejected by) the other agencies of social welfare: this may persuade practitioners that they automatically qualify for the community's esteem and gratitude (Olivetti Manoukian, 1998). By contrast, the community bases its judgement on the 'competence' of the practitioner, on their 'superior skill' as a 'professional', and on the tangible results achieved (and we know that the criteria used to assess them differ from actor to actor (see for example Donabedian, 1980)). Therefore, it is not so much the nature of the problem taken on by the practitioner that guarantees the community's appreciation of a service, but rather the quality of their action in terms of effectiveness.

As a consequence, it cannot be taken for granted that the public will feel 'safer' from petty crime merely because it knows that the local social services are working with drug addicts or with deviant minors and juveniles 'at risk'. If the latter cause social alarm, the fact that they are being 'looked after' by a network of services does not make them automatically less threatening in the eyes of the general public.

Reassurance as explicit control

A second view of social reassurance, closely connected with the one just discussed, centres on the explicit social control that the services agree to exercise over their users.

It is obvious that the function of services is not restricted solely to care and rehabilitation. Services also undertake surveillance duties, and they indirectly restrict the freedom of action of members of the community who may be the cause of social alarm. The actions of 'labelling' and 'diagnosing' serve to locate individuals on one or other side of the line that defines 'normality' and 'acceptability' by the community. This results in a constant process of definition of social norms and the negotiation of their application to individuals or social groups. Society is thus assured that social control is being exercised in not only the application of the norms but also their definition in the practice and relations of everyday life, thereby 'continually' reaffirming the value and re-legitimating the role of authority and, hence, of social control (Scott, 1992).

An interesting example is provided by the application in Italy of a law enacted in 1990, which, with regard to services for drug addicts, has imposed forms of co-operation between the police, magistrates and health and social services which have explicitly reinforced the social control and repression performed by social workers. Thus, the services have been obliged to 'substitute' for the institutional agencies of control. The type of relationship that has consequently arisen with users reflects the ambiguity of a situation in which care and rehabilitation are alternatives to judicial provisions. The mechanisms of referral by this type of users to services effectively undermine the voluntary nature of engagement with social work. This heavily conditions the terms of contract stipulated between user and practitioner in the helping relationship. The practitioner's power to sanction the user inevitably gives rise to an asymmetry, which makes the relationship ambiguous, and in constant danger of lapsing into suspicion or indifference on the part of the user.

However, it is not only explicit collaboration with the institutional agencies of control that engenders a repressive role performed by social workers. In work with minors, immigrants or the socially excluded, reintegrative social work may operate on the one hand through the transmission of norms or 'appropriate' patterns of behaviour, or on the other, by suppressing the 'deviance' from social rules that often causes social alarm. Particularly in the case of minors, pressure is applied proactively, in the sense that it anticipates and represses behaviour by minors that may have serious consequences on their life-courses or on their chances of success in the social system. The objective here is to forestall specific behaviour by well-identified individuals.

In their everyday practices as a whole, the discretion exercised by social workers in allocating awards and resources is in any case an instrument of social control. For some practitioners this mandate is clear and is explicitly assumed. The community's social cohesion, understood as the absence of conflict and the control of deviance, is therefore deliberately employed as a criterion in evaluation of the quality of their work.

Reassurance through social reintegration

A further way to view social reassurance relates to the work of social services in maintaining or restoring their users to full membership of the community, from which they have been, or risk being, excluded because of their deviant behaviour or the threat that they raise to social harmony. If we consider the phenomenon of drug addiction, for example, people perceive the drug dealing and use, that takes place before their eyes, as signals of social disorder and degeneration (Skogan, 1990). A case in point is programmes for the social reintegration of former drug addicts; those, that is, who have reached an advanced stage of rehabilitation. These programmes involve vocational training or work re-entry schemes targeted on small groups of ex-addicts, selected because their detoxification is nearing completion, or the setting up of halfway houses before ex-addicts completely detach themselves from the care and rehabilitation services. In addition, within this category are projects organised in prisons to encourage drug-addict inmates to undertake courses of therapy or join communities on their release.

In progress for some time there have been similar schemes designed to deal with street prostitution and its attendant extensive problems of exploitation and abuse. As regards minors, the aim in the majority of cases is to keep them below the subtle line that divides legality from illegality, social acceptance from rejection, membership of the community from exclusion; whether by choice of the minors themselves (Elmer and Reicher, 1995) or through imposition.

In some way, the community is called upon to 'resume' responsibility for situations, to embrace individuals once again, or in other words, to share problems that tend to be pushed aside.

Social reassurance is thus indirectly pursued though the strengthening of the social bonds and community solidarity which not only provide support in critical situations but also exercise more efficacious control over subjects at risk precisely because they accept it.

Reassurance as cultural action

In the intentions of social service workers and managers, initiatives for prevention and information should also serve to combat stereotypes, prejudices and ignorance about the social problems that the services deal with on a daily basis. There are probably very few who still believe that it is possible to 'convince' people with the force of scientific evidence and by rational argument. Nor is it possible to overcome suspicion and fear simply by bringing the two sides together. Moreover, the availability of more accurate knowledge, less polluted by stereotypes and prejudices, does not necessarily reduce hostility towards situations and persons deemed to be morally corrupt or socially dangerous.

Less ingenuous, therefore, is an approach that seeks to show the social and therefore conventional nature of the community's attribution of the labels 'deviant' or 'dangerous'. More pragmatically, the aim may to be to reveal the mechanisms by which the images of social problems and deviance that circulate in a community are socially constructed. However, in this case, will the result not be 'understanding' (not only knowledge but also empathy or emotional sharing) of problems. None the less, it may be possible to 're-negotiate' the image and conception of 'social deviants', taking the concerns of the community as a matter of fact and not as a simple cognitive 'dysfunction' or morally reprehensible attitude. The role, aims and working methods of the services may be part of these campaigns of discussion and explanation, where knowledge is not an end in itself and a guarantee of reconciliation, but only one stage in a process of dialogue and negotiation in which the various parties concerned (citizens, practitioners, users) are hopefully able to express their motives and state their needs.

Reassurance as harm reduction and the containment of deviance

Services that adopt policies of harm containment find it particularly difficult to reconcile their work with the expectations of the community. In fact, it is likely that the community will see the services' conception of and approach to situations like drug addiction, juvenile delinquency or prostitution as substantially the acceptance of these forms of deviance, and as renunciation of the endeavour to bring these situations and individuals back to 'normality'. Working as 'detached workers on the street' and in 'drop-in' centres, requires social workers to establish and maintain contacts with individuals whose behaviour is openly deviant, sometimes even criminal. The aim of social work practice is to form a trust relationship with them, so that the gravity and dangerousness of their behaviour can be reduced. However, their restoration to normality cannot be the immediate priority of the intervention. Only as a consequence of gradual changes will this occur: changes that necessarily take a long time to introduce. The option of seeking to contain, rather than to eliminate, forms of deviance almost inevitably lead to some sort of 'complicity' between practitioners and users. The need to maintain a bond, however fragile and ambiguous, with users entails tolerance of behaviour that may lapse into the unlawful. This attitude by practitioners may be disconcerting to the community where they work, which may fail to grasp the sense or importance of the decision not to perform 'care' functions with more marked connotations of control. Misunderstandings and hostility may arise in the practitioners' dealings with the formal control agencies (especially law-enforcement agencies) and also with other practitioners and social services, in particular where the prohibitionist culture still predominates, or where social alarm is particularly severe. More or less deliberately, practitioners who opt for this approach seem to take account of this risk of incomprehension and conflict. In their contact with vulnerable people or those at risk, social workers, by prioritising the trust relationship with users, appear willing to sacrifice the social consideration, esteem and appreciation of the community.

Rejection of social reassurance as the task and goal of social services

In addition, there are the arguments advanced by those who explicitly and with greater or lesser vigour claim the right, or even the duty, to exclude reassurance of the community from the ends to be pursued by the social and health services.

Four main mechanisms are used to justify the assertion that social reassurance is not the task of services:

- Playing down the level of social alarm: obviously, opinions differ among services and practitioners as to how the community perceives the level and seriousness of such problems as drug abuse and juvenile delinquency. Probably, frequently there are cases in which the term 'social alarm' is partly or wholly inapplicable to the way that the problems addressed by practitioners are interpreted and described. In other cases, there is an understandable effort to play down, rightly or wrongly, the local situation and to restrict social alarm to social categories or groups whose good faith cannot be taken for granted. In addition, frequently and largely justifiable, is the accusation that the mass media exaggerate episodes of deviance and foment social tension.

- Redefining the phenomena that provoke social alarm: the context of the images and analyses offered to the community by practitioners, whose purpose is to minimise or even deny the 'abnormality' and 'illegitimacy' of certain behaviours removes the basis and therefore the justification for social alarm. The causal mechanisms cited by practitioners to explain deviance often places blame on collective or social factors that reveal 'hypocrisy' in the community's attitude.

- Specification of role and restricting the categories of recipients: even more direct and pertinent is the argument that the professional and institutional mandate and duty of the social worker are incompatible with the functions of social control and reassurance. There are those, therefore, who question the efficacy itself of the mechanisms of control and repression, together with those who express great reluctance to accept and perform those functions.

- Delegating responsibility to other agencies: just as the role of providing social control (and reassurance) can be refused outright, so it can be delegated to other agencies institutionally charged with exercising control and repression; in this way a more precise, and traditional division of roles can be restored.

Concluding Remarks

The foregoing classification confirms that the tension between the functions of both care and control performed by social workers is irremediable. The greater emphasis placed by the various points of view discussed above concerning care rather than on control seems, in fact, to be ideologically motivated, rather than grounded in any other obvious factors. The assumption that treatment of people also involves social control seems to be a feature intrinsic to the helping professions. Here, it is not a matter of choosing between care and control: both these functions are inherent in social and health work; it is the nature of the problem addressed and the features of the social setting in which the social worker operates that determine the weight that control assumes in practice alongside caring functions.

If one accepts the inevitably 'ambiguous' or ambivalent nature of social work, social alarm should be included among the factors that are more or less directly or deliberately brought to bear in determining the nature of practice, given that the level of social alarm is one of the characteristics of the environment in which the social services operate. As such, its influence, the fact that it conditions and constrains the action of services, seems difficult to deny. The degree of acceptance or recognition of the work of the social services also depends on the social climate. The quantity and quality of the resources made available by the community, also in terms of social legitimacy, inevitably reflect the amount and nature of 'disquiet' abroad in the community.

Consequently, there must be the maximum amount of transparency and precision in the definition of the aims to pursue, and in the presentation of the means and resources that the services intend to use. The mandate that the community gives to the social services is not entirely predetermined; it must be negotiated and defined with the other actors operating in the system and representing the community's interests.

Hence, the evaluation of results must take account of social alarm. This is not a matter of taking on the community's fears and preoccupations, but rather of considering the effects of social work, irrespective of the results achieved with users or in the social group targeted. Efficacy should also be measurable with regard to social alarm, but this does not imply that it is the duty of the social services to reassure the community directly. Instead, the effects on social alarm exerted by the services should be included among the indicators used to assess the quality of results, even if, paradoxically, it may be decided that tension or alarm over certain social problems should not only be maintained but even reinforced.

This is therefore not a matter of perverting the mandate of the social services, of bending it opportunistically to gain acceptance by public opinion. Instead, social alarm does not lie outside the range of action of the social services but is an important part of it. It is up to the services to decide what action to take in its regard on the basis of explicit definition of their role and their objectives, which should be negotiated with the other actors and agencies concerned.

Questions for Further Consideration

1. Should the purposes and interests of social work actions be directed by and towards individuals and groups who are the targets of their interventions or by the opinions of the wider society, i.e. should the political in contrast to therapeutic aspect of social work be given greater recognition?

2. To what extent should organised responses to social needs and problems remain located solely within the purview of social work agencies, i.e. to what extent should social work acknowledge the limits to its effectiveness in an increasingly complex and fragmented society?

Chapter Ten

Social Work Education and Training: The Spanish Experience

Jordi Sabater

Introduction

In order to examine the situation, needs and challenges facing providers and consumers of education and training for social workers, it is necessary to appreciate and understand the particular cultural, institutional and legal frameworks of the country where that education is located. The reality of any particular educational system and more specifically, the approach to education and training remains deeply embedded in the political and administrative structures, procedures and arrangements that exist for welfare and social protection. The enduring influence of historical and national contextual factors should not be under estimated. Only by reference to the particular and concrete, will we be able to understand the common ground from and to which the individual trajectories of different countries relate.

However, in spite of differing models of welfare provision, varying degrees of development in social and educational policies and different academic traditions, European countries increasingly tend towards having more in common, than features that divide them—at least in matters such as the education and training of social workers. It is also true, that in spite of the differences, European countries share a similar context of rapid economic, social and even cultural change that demands a continuous effort to find flexible strategies that will achieve the objective of developing autonomous professionals—practitioners who are able to face a dynamic social reality in a considered and rigorous manner and who are able to intervene with a clear understanding of complex and changing situations, needs and problems.

There is little doubt across Europe a sense of shared social problems are leading to similar and convergent trajectories in respect of the nature of social work education and training. Here we will explore the needs and future prospects of social work education and training. Accordingly, this chapter presents, as an example, material with which to work and as a starting point for debate, an historical view of social work studies in Spain,

concluding with a brief overview of the current situation and a list of the more significant challenges to be faced in Spain and elsewhere in Europe.

A Different History but Familiar Story

Patronage and Regulation

Social work education and training in Catalonia, and other parts of Spain was first established in the 1930s, during the Second Spanish Republic. The basis for the founding of the first social work school in Spain (at Barcelona in 1932) was a result of the combined effects of : a new social and educational climate; the impact of influences from other European nations, especially via Brussels; and, most of all, the need felt by 'social Catholicism' for suitable vehicles with which to strengthen their presence amongst the working and underprivileged classes. The School of Welfare for Women which was linked to the Women's Committee for Social Improvement, had already in 1929, at the National Welfare Congress, established the need for a dedicated training centre for social work. This was an explicitly Catholic institution, whose aims were to educate the working classes and provide knowledge and technical training to those wishing to be involved in improving society.

The syllabus adopted for educating social workers was similar to that of other European schools at that time: the training course offered was for a period of two years—with the majority of teachers coming from the University sector or from Colleges of Further Education. In the first year, the program sought to reinforce and consolidate the 'female' nature of the institution and profession, by providing a focus on civic and moral duties. While the economic and social teaching at the school aimed at inculcating highest levels of general knowledge and a clear understanding amongst students of a woman's 'correct place' in respect of the family and society. During the second year, students specialised in the field of employment or health. On finishing, students had to present a practical piece of work on a social topic. The school was initially attached to the International Catholic Union of Social Service - until 1935 when it was officially recognised by the Department of Social Welfare of the autonomous Catalan government.

The Spanish Civil War and beginning of the dictatorship disrupted the process that had been started with the initial development of social work education. It must not be forgotten that in Spain the consequence of depression of the thirties and the experience of the Second World War did not culminate in a post - war Welfare State, but in a decidedly interventionist, dictatorial, authoritarian New State with strong fascist roots. A state that was completely distanced from the liberal social developments taking shape in much of the rest of Western Europe. Within this framework of dictatorship, a social policy reflecting the ideological mixture that characterised the Franco regime came into being. This was the case especially in the initial phase of the regime, which was characterised by traditional conservatism, ultra-conservative Catholicism, corporatism and fascist symbolism. In this way, the prevailing charity-welfare orientation was driven by a strong ideology of paternalism combined with authoritarianism. The aim of this orientation was to maintain the Spanish capitalist structures and control the population. Hence, 'social Catholicism' was replaced with 'national Catholicism' - whereby the state defined itself as being Catholic and simultaneously attempted to end social and political pluralism.

It is therefore, of little surprise that under such a regime the schools for social workers were linked either to the Church or to the networks of the totalitarian regime. For example 1939 saw the creation in Madrid of the *'School for Family and Social Training'* under the patronage of the Primate Cardinal and later, the *San Vicente de Paul College for Social Workers* by the Daughters of Charity. In Barcelona, the social work school founded in 1932 underwent profound changes. It came to be called the *'School for the Home and Female Social Work'*; subjects such as religion and morality were added to the course syllabus with apostolic objectives replacing the former social concerns. However, later, in 1944, the school was consolidated as the *Catholic School of Social Education*, dependent first upon the *Diocesan Department of Welfare* and subsequently upon the *Promotion of Social Action*. Parallel to this, the second school in Barcelona and the fourth in Spain was created in 1953 the *Women's School of Psychiatric Social Workers*. This school was linked to the institutions of Franco's single Party system

and to the hospitals. The school maintained its eminently psycho-social nature, with subject emphasis on psychiatry and psychology.

Hence, until the late fifties, social work education and training in Spain was clearly associated with a social and political context of material and academic poverty, international isolation, markedly ideological connotations, technical training and scientific research related to religious values and embedded in a regime of paternalistic and controlling welfare practices. The purpose of social work and of social work education was grounded in the reproduction of an approach to practice centring on a particular view of the family (patriarchal, hierarchical, conservative) and especially of the construction of the role of women (carer, maternal, dependent). All this occurred within a climate of relative social and economic underdevelopment .

The professionalisation of welfare

The end of the fifties saw the beginning of a new era. In general, those in favour of promoting economic growth without democratising the political system came to influence the regime . Boosted by general European economic growth, a new model of development was constructed. This model, despite its limitations and contradictions e.g. the State's requirements for low cost labour; very little pressure to pay taxes; and the emigration of hundreds of thousands of Spaniards, gave rise to strong industrial growth that was to modernise the capitalist structures. This economic growth marked the switch from a fundamentally agrarian society to one based on industry and services, from underdevelopment to consumerism. These economic changes, in turn, brought about a restructuring of various state institutions and the modification of the social security system. Thus for example, in 1958 Unemployment Benefit was introduced and the General Wages Law was passed allowing for some development in wage negotiations (albeit controlled from above). In 1963 the Social Security Income Law was announced, this ended the lack of co-ordination between the various protection systems that had developed since 1939. These developments progressed, partially along universal lines and, as of 1964, with the approval of an extensive economic development plan, public services were extended, although unequally, with considerable increases in education and health services.

All of these developments constituted a qualitative change in direction of social policy. In general, it can be stated that the 1960s saw the creation of a welfare system that, although limited and authoritarian formed the basis for later developments in the social policies of democratic Spain. During this period, a marked development of social protection systems and public services could be observed. Even with all its many ambiguities, this system contrasted with what had existed previously. It must be stressed that these developments were closely linked to the demands and impact of the process of capitalist industrialisation. These important economic, social and cultural changes, along with the new but ever more conflicting socio-political circumstances and the changes undergone by the Catholic world on an international scale, could not but affect the situation of the profession and the training of Spanish social workers.

Firstly, we see a spectacular rise in the number of schools of social work. Up until 1957 there were only five in the whole country, by 1969 there were forty-two. Of these, twenty-nine were accountable to the Church, nine were state-run or semi-public and four were private. However, the growth in social work education and training was relatively disorganised. Social work education sought to respond to the growing and complex problems generated by industrial development. Problems ranging from accelerated urbanisation resulting in the development of significant migratory movements, to changes in structures of employment and large deficits in the social and health infrastructure. Nonetheless, social work education was unable to provide a sufficiently efficient and effective response. The number of qualified professionals was low and social institutions were reluctant to take on newly educated professions.

The new situation was consolidated by the recognition and regulation of education and training by the public authorities. In April 1964, a decree by the Ministry of Education and Science officially established the Certificate in Social Work and laid down the regulations for schools including access for intending students to those schools. As of that moment, the academic qualification became a requirement for professional practitioners. It was stipulated that the length of the course could be not less than three years, encompassing both teaching of theory and practical training. In order to embark on a course applicants were required to have a Higher School Leaving Certificate or a nursing, teaching or technical qualification. Graduates from these programmes were classed as ' semi-professionals' (Friedson, 1986). Official

recognition, did not bring the conversion of training into a university or higher degree. Two later ministerial orders, one in 1964 and another in 1966, laid down details of the syllabus, time-tabling and examination papers for social work programmes. The new syllabus focused mainly on the practical side, and confirmed religious, physical and moral training and political indoctrination as essential elements in the teaching programme. In 1967, this process of state control of education culminated in the creation of the only Official School for Social Workers in Madrid which also served as an Examination Board for students from other schools and those who had previously qualified under earlier arrangements. These arrangements established a system characterised by rigorous oversight and extreme centralism.

The initial isolation of social work education in Spain began to break down as schools of social work developed more and more contact with foreign professionals. Some social workers completed their studies in other European countries and the professional associations within Spain began to mobilise. In 1967, the *Spanish Federation of Associations of Social Workers* (FEDAAS) was created. In 1968, the first national congress of social workers was held in Barcelona. This congress proposed the creation of a university degree in social work by the faculties of social sciences. Moreover, in 1969 proceedings began for the creation of a constitution of officially approved professional colleges and associations. Conferences and seminars were also arranged on the topics of professional dynamics and training needs. In general, and in spite of the fact that from a methodological point of view the approach to practice was quite traditional, there was growing concern to give social work a more scientific orientation.

During the final phase of the Franco dictatorship, there was a growing modernisation of Spanish society, an opening-up of new opportunities due to the enormous needs, inequalities and geographical imbalances of a country suffering from the effects of accelerated and uncontrolled growth, with few corrective measures or inadequate forms of intervention. However, an extremely important stimulus for change also came from outside, the Second Vatican Council. Already since the 1950's, the Spanish Catholic charitable society, *Caritas*, had begun to replace charity work with social action. This organisation had set itself the objectives of social promotion and development. However, during the 1960's with the coming of age of a generation that had not lived through the Civil War and coinciding with the new post-conciliation atmosphere there was an opportunity for the consolidation of social work as a profession and the development a new approach to training.

University and Universality

In Spain, the difficult transition from a dictatorship to a democratic regime, coincided with both the global economic crisis and the wide ranging social developments and changes of the 1960s. In addition to the political uncertainty and sometimes very complex adaptation to democratic institutions, were added the serious effects of the economic recession from which Spain suffered particularly severely. However, in Spain these economic and social pressures impacted upon the political process of democratisation in such a way that they led to a significant increase in public and social expenditure. As a result a Welfare State was established, financed through general taxation. Whilst in the rest of Western Europe welfare services were entering a phase of retrenchment, in Spain, welfare services were expanding.

The Spanish Constitution of 1978 designated Spain a Social and Democratic Constitutional State. There was a certain consensus among the political classes and interest groups around a project to modernise the country linked to the processes of democratisation. This project encompassed, among other features, an extension of the public sector and various public income distribution policies. In other words, political transition involved the building of a democratic state with the structures, capabilities and policies of a Welfare State, a consequence of both the democratic obligations and the social pressures that arose within an unfavourable economic climate. In addition, the fact that Spain comprised several nations and the demands that this generated, led to the transformation of the old centralist and unifying state. The result was a new territorial structure based on autonomous regions that, although far from a federal model, implied significant decentralisation. For example, from then on Catalonia had extensive powers in social and educational matters. In this context, the old framework of Charity and Social Assistance was replaced by a new system of social services. The development of these services and their implementation gave rise to a demand

for new professional technical and training requirements.

The ending of the Franco dictatorship and the beginning of democracy brought a period of substantial political and social agitation. The opposition to centralised control, patronage and charity, together with the renewal of catholic interest in social topics, brought about a re-conceptualisation of the nature and purpose of social work that was reflected in social work education and training. This lead to the development of a model of social work which supported the active involvement of professionals in the field of political and social struggles of the day. Hence, the role of 'social worker' was formulated as an agent of change who contributed to the processes transforming social structures. In the midst of a great wave of popular demands, this approach, 'social transformation' - imported from Latin America - offered political meaning and a radical approach to social work. In accordance with the expectations and sensibilities of the time, these developments provided the driving force and the theoretical foundations for a community-based form of intervention. These themes converged in a long-standing vindication of the need for a social work qualification to be established at the university level.

The General Law of Education of 1970 had opened the door to this form of recognition. This Law offered the possibility for social work studies to be located within the university schools. Previously social work courses had been created specifically as higher education diploma courses outside of universities. However, the 1970 Law did not, as yet. include social work as a subject in its own right, but rather as an example of those disciplines whose classification was yet to be determined. From that moment, there was an ever-increasing mobilisation by the schools and the profession to attain university certification through such measures as strikes, assemblies and student lock-ins.

The writing of the Spanish Constitution in 1978 recognised the need to provide social workers, as professionals directly involved in social action, with professional training appropriate to the constitutional intentions regarding social rights and in accordance with the existing training in our cultural environment. In 1979, the Spanish Federation of Associations of Social Workers drew up a program to set up a degree in the subject. This proposal was presented to the Ministry of Education and Science, albeit suggesting the need for a period of adaptation, by establishing a diploma. In February 1980, the House of Representatives passed a motion on the conversion and classification of social work studies as a university qualification, through the creation of the Diploma in Social Work and the transformation of the Schools of Social Work. This was the preliminary step to definitive recognition, which arrived with the Royal Decree (1.850/1981 on the 24th August), which officially established the Diploma in Social Work. The Decree ordered that the teaching of social work take place as part of university education through the University Schools. Students passing the course would obtain a degree in social work. The new name, 'Degree in Social Work', reflected the desire of professionals in the field to break away from previous concepts of social assistance.

The attainment of university status was achieved in the 1982 law creating the Official College of Qualified Social Workers. In April 1983, a Ministerial Order laid down the directives for drawing up a syllabus, requiring that teaching be spread over the following three areas: core sciences, social work and supplementary sciences.

- Core Sciences integrated the disciplines dealing with human behaviour, psychology, sociology and law, both from an individual and a social perspective as well as fundamentals of the legal system and social relations. These core sciences aimed to provide tools to analyse society through an understanding of social dynamics and interactive mechanisms.

- The field of social work consisted of social work, social services and social policy and attempted to provide the theoretical and conceptual framework for social work and a methodology and specific techniques for social intervention, at the level of individuals, groups, institutions and communities.

- Supplementary sciences included statistics and techniques of social research, public administration law, economics, social and cultural anthropology and ethics, which meant to improve understanding of the other two areas.

The Order also laid down that the maximum number of subjects would be 20, fifteen compulsory and five optional, and the total volume of lecture hours would be 3,200, of which 40 per cent would be assigned to practical training. Special emphasis was therefore given to theory-for-practice , with compulsory fieldwork

with working professionals, provided and supervised by the colleges. This gave students some knowledge of the relationship between the social worker and the client or user, and specific skills and awareness necessary for them to enter the professional world. The new arrangement therefore confirmed the university status of social work studies, putting them on a par with any other mid-level professional qualifications. In addition, these changes consolidated the field of social work as the backbone of the course, but at the same time establishing the social and human sciences as a fundamental element of the course. Moreover, religious or moral teaching were eliminated as taught subjects, which, from now on, only referred to clinical models.

In 1983, the University Reform Law was also passed, and this started a long process of re-evaluating university studies in general and the renewal of their respective structures and curricula. The new model introduced a more flexible and autonomous view of higher education, which gave faculties and schools more room for manoeuvre and greater opportunities for students to choose their subjects. A Royal Decree of 1990 instituted the official university Diploma in Social Work and laid down general directives on the syllabi. The new legal framework ratified the maximum duration of the course as three years and its designation as a university diploma. Lecture hours could be no less than 180 credits (each credit being equivalent to 10 hours) and no more than 270, spread between 20 and 30 hours per week, including practical teaching, with theory work not superseding 15 hours a week. The reform of university syllabi laid down four kinds of subjects:

- the core subjects, common to all colleges;
- the compulsory subjects decided by each university;
- the optional subjects to be decided by the students.

In the case of the Degree in Social Work, the 1990 Decree listed as core subjects the following: law; methods and techniques of social research; social policy; psychology; public health and social work; social services; sociology and social anthropology; and social work.

The new course format was complemented by a decision of great importance and significance: the creation of the field of knowledge of social work and social services. With this, the discipline not only consolidated its academic status, but also gained an identity and gave educators an ability to defend the subject within the university structure.

As regards entrance requirements, current legislation recognises five access routes:

- passing University entrance exams after having completed secondary education;
- holding a university degree or diploma;
- passing the entrance exam for mature students over 25 years of age;
- holding an advanced level certificate of secondary education; or
- holding a Level II Vocational Training Certificate in one of the following branches: administration and Commerce, Health and Community Service.

The current conception of social work education and training

To be and to know

Now, the syllabus of Barcelona's University School of Social Work (EUTS-ICESB) will be presented as an illustrative example within this general framework. The current syllabus in this school (although, it is being revised) was approved in 1994. The aims of the syllabus are to provide students with:

1. tools for the analysis of social reality and thereby understand its dynamics.

2. the theoretical and conceptual framework and the necessary methodology and techniques with which to practice the profession of social work.

3. the capacity to act in a critical, responsible, creative and committed manner and work in multi- and inter-professional teams.

The education of social work students seeks to give priority to assistance, counselling and personalised support to students, with the aim of enhancing the skills and abilities necessary for entry into a changing workplace. The social work programme therefore adopts a model of learning that values not only results in terms of academic qualification, but also in relation to the learning process and experience of each student. This model takes the form of group work, with students undertaking: seminars in the first year, technical subjects in the second year and their chosen subjects followed by practical work in the final year of the course.

The curriculum

In the first year, alongside general subjects, four hours a week are devoted to seminars. The seminar is a teaching space for a small group of a maximum of twelve to fourteen students. The group, guided by the teacher-tutor, undertakes both individual and group activities.

In the second year, the main objectives are to focus on in depth exploration of the various subjects, deepen students' understanding of skills, theoretical models and methodologies through coaching in the use of various techniques. It is also during this year that a wide range of optional subjects are offered. These allow each student to develop a particular area of interest.

In the third and final year theoretical and practical subjects complement each other. The practical work is an independent subject structured around three essential components: incorporation of the student into the practice work place; supervision provided in college; and a model of evaluation that integrates the whole experience. In total, the student must spend 400 hours in a public or private welfare service with the aim of becoming part of the agency and learning about the professional practices of social work alongside a professional expert. This individual plays a fundamental role in the students training and gives an opportunity for direct contact with the professional arena. In this sense, they are not only the first 'close-up image the student receives of the profession, but it is also through this person and their presentation of the services, way of working and personal attitude, that the student comes to learn a professional style and model of practice.

Group supervision of students is a dimension of learning through which the student's progress is evaluated by exploring their ability to undertake situational analyses. In addition, the students' understanding of the relationship between knowledge provided in college and its application to practice is also tested using these groups. Supervision is also intended to support the students so that they progress with practical work in a satisfactory manner.

The Syllabus

In detail the syllabus unfolds by incorporating the following core and compulsory subjects (Table 10.1) (credits for each subject are given in brackets).

Additionally students must take 25 credits in chosen subjects and 21 in free subjects. The latter can be taken in the college or in other centres.

Future Imperfect

Training social workers requires ongoing thought and the constant development of new approaches to meet the needs of both society and the market. Analytical tools that give autonomy, flexibility and initiative to a professional group must be developed to enable social work practice to be ever more multifunctional and adaptable to the demands of an ever-changing reality. However, we do need to offer an outline of the professional profile we want to develop for the future. The University cannot simply be dragged along by external demands, which are often ad hoc and contradictory. The University has a responsibility to pioneer new initiatives. This not an easy task at a time when the role and even the identity of the social worker is ill defined; even though, in Spain at least, it must be stressed that social work is now an established profession. Now, more than ever, it is necessary to provide

new responses to emerging needs and problems, to better understand the significant transformations that societies across Europe are experiencing.

Following Manuel Castells' (1998) analysis of the new problems and challenges for those working in the field of social intervention, a new social era - the Information Era is emerging, characterised by:

- Demographic changes, such as an ageing population, trans-national migration and changes to family structure;

- Changes in the labour market, such as the move to a post-Fordist model of production, the end of mass employment and insecure, flexible working conditions and contracts and the internationalisation of production and labour;

- Changes in social structure and in social relations, such as diversification and segmentation of society, the advent of new forms of social exclusion;

- Identity problems and conflicts; the domination of market forces and the

Table 10.1: The Syllabus

First Year	Second Year	Third Year
Social Anthropology 1 (2)	Social Anthropology 11 (5)	Social Medicine (4)
Economics applied to social work (6)	Law applied to social work (5)	Practical Work (28.5)
Statistics and IT (4)	Social Structure (5)	Social Services III (4.5)
Fundamentals of Law (8)	Social Policy (6)	Social Work III (6.5)
Social History (6)	Social Psychology (6)	Research Project (12)
Introduction to Family Work (3)	Social Services II (3)	Social Sciences (22)
Social Research Methods (4)	Social Work Methods I (3.5)	Health and Welfare (10)
Psychology (7)	Social Work Methods II (2.5)	Social Interventions (34)
Social Services I (8.5)	Social Work II (9)	Intervention Techniques (16)
Sociology (6)	Professional Ethics (6)	European Social Policy (12)
Social Work I (13)		Social and Welfare Policy (12)

subsequent limitation and deterioration of politics;

● The erosion of state sovereignty and the emergence of a new geopolitical situation.

All these factors, in addition to pre-existing social problems, call for a redefinition of the aims and priorities of social welfare and protection systems, a restructuring of our services and new demands on social workers.

These changes in social work practice are also encompassed in a wider process of de-legitimisation of social interventionism by the State and the growing hegemony of an individualistic view of society and social problems, all of which fosters de-politicisation and *individuals'* social rights and needs, rather than communities. Meanwhile, not so paradoxically, the economic and social processes reduce personal autonomy and state sovereignty, forming a new coalition of forces that do not favour the working classes. Therefore, social work suffers from growing and sometimes contradictory pressures, not only to define some realistic goals, but also to forge its own professional identity.

Social work education and training— the future

These recent developments have noticeable effects on the foundations of education and training for social work. The new demands mingle with ' old' problems, linked to what we could call the nature and construction of the profession . The challenges that must be faced, that *are* being faced by social work colleges are many. They range from the general challenges affecting the education system as a whole (one of the fundamental responses to the impact of globalisation and the formation of a knowledge-based society is the redirection of educational policy) to meet the specific challenges of a profession and a developing field of study.

In the space available here, it is not feasible to discuss all the issues that must be raised in respect of social work training. What is really impossible is to provide *answers* that address all the issues. Yet it is possible, and surely necessary, to formulate courses of action, a focus for the future, priorities and minimum prerequisites, even doubts and concerns. It is preferable to do this collectively ; sharing our thoughts based on our different experiences, each with our own convictions and history.

Some of the issues that seem particularly important are as follows.

1. It is necessary to raise the status of research in social work, to deepen knowledge, in order to develop the discipline as a profession and as a taught subject. Here, I refer to the need to both develop and formalise scientific knowledge and to prepare students to be able to use analytical and research tools in an exacting and sound way. Also, for the academic world to interact with the professional one, in a vital synergetic relationship between action and knowledge. By way of example, I will describe a study that was undertaken into the development of social work in Catalonia in Barcelona, this year:

   The aim of the study was to identify and examine the current situation and future prospects of social work. The study comprised a series of interviews with social workers of considerable, proven experience, which were conducted by students who were guided and tutored by a team of lecturers. The essence of the study was to capture the subtle elements and show the richness of the social work process and practice that allows the profession to locate itself within current social changes. As such its aim was to construct a thought process and a logic that would both transcend and encompass academic life by acknowledging and transforming the day-to-day know-how of practitioners into knowledge. A knowledge that could inform the training of new professionals and, by extension, the profession itself.

2. We must not confuse the applied nature of our studies with the need for a purely practical model of training. If theory is disconnected from practice it becomes sterile, but practice that is separated from theory leads to blind activism. We must take care not to fall into an excessive emphasis upon practice and the acquisition of mere technique. Techniques may be necessary, but if they are not grounded in solid frames of reference, they are reduced to simplistic and uncritical accumulations of different experiences that are unexacting and lead to the erosion of professional judgement and autonomy.

3. Fieldwork is and should remain an essential part of the learning process of future social workers. It is a necessary dimension, which

allows for the integration of knowledge and skills and requires students to confront the professional world and so mature as practitioners. The role of 'practice teacher' is vital to this dimension of the student social worker's learning experience.

4. Social work education necessarily includes a grounding in the Social and Human Sciences. However this must be organised with due regard to the core demands that are made on the profession. A critical debate, at least in Spain, is required within the university sector regarding the relationship between social work and the social sciences : a critical dialogue that allows for cross-, inter- and multi-disciplinary communication that informs and extends rather than narrows and divides the knowledge base of social work. In particular, we need to relinquish the opposition between a psychological and sociological perspective in social work. It is unhelpful to have to choose between social or individual theories of causation and models of intervention if social workers are to be equipped with the conceptual tools for intervening at both the psycho-social and social- policy levels.

5. The present crisis of national welfare systems necessitates the education and training of social workers to equip students to work in a range of settings other than state bureaucracies. Across Europe, economic, social and political changes are leading to a greater involvement of the private and voluntary sectors in the welfare system. Additionally employment patterns and conditions are generally becoming less certain and secure - leading to social workers having to adapt to a situation where there undertake temporary or part-time work, short-term and project based contracts and self-employed status. The education and training of social workers needs to take account of such contingencies by training enterprising professionals, who are capable of adapting to different and changing contexts, undertaking continuous professional development and transferring their knowledge, values and skills to a variety of tasks and settings.

6. In the case of social work, the development of distance learning models is clearly a route to follow in the future. Here, we suggest that these should adopt more of a semi-attendance than a non-attendance mode. Additionally students will have to widen, review and even change their knowledge base during their professional careers. This new situation means refocusing teaching content, methods and strategies away from a 'closed' way of imparting knowledge towards an 'open' curricula that facilitates the access, selection and utilisation of an expanding information base. In particular the educational dimension will need to reflect the changes in the professional world and organisational demands for quality and competition. These demands influence practitioners, in respect of, for example increased levels of personal accountability, stress and professional mobility.

7. The education and training of social workers must promote the European dimension more actively. Social work programmes should encourage co-operation between study centres through facilities, such as learning foreign languages, to enable student and teacher mobility, the participation in cross- national research projects and the joint authorship of literature and the recognition of qualifications between countries. The future for education, including that of social workers, means accepting, as Ulrich Beck (1992) has argued, globalisation, which calls into question one of the assumptions of modernity: methodological nationalism. Globalisation breaks the unity of the nation state through establishing a trans-national space in which events, problems, conflicts and even personal narratives can be located. Both university education and social work practice must become trans-national by utilising Europeanisation as a platform from which to develop their legitimate interests and purposes. Trans-nationalisation does not however imply uniformity or standardisation. The global and local do not cancel each other out. Awareness of and exchange of cultural differences are not a hindrance but a resource through which diversity can be celebrated. Indeed, it may well prove that it is only through maintaining cultural and educational heterogeneity that we can resist the imposition of market forces in our social relations.

It has not been possible here to deal with the subject of the education and training of social workers exhaustively, nor to close a topic that must remain open. Rather, the aim has been to develop a dialogue that will encourage universities to be one of the engines of society and not mere 'producers' of graduates; and in so doing allow the social work profession to play a full and effective role in citizens' efforts to improve their quality of life, their opportunities and their welfare.

At Ramon Lull University in Barcelona we are engaged in debate over the issues outlined here, we firmly believe that this debate should be inclusive and extend beyond national boundaries. In any event, whilst the future will always be imperfect, it is for us to take responsibility for our own actions in the present.

Questions for Further Consideration

1. What are the professional characteristics of social workers and what academic qualities and attributes are required of them in your country?

2. Social workers respond to individual problems, but are not only concerned with individuals. Needs and problems are also collective and are related to social structures and processes. How can we enable professionals to be no mere instruments of policy delivery, but people who can critically engage with and are equipped to design, manage and implement social policies?

3. By what means and in relation to which models and approaches is it possible to stimulate a critical spirit, initiative, ability to propose alternatives, adaptability and responsibility amongst social work students?

4. The acquisition and demonstration of competence is still a fundamental objective. However, are we in danger of diluting the intellectual qualities required of social workers and reducing the applied nature of the education to a form of vocational training and loosing sight of important knowledge, methods and techniques?

5. What possibilities exist in your country for developing international standards and establishing new strategies for inter-disciplinary participation in wider forums of debate?

Chapter Eleven

Social Work as a Career: Choice or Accident? The French Example

Emmanuel Jovelin

Introduction

In spite of current circumstances, characterised by a decline in recruitment and difficulties in retention of social workers within a rapidly changing political and organisational context, social work remains a potentially attractive occupation for a considerable number of people. As the field of social care becomes increasingly subject to global processes and national welfare regimes are reconstructed by the impact of both market forces and new social movements (see Adams *et al.*, 2000), so the question of the identity of social workers becomes amenable to different forms of analysis. At one level the changing relationship between the state, the private and the not-for-profit sectors is reconfiguring the variety and availability of different forms of social work. This allows for a contrast between either the regulatory or therapeutic nature of practice and career prospectus and competition within the labour market which determine the different capacities in respect of knowledge, skills and ethical orientation required of practitioners in different settings and roles. These factors will in turn interact with the personal biographies and motivations of individuals who have or who are intending to enter social work.

The purpose of this chapter is to identify significant factors that influence the individual's decision to enter the profession of social work, with particular reference to the context of French social work. The central hypothesis presented is that under the prevailing economic situation and associated high levels of unemployment, the choice of social work as a profession is increasingly a matter of occupational necessity rather than a matter of vocation. This argument is based primarily on the findings of a study by Jovelin (1998) consisting of interviews of 254 social workers in France (of whom 133 were of French origin and 121 of foreign origin).

Studies of the choice of occupation

Whilst there is a considerable body of literature on the nature of professions, (for example

Larson, 1997; Dingwall and Lewis, 1983; and Friedson, 1986) there exists limited research on the motivation or occupational identity of social workers. In the UK, Munday (1972) and Pearson (1973), drew attention to the accounts of social workers themselves and how these exposed the tensions that may arise between the motivational and organisational components of social work and the extent to which the choice of social work as a career may serve the individual in his, or more usually her, project of aspirations in as much as:

> He hopes to find something in himself and for himself in the act of helping others to find things in and for themselves.
>
> (Pearson, 1973: p 213)

Studies in France, where the particular forms of social work intervention arose from the historical interplay and connections between three principle disciplines:

- *Social Assistants* (who provide support for the family)
- *Social Animators* (socio-cultural educators)
- *Specialist Educators* (who provide education for maladjusted youth)

have examined more closely the relationship between personal biography and professional identity (see Adams *et al.*, 2000). Dubar has argued that one cannot consider the motivations behind the choice of occupation of specialist educators from a purely sociological perspective:

> It is not sufficient for the sociologist to identify the impact of socially determined constraints alone in order to explain the effective behaviours of an individual's choice of profession; rather one must also try to explain why these constraints usually impact at an unconscious level and more particularly, why more or less coherent subjective justifications are often substituted by justifications grounded in explicit social determinants.
>
> (Dubar, 1970: p 6 editor's translation)

The findings of the study by Jovelin (1998) concur with Dubar's analysis, in that satisfactory explanations of the choice of a profession can only be arrived at by reference to both psychological and social factors.

Dubar refutes the commonly held and well-established hypothesis that some individuals have an innate inclination and aptitude towards a particular vocation and that an awareness of this vocation is sufficient to direct them towards the particular profession. Rather, he follows the analysis of Naville, who concluded that:

> ...*the very notion of professional aptitude is illusory and sterile.*
>
> (Naville, 1957: p 194)

Further, Dubar argued that an innate aptitude or inclination towards a particular vocation cannot be empirically established. Moreover, the choice of profession is dependent upon the availability and variety of jobs existing at any given time.

Dubar's studies have demonstrated that the process of job selection in the case of 'specialist educators' is complex. He found that orientation towards this form of employment was closely linked to an individual's family history. Particularly, he emphasised the importance of childhood experiences, family values and attitudes and the discrepancies between parental aspirations and expectations regarding their children's careers and their subsequent choice of occupation. In his study of specialist educators in the North of France, Dubar identified that a high proportion were of middle-class origin, that the majority came from large families within which there were strongly held religious and social beliefs with some 90 per cent being Catholic—almost half practising Catholics. Typically, amongst this sample, their school record and progress was chequered by successive failures up to and including the baccalaureate—as well as to other levels of the training, and that parental aspirations for their children's future occupation did not correspond with their subsequent employment as a specialist educator.

From these findings, Dubar developed the hypothesis that the choice of occupation, in particular that of a specialist educator, was primarily determined by 'class factors', here defined by the relationship between family values and aspirations and school achievement. Thus, for specialist educators of working-class origins, the choice of profession represented a conscious but limited rise in social status, achieved through successes in extra curricula activities, such as membership of a youth club and a limited educational achievement. For those of upper middle class origin, the choice of employment represented a compromise with respect to social aspirations, whereby the failure to achieve high levels of educational success and their subsequent occupation was rationalised and legitimated by reference to family values and attitudes. For those of middle class origin, a population whose boundaries are more difficult to establish due to the diversity of family situations from which they originate, justification of their choice of occupation was made by reference to explicit criticism of their poor school experience and level of achievement. Hence, for example, in Dubar's study one respondent commented:

> *The education system is badly organised, and failed me. Specialist education is a better formulated and developed concept, that is why I've chosen it as a profession...I could have been a teacher but I was put off by my experience of schooling. Being a specialist educator is more dynamic and it corresponds more closely with how I prefer to work with children.*
>
> (Dubar, 1970: p 99)

Such criticisms of the school system were accompanied by reference to involvement and experiences in extracurricular and leisure activities such as membership of youth and community groups that provided an orientation towards and socialisation into specialist education. Thus, choice of a career arose from the consequences of limited success in educational achievement coupled with an orientation towards the norms and values associated with specialist education:

> *There exists a continuity between the kind of education received in the family, the youth movements and the conception of the profession chosen, or in other words a certain conformity between the ideologies of the social group of origin and those of the profession of worker.*
>
> (Dubar, 1970: p 135)

Dubar concludes that the choice of occupation of specialist educator is a result of several combined factors, in particular: family education, attitudes towards school and levels of contacts and involvement with youth and community groups. However, the impact of each of these factors varies according to an individual's social class origins. A predisposition towards the choice of profession arises primarily because of attempts to accommodate and rationalise the relationship between parents' and their children's social status and aspirations.

Dubar develops his hypothesis by arguing that the process leading to choice of occupation can be divided into two main stages. First, there is the preparatory stage in which specialist education is identified as a possible career.

Second, there is a realisation of this choice of career grounded in the individual's concrete circumstances:

> *The origin of the professional choice is a direct or indirect result of ideological, school and social determinants from the individual's childhood and the mechanisms by which the former have influenced the professional choice. Thus the immediate circumstances of entry into the profession are most often understood as contingent and independent of general influences and are represented without necessarily referring to the more general causal and motivational factors.*
>
> (Dubar, 1970: pp 142–143)

This argument, although an essential contribution to the understanding of the manner in which individuals entered the profession, has not been verified empirically. However, it draws similar conclusions to those of Muel-Dreyfus (1983), who analysed the social determinants of becoming a teacher as a choice of occupation, through a study of individuals' narratives of their different social trajectories arising from different social origins. Here, Muel-Dreyfus explores the connections drawn by the subjects of the study between the nature and value of the occupation and their justifications for becoming a teacher in the context of their own and their parents' social status, values and aspirations.

Muel-Dreyfus (1983: p 151) argues that these accounts of the personal and professional life projects of teachers can be understood in the context of a gap, between the opportunities and achievements provided by the school system, the social aspirations of the families and the realities of the labour market, that occurred during the 1970s. His analysis suggests that the decisions regarding this choice of the career arose at a particular point in the individual's career as a 'biographical accident'. Further, that this accident coincided with a rupture with the family aspirations and school achievement:

> *Entry into the profession arose from the successful alignment at a particular moment between individual circumstances and the social positions to which they gave rise…This can only lead us to speculate on whether the choice of occupation as a teacher was in fact not a preferred option, but one that has been rationalised in the light of their failed aspirations and lack of achievements.*
>
> (ibid: p 151)

Muel-Dreyfus's study of teachers' accounts is organised within the context of their personal family history. The reconstruction of the family's social trajectory thus serves to explain the individual's career trajectory, and the necessity of considering: family history; assessment of parental economic and social achievements, norms, values and attitudes along with the opportunities afforded by the school system in creating possible social futures.

Muel-Dreyfus's analysis is compatible with that of Lapauw (1969) about 'the moment of choice and the difficulty in making a choice', that arises for the prospective teacher, who by reference to their own life trajectory, begins to reflect upon their motives for embarking upon this particular career. Such a process gives rise to a conscious recognition and often painful realisation of the impact of past family circumstances and aspirations and personal achievements and failures upon the present. It is the understanding of the inter-relationship of past and the present realities, embedded in family structures, childhood and affective relations that characterise this process and to which Muel-Dreyfus refers.

When applied to Dubar's samples of specialised educators, the work of Muel-Dreyfus, relating to the choice of profession amongst teachers is methodologically limited, as it is not representative of the full range of roles within the field of specialist education (Autès, 1983). However, Muel-Dreyfus' work does provide a basis for further inquiry, particularly in the light of the earlier findings of Naville and Lapauw. Further, Muel-Dreyfus's findings are supported by the more recent work of Vilbrod (1995), who interviewed over 800 teachers to explore their expressed reasons and motivations and to identify the predisposing social conditions for their entry to the profession. Vilbrod's study confirms the findings of Muel-Dreyfus, but this later study provides information about an additional dimension to the influence of family history on the choice of career amongst teachers. Here, the 'generation effect' is identified as being the fact that entry to the profession is a response to failures in academic achievement. A significant proportion of those entering the profession had experienced failures, relegation and repetitions throughout their school careers. Furthermore, in the study it was apparent that previous generations within their families had turned to teaching as a result of similar compromised schooling, often following failed aspirations to pursue other more highly valued or highly paid careers.

Finally, Verba provides an insight into the process of career choice amongst primary school teachers. This study identifies two common experiences amongst the sample and reinforces the findings of Dubar and Muel-Dreyfus. In the first type of experience, the teachers gave accounts of a painful family history and characterised their education as dysfunctional and contradictory. Their stated motivation to subsequently become teachers themselves arose from:

> *...a desire to provide children with an experience that they had been denied during their childhood.*
>
> (Verba, 1995: p 64)

In the second type of experience, 68 per cent of primary school teachers acknowledged that they had only achieved an average school performance with 67 per cent having had to repeat at least one year of their schooling, (which occurred for 20 per cent in their upper sixth form).

Implications for the career choice of social workers

The findings from these studies of factors influencing career choice amongst teachers and special educators, echo those identified in the work of Simonot (1974) in relation to social work. This study, which examined the motivation of trainee socio-cultural animators, similarly identified that their choice of career was related to the interrelationship between their family history and socio-economic status and their own school career and involvement in youth and community activities. However, in spite of these recurring patterns across family histories and school careers as causal in selection of a career amongst both special educators and social animators, there persists, in the accounts given by the subjects of these studies, reference to the vocational aspect of these occupations. Helping and caring provide the overt justification for entering this occupational field.

Turning to the accounts given in Jovelin's (1998) study of social workers, these show a marked similarity to those reported by Simonot. For example, Jovelin's (1998) study reveals that the social role attributed to the occupation of social work by the respondents is one where social work is characterised as an activity or occupation that demonstrates a moral commitment to combat poverty, inequality and oppression. Further, social workers are expected to have a desire to make a personal contribution to combating these social

ills and that social workers expect to be of use to society (1974: p 160). For example, as one respondent stated:

> *I wanted to help the destitute in a society where the rich become richer and the poor become poorer. It is a need to feel useful to society.*
>
> (Jovelin, 1998: p 269)

However, reference to the process by which this individual chose a career as a social worker, reveal the relationship of this choice to their own biography:

> *After the upper sixth form, I was registered for a D.G.U.S. (Degree of General University Studies) but instead I opted to enrol on the program of Social and Socio-cultural Animation at the University Institute of Technology. I made that re-orientation because I was not satisfied with following a career as a teacher and the university studies did not suit me. The choice of social work as a career is a need, a will to help people in difficulty, to advise them, and enable them to develop, evolve and overcome their problems and failures through support and assistance, but above all, to become self determining and autonomous individuals.*
>
> (ibid: p 270)

These stories fit with the traditional evocations of social work as a vocation. In other words, the justification of the choice of career by reference to a personal commitment of service to others is based upon ethical principles and collective values (Morand, 1992: p129). Such narratives suggest a sense of mission and salvationist overtones, where proponents assume, in the exercise of their function, the expression of a system of values that privileges equality at the cultural, economic, social and political levels:

> *I want to help with a purpose, to change things...it is the need to feel useful to the society...the need to reach out to others in the struggle against exclusion.*
>
> (ibid: p 271)

Such a mission, aimed at reducing inequality, is conceived as a form of intervention where social work has an 'orthopaedic function' (Besnard, 1980), towards a 'sick social body' in which social work plays the role of re-integrating, re-adjusting, re-orienting and correcting deficiencies of the socially excluded. It is a scenario of normalisation, wherein social work is a means at the service of individuals, the aim of which is to restore individual identities and social relationships through the giving of assistance and proposing new frames of reference for individuals.

However, in Jovelin's sample it was apparent that an orientation towards social work, associated interests and the choice of social work as a career occurred relatively late in individuals' personal accounts of the motivation to enter social work. Thus, such an orientation was realised only in the context of individuals' unique biographies and was associated with particular events such as family problems, disillusionment, failure or abandonment of school or university studies, unemployment or lack of success in a former career. For example, see the case of Mr L.

Case example: Mr L

Mr L was born in 1953 into a family of eight children. He is married and has two children. At school, he obtained a technical qualification and from 1969 was employed as a 'fitter' in a company until its closure in 1991. He cites as his motives for entering social work, a desire to help young people and was encouraged to pursue a career in social work on the advice of a friend, rather than as a direct result of his experience of becoming unemployed.

A considerable number of the respondents stated that they turned towards social work, as a career, on the advice of friends or parents, who were themselves working in this field. This finding raises the question of the extent to which entry into the profession of social work is a matter of 'professional proximity'. For example, many of the parents who advised their children to enter social work as a career were not necessarily specialist educators or social animators themselves, but were working in associated jobs as carers and social assistants. Others reported that they had previously belonged to a community or collective association or union. Although involvement in a trade union appears less important in the profiles of social workers than during the 1970s, union membership is suggestive and representative of a loose collection of interests rather than a general commitment to collective issues and action. It should also be recognised that since the late 1970s disruptions to the labour market have weakened militant tendencies in the Trade Union movement. Increasingly, young people no longer identify themselves with the working class as an entry into adult life and adult status: socialisation through industrial work is no longer assured (Dubet, 1987).

In Jovelin's sample, there were individuals who expressed a militant attitude but this was not translated into formal activity. This accords with the difficulties of combining a militant stance and a professional role, particularly in an occupation such as social work where the worker acts, in effect, as a mediator between the population and the political-administrative system. Here a militant attitude is seen as problematic and inappropriate.

The chequered biography

A central argument generated by Jovelin's study is that the choice of career as a social worker represents one of adjustment to biographical events. From a sample of 254 social workers, the life stories of some 148 fitted this hypothesis. Here, the adoption of a social work identity came about as a reaction to other events, such as lack of success in academic attainment, redundancy or failure in other forms of employment. As such a social work career constitutes the abandonment of a previous life project and a readjustment or reorientation of interest and aspirations. From an analysis of the accounts presented in this sample population, over half of the reconstructed life stories represent what can be referred to as chequered biographies. Of these three particular patterns or biographical trajectories can be discerned:

First, the *professionally vulnerable*: whose careers have been unstable and who have been employed in a number of occupations and who have experienced redundancy and periods of unemployment. These are people whom Demasiere has termed 'the discouraged unemployed' and who have internalised their exclusion from the workforce. A consequence of which is that their chances of finding employment in the chosen area are very weak and they have turned to social work as an alternative career opportunity. The example of Mr T illustrates the professionally vulnerable career history and motivation to enter social work.

Case example: Mr T

Mr T was born in 1959 and is married with two children. His father was a foreman in the metallurgical industry; his mother did not have paid employment. After obtaining his school-leaving certificate, he left school in 1977 to work as a metallurgist. Two years later he went to work for Renault. Following the restructuring of the car manufacturing industry he subsequently moved in 1980 to Monaco to work once more in the metallurgical industry. From 1981, he worked in the hotel business in Menton and Roquebrune and subsequently returned to the North of France where he worked in a printing works and then as a shop assistant in a supermarket. During this period, he encountered social workers through his activities as a member of a political party. He then undertook occupational training and gained a technical qualification that enabled him to enter Technical University to undertake a degree in social work. However, when asked as to his reasons for choosing a career in social work he made no mention of his 'chequered career', rather he referred to his interest and commitment to trade union and political activity and a desire to help young people.

Second, the *academically frustrated*: are individuals whose academic ambitions and careers have been subject to disruption, curtailment and general lack of progress. Some of this disruption may be accounted for as part of an individual strategy and choice to voluntarily end and later continue general university studies prior to opting for social work: often predominantly in the juvenile protection and justice services.

Case example: Mr S

Mr S is a 29-year-old educator. He has a *baccalaureat*, a *licence de sociologie*, a *maitrise d'économie*, a *licence d'administration publique* and a *diplome d'études approfondies en science politique*. After a period of unemployment, he accepted a job as a social worker, as an interim measure until some other opportunity presented itself.

Third, there are the *university drop-outs*: graduates who obtained a university degree but who failed to obtain a professional diploma. Their career development often seems to have been hampered within the limits of their academic achievement. Their career aspirations are frustrated due to the lack of an appropriate and recognised qualification. They openly acknowledge that the choice of social work as a career is one that has been imposed on them through circumstance.

Case example: Ms S

Ms S is 21 and single. Her father is an artisan and her mother is unemployed although she had previously worked in a textile factory. In 1988, she was awarded the *baccalaureat électronique*, and later enrolled in the first year of *brevet technicien superieure*. Having failed in the first year examinations she left this course and enrolled in the first year of the *diplome d'études universitaires générales*. However, following exam failures in the second year, she ended her studies and obtained work as a social worker.

A general characteristic amongst all these groups is that their entry into social work represents a strategy in their own struggle against exclusion (Castel, 1996). For these entrants then, social work constitutes a solution to their own difficulties. In much the same way the minimum wage or income support provides a means for survival for those on the margins or excluded from employment. The choice of social work as a career thus offers a double benefit, in as much as it offers both a meaning and purpose and means of livelihood to those whose personal and occupational careers were disrupted and vulnerable.

Implications for those who enter social work as a matter of necessity rather than choice

A significant proportion of the social workers interviewed were unwilling to recognise or acknowledge that their choice of career in social work came about as a result of their own vulnerability and experience of misfortune or lack of success in achieving their ambitions and aspirations. Rather they preferred to emphasise their commitment to the espoused values and interests of the profession, which suggests that there is an essential ambivalence towards their choice of social work as a career. Although, amongst those individuals who entered the profession by necessity, rather than choice, a significant number made claims to a subsequent conversion and commitment to the ethics and purpose of the profession, for example as one respondent stated:

> Finally, now I am in practice, I cannot see myself working anywhere else, I like what I do. I think that even though I may find a better job, it will be close to social work.

> (Jovelin, 1998: p 218)

For these individuals, the 'hidden causes' of their choice of social work as a career have been rationalised and resolved. This acceptance of the vocational dimension to social work demonstrates that for these individuals the meaning of their investment towards the recipients of social welfare service has taken on a new importance. For them, the adoption of the ethical position, implied by social work as an activity, provides the rationale for not only the way in which they behave towards other people but also as a means through which they have come to terms with their own chequered

biographies. For those who have not been able to make this transition to an alternative view of their own histories and disappointments, social work remains a temporary relief and transient activity, as indicated by the comments of this respondent:

> Social work is a temporary job for me. With my qualifications, I don't know what I am doing here, but I know that I will leave one day because I am not suited for this job although I am competent to do it.

> (ibid: p 379)

For these people the purpose, values and interests of social work cannot compensate for their sense of disappointment and thwarted aspirations. The ambivalence remains in as much as they are unable to make a commitment to social work, but are unable to find an alternative career. Amongst such individuals, there is evidence of burn-out, which arises not from over-commitment but from a sense of frustration.

Implications for the selection of individuals to social work education

The regional commission for the organisation of selection procedures in the North-Pas-de-Calais Region of France is currently considering mechanisms by which candidates who present as ambivalent or lacking in insight about their motivation for entering the profession may be screened out. However, adopting such a strategy and developing criteria and procedures aimed at avoiding the selection and recruitment of such individuals has wider implications for the profession.

This research suggests that the hidden motives of individuals who 'choose' social work as a career need further exploration and emphasis. The capacity to acknowledge and reflect upon one's own personal history and experiences is central to the ability to develop an orientation towards the values, interests and purpose of social work; just as the recognition of one's own vulnerability and experiences of loss and frustration are essential components in the development of an empathetic and enabling stance towards others. That an individual arrives at a decision to enter social work as a result of 'set backs' in their own career is not of itself problematic. Rather it can be beneficial both to their own development and in developing abilities to assist others. However, in a society that values success, achievement, advantage and competition, both the individuals who are considering entering the profession and those who represent the profession of social work need to be able to work through and acknowledge that the purpose of social work derives from the realities of sickness, misfortune, loss, disappointment and hurt.

Conclusion

The analysis presented here demonstrates that the motivation to pursue a career in social work is a complex and often ambivalent process. Often the decision to become a social worker is as much a matter of necessity as of choice. As such, the choice of social work as a career often constitutes an experience of adjustment and reconciliation closely associated with an individual's biography and as a consequence of unforeseen events (Jovelin, 1998 and 1999). Ironically, it may well be that such awareness provides a foundation for the individual's adoption of the ethics and purpose of social work, in as much as it relates to the concepts of emancipation, empowerment, and self-determination. Moreover, such experiences evidence the possibility for overcoming experiences of loss and oppression. However, painful biographical realities need to be acknowledged rather than denied or hidden if those involved in social work are to realise the potential of social work both for themselves and also for others who receive a service.

Questions for Further Consideration

1. What is your motivation to work as a social worker and do you know of any research in your own country about the reasons why social workers enter and remain in the profession?

2. Are the selection criteria for aspiring social workers that are currently being developed in France similar to those in use in other countries in Europe?

3. On what basis should selectors determine a candidate's suitability for social work?

4. What characteristics and qualities are necessary for those involved in the selection of candidates?

Postscript

Adrian Adams, Peter Erath and Steven M. Shardlow

Differences in welfare policies and services that have developed, since the end of the Second World War, in the different nation states of Europe may be accounted for by reference to different historical, political, economic and cultural reasons. Increasingly, across Europe, social welfare policies and services aimed at promoting social protection and social inclusion, are undergoing major changes. These changes can be accounted for by reference to the influence of and re-alignment towards: market forces in the forms of commodification and the individualised consumption of care, the privatisation of care services and an emphasis on the relationship between welfare and work (Pillinger, 2000); and geo-politics: the re-drawing of boundaries of nation-states and the emergence of supra-national boundaries such as the EU (Williams, 2000).

The breaking of the post-war period of consensus between the interests of the political left and right, the public and the private and the general and the particular that characterised welfarism, and the advent of a mixed economy of welfare wherein both providers and consumers must compete for limited resources by reference to, on the one hand, criteria of efficiency and effectiveness, and on the other, to claims for recognition and entitlement, has given rise to the necessity for social work to re-invent and re-locate itself within the politics of welfare and identity. Here, the problem for social work is that:

> The pursuit of an ideal consensus is seen as misguided, for what we need is a more accepting attitude towards contingency and particularly the various 'language games'. A primary goal of social theory, and I would suggest social work, in the (post) modern era is to try and enhance intelligibility between different cultures. It is not, however, that we should subscribe to the view that whatever is, is sacrosanct. Quite the reverse! We should praise innovation. The problem is that we cannot evaluate according to any absolute standards of progress. While trying to differentiate between accept-able and unacceptable practices and positions we must recognise that this is always necessarily contentious and incomplete.

(Parton, 1994: p 110)

Social work, by reference to its genealogy, as a response to mass industrialisation and urbanisation in the nineteenth century and more recently as the professional embodiment of post-war welfarism, is challenged by the impact of market forces and geo-politics upon attitudes towards, and structures of, public welfare policies and services. In response to this challenge, to its role and purpose in the face of changing political and economic imperatives, new forms of practice have emerged. However, in seeking to maintain its legitimacy within an emergent redefinition of welfare, a fundamental dilemma has re-surfaced:

> In whose interests and for what purposes does social work act: the institutions and agents of government or the needs of citizens?

Each of the preceding chapters has explored an important theme in both the traditional and current re-constructive phases of social work. In so doing they offer a perspective from which the purpose and interests may be constructed. Collectively they offer a wider horizon for understanding and action in a post industrial/reflexive society, in which: 'intensification and individualisation of social inequalities interlock' (Beck, 1992: p 89) and wherein the recipients of social welfare, the 'socially excluded fall-out' from the economic and political imperatives of society, are thus additionally disadvantaged and perceived as failing to achieve social competence:

> As a consequence, the problems of the system are lessened politically and transformed into personal failure. In the detraditionalised modes of living, a new immediacy for individual and society arises, the immediacy of crisis and sickness, in the sense that social crises appear to be of individual origin, and are perceived as social only indirectly and to a very limited extent.

(ibid.)

From this perspective, social work clients, whilst classified as vulnerable or dependent (and thus implicitly as deficient individuals), may perhaps be better understood as those who cannot secure or maintain a *social identity*-recognition, and *status*-respect, within established or emergent communities. As such they are people who are: *excluded* from and denied access to economic, political, legal and administrative institutions, processes and activity through which they have access to influence and justice, state benefits and services, and for whom the means of life may be secured, and who are *alienated* from social norms and values and the rights and responsibilities of citizenship. For such groups and individuals, *life chances* are constrained through conditions of deprivation, exploitation, inequality and discrimination. So too are opportunities to engage in self-actualisation through: *life planning*—the reflexively organised trajectory of the individual in the context of risks, or in *life politics*—engagement in autonomous collective action, and thus acquire the generative power necessary to influence social institutions.

References

Preface

Ricoeur, P. (Translation Brennan, E.) (1995). Reflections on a New Ethos for Europe. *Philosophy and Social Criticism*, 21(5/6):12.

Introduction

Bourdieu, P. (Translation Nice, R.) (1977). *Outline of a Theory of Practice*. Cambridge: University Press.

Cantell, T., and Pedersen, P.P. (1992). Modernity, Post-modernity and Ethics: An Interview with Zygmunt Bauman. *Telos*, 93: pp 133–145.

Cooper, A., and Pitts, J. (1994). Ironic Investigations: The Relationship Between Trans-national European Social Work Research and Social Work Education. In Gehrmann, G., Muller, K.D., and Ploem, R. (Eds.). *Social Work and Social Studies*. Weinheim: Deutscher Studien Verlag.

Foucault, M. (1970). *The Order of Things*. London: Tavistock.

Gadamer, H.G. (Translation Barden, G., and Cumming, J.) (1975). *Truth and Method*. London: Sheed and Ward.

Habermas, J. (Translation McCarthy, T.) (1984 and 1987). *The Theory of Communicative Action* (2 vols.). Boston: Beacon Press.

Chapter 1

Adams, A., Erath, P., and Shardlow, S.M. (Eds.) (2000). *Fundamentals of Social Work in Selected European Countries*. Dorset: Russell House Publishing.

Bailey, J. (1992). *Social Europe*. London: Longman.

Berg-Schlosser, D., and Müller-Rommel, F. (Eds.) (1991). *Vergleichende Politikwissenschaft*. Opladen: Leske Verlag und Budrich GmbH.

Bourdieu, P., Accardo, A., Balazs, G., Beaud, S., Bourdieu, E., Broccolichi, S., Champagne, P., Christin, R., Faguer, J-P., Garcia, S., Lenoir, R., Oeuvrard, F., Pialoux, M., Pinto, L., Podalydès, D., Sayad, A., Soulié, C., Wacquant, L.J.D. (1993). *La Misère du Monde*. Paris: Editions du Seuil.

Cannan, C., Berry, L., and Lyons, K. (1992). *Social Work in Europe*. Houndmills, Basingstoke: Macmillan.

Castles, F.G. (Ed.) (1993). *Families of Nations: Patterns of Public Policy in Western Democracies*. Aldershot: Dartmouth.

Chamberlyne, P., Cooper, A., Freeman, R. and Rustin, M. (1999). *Welfare and Culture in Europe*. London: Jessica Kingsley.

Deacon, B., Hulse, M., and Stubbs, P. (1997). *Global Social Policy. International Organisations and the Future of Welfare*. London: Sage.

Esping-Andersen, G. (1990). *The Three Worlds of Welfare Capitalism*. Cambridge: Polity Press.

George, V., and Taylor-Goodby, P. (Eds.) (1996). *European Welfare Policy: Squaring the Circle*. Houndmills, Basingstoke: Macmillan.

Habermas, J. (Translation McCarthy, T.) (1987). *The Theory of Communicative Action Volume 2: Lifeworld and System*. Cambridge: Polity Press.

Habermas, J. (Translation Rehg, W.) (1996). *Between Facts and Norms: Contributions to a Discourse Theory of Law and Democracy*. Cambridge: Polity Press.

Hantrais, L. (1995). *Social Policy in the European Union*. Houndmills, Basingstoke: Macmillan.

Hartmann, J. (1995). *Vergleichende Politikwissenschaft*. Frankfurt: New York Campus Verlag.

Heckhausen, H. (1972). *Discipline and Interdisciplinarity, in OECD: Interdisciplinarity: Problems of Teaching and Research in Universities*, pp 83–89. Paris: OECD, Centre for Educ. Research and Innovation.

Hetherington, R., Cooper, A., Smith, P., and Wilford, G. (1997). *Protecting Children: Messages from Europe*. Lyme Regis: Russell House.

Kiely, G., and Richardson, V. (Eds.) (1991). *Family Policy: European Perspectives*. Dublin: Family Studies Centre.

Kohl, J. (1992). Armut im internationalen Vergleich. Methodische Probleme und Empirische Ergebnisse. In Leibfried, S., Voges, W. (Eds.). *Armut im modernen Wohlfahrtsstaat. Sonderheft der Kölner Zeitschrift für Soziologie und Sozialpsychologie*, pp 272–299. Opladen: Westdeutscher Verlag.

Lefebreve, H. (1994). *Everyday Life in the Modern World*. London: Transaction Publishers.

Lorenz, W. (1994). *Social Work in a Changing Europe*. London: Routledge.

Luhmann, N. (1995). *Gesellschaftsstruktur und Semantik*. Frankfurt/M: Suhrkamp.

Luhmann, N. (1995). Das Paradox der Menschenrechte. In ead. *Soziologische Aufklärung*, 6: pp 129–236. Opladen: Westdeutscher Verlag.

Lyons, K. (1999). *International Social Work. Themes and Perspectives*. Aldershot: Ashgate.

Ritter, G.A. (1991). *Der Sozialstaat. Entstehung und Entwicklung im internationalen Vergleich*. München: R. Oldenburg Verlag.

Shardlow, S.M., and Payne, M. (Eds.) (1998). *Contemporary Issues in Social Work: Western Europe*. Aldershot: Ashgate.

Trevellion, S. (1996). Towards a Comparative Analysis of Collaboration. *Social Work in Europe*, 3(1): pp 37–39.

Weber, G. (1999). *Soziale Hilfe: ein Teilsystem in der Gesellschaft?* Opladen: Westdeutscher Verlag.

Chapter 2

Abrahamson, P. (1997). The Scandinavian Social Service State in Comparison. In Sipilä, J. (Ed.). *Social Care Services: The Key to the Scandinavian Welfare Model*, pp 156–177. Aldershot: Avebury.

Adams, A., and Shardlow, S.M. (2000). Social Work Practice in the United Kingdom. In Adams, A., Erath, P. and Shardlow S.M. (Eds.). *Fundamentals of Social Work in Selected European Countries. Historical and Political Context, Present Theory, Practice Perspectives*, pp 119–137. Lyme Regis: Russell House.

Anttonen, A., and Sipilä, J. (1995). *Five Regimes of Social Care Services*. Mimeo. University of Tampere, Department of Social Policy and Social Work.

Bergmark, Å. (1996). Individual Morality and Incentive Structures: A Problem for the Swedish Social Assistant Scheme? In Hämäläinen J. and Vornanen R. (Eds.). *Social Work and Social Security in a Changing Society*, pp 33–47. Festschrift für Prof. Pauli Niemelä. Augsburg: MaroVerlag.

Deacon, B. (1998). The Prospects of Global Social Policy. In Deacon, B., Koivusalo, M. and Stubbs, P. (Eds.). *Aspects of Global Social Policy Analysis*, pp 11–39. Helsinki: National Research and Development Centre for Welfare and Health.

Deacon, B., Hulse, M., and Stubbs, P. (1997). *Global Social Policy. International Organisations and the Future of Welfare*. London: Sage.

Esping-Andersen, G., and Korpi, W. (1987). From Poor Relief to Institutional Welfare States: The Development of Scandinavian Social Policy. In Erikson, R., Hansen, E.J., Ringen, S., and Uusitalo, H. (Eds.). *The Scandinavian Model. Welfare States and Welfare Research*, pp 39–74. New York: M.E. Sharpe.

Evers, A. (1990). Shifts in the Welfare Mix: Introducing a New Approach for the Study of Transformations in Welfare and Social Policy. In Evers, A., and Wintersberger, H. (Eds.). *Shifts in the Welfare Mix. Their Impact on Work, Social Services and Welfare Policies*, pp 7–30. Boulder: Westview Press.

Friedman, M. (1981). *Free to Choose: A Personal Statement*. New York: Avon Books.

Hausgierd, H. (1991). *Social Security in Norway*. Produced for the Ministry of Foreign Affairs by NORINFORM. Oslo.

Hayek, F.A. (1990). *The Road to Serfdom*. London: Routledge.

Holmes, S. (1988). Liberal Guilt: Some Theoretical Origins of the Welfare State. In Moon, J.D. (Ed.). *Responsibility, Rights and Welfare*, pp 77–106. Boulder: Westview Press.

Huxley, P. (1993). Case Management and Care Management in Community Care. *British Journal of Social Work*, 23(4): pp 365–381.

Kaufmann, F.X. (1985). Major Problems and Dimensions of the Welfare State. In Eisenstadt, S.N. and Ahimer, O. (Eds.). *The Welfare State and its Aftermath*, pp 44–56. Ottowa: NJ Barnes and Noble Books.

Lorenz, W. (1994). *Social Work in a Changing Europe*. London: Routledge.

Lyons, K. (1999). *International Social Work. Themes and Perspectives*. Aldershot: Ashgate.

Niemelä, P. (1994). Peruspalvelun käsite ja hyvinvointipalvelujen tuottamisen subjektit—tarkastelukehikko. In Niemelä, P., Knuutinen, M., Kainulainen, S., and Malkki P. (Eds.). *Peruspalvelut. Mitä ne ovat ja miten ne tulisi tuottaa*. Kuopion yliopiston julkaisuja E. Yhteiskuntatieteet, 23: pp 11–24. Kuopio.

Niemelä, P., Knuutinen, M., Hyvärinen, S., Kainulainen, S., Myllykangas, M., and Ryynänen, O-P. (1995). *Sosiaali- ja terveydenhuollon priorisointi. Tutkimuspriorisointiprosessista ja -näkemyksistä kunnissa*. Sosiaali- ja terveysalan tutkimus-ja kehittämiskeskus. Raportteja, 174: pp 38–41. Helsinki.

Nilsson, L., and Wadeskog, A. (1990). Local Initiatives in a New Welfare State: A Fourth Sector Approach. In Evers, A., and Wintersberger, L-L. (Eds.). *Shifts in the Welfare Mix. Their Impact on Work, Social Services and Welfare Policies. European Centre for Social Welfare Policy and Research*, pp 33–61. Boulder: Westview Press.

Riihinen, O. (Ed.) (1992). *Sosiaalipolitiikka 2017: näkökulmia suomalaisen yhteiskunnan kehitykseen ja tulevaisuuteen*. Porvoo: WSOY.

Simonen, L. (1995). From Public Responsibility to the Welfare-Mix of Care. Private Producers of Social Services. Finnish Local Government Studies 4. Special issue in English edited by Lasse Oulasvirta. *Finnish Local Government in Transition*, pp 325–332. Helsinki: The Finnish Association of the Local Government Studies.

Sipilä, J. (1989). *Sosiaalityön jäljillä*. Helsinki: Tammi.

Sipilä, J. (1999). *How Does the Finnish Welfare State Manage to Solve Social Problems?* Paper presented in the conference of the European Association of Schools of Social Work. 'European Social Work: Building Expertise for the 21st Century'. Helsinki: June 10–13, 1999.

Sipilä, J., Andersson, M., Hammarqvist, S.E., Nordlander, L., Rauhala, P.L., Thomsen, K., and Nielsen, H.W. (1997). A Multitude of Universal, Public Services: How and Why did Four Scandinavian Countries get their Social Care Service Model? In Sipilä, J. (Ed.). *Social Care Services: The Key to the Scandinavian Welfare Model*, pp 27–50. Aldershot: Avebury.

Titmuss, R.M. (1974). *Social Policy. An Introduction*. Edited by Abel-Smith, B., and Titmuss, K. London: George Allen and Unwin.

Øyen, E. (Ed.) (1986). *Comparing Welfare States and Their Futures*. Aldershot: Gower.

Chapter 3

Bauman, Z. (1978). *Hermeneutics and Social Science*. London: Hutchinson.

Bertalanffy, L. von (1950). An Outline of General Systems Theory. *British Journal of the Philosophy of Science*, 1.

De Maria, W. (1992). On the Trail of a Radical Pedagogy for Social Work Education. *British Journal of Social Work*, 22(3): pp 231–252.

Dewe, B., and Otto, H-U. (1996). *Zugänge zur Sozialpädagogik. Reflexive Wissenschaftstheorie und kognitive Identität*. Weinheim, München: Juventa.

Dilthey,W. (1888). Über die Möglichkeit einer

Allgemeingültigen Pädagogischen Wissenschaft. In Dilthey, W. *Gesammelte Schriften VI. Bd. Die geistige Welt. Einleitung in die Philosophie des Lebens. Zweite Hälfte. Abhandlungen zur Poetik, Ethik und Pädagogik*, pp 56–102. 6. Aufl. Stuttgart-Göttingen 1978.

Durkheim, E. (1952). *Suicide: A Study in Sociology*. London: Routledge and Kegan Paul.

Foucault, M. (1970). *The Order of Things*. London: Tavistock.

Freire, P. (1985). *The Politics of Education. Culture, Power and Liberation*. Massachusetts: Bergin and Garvey.

Gambrill, E. (1977). *Modification: A Handbook of Assessment, Intervention and Evaluation*. San Francisco: Jossey-Bass.

Germain, C.B. (1981). The Ecological Approach to People-Environment Transactions. *Social Casework*, 62(6): pp 332–341.

Giesecke, H. (1973). *Offensive Sozialpädagogik*. Göttingen. Vandenhoeck and Ruprecht.

Greit, G.L., and Lynch, A.A. (1983). The Eco-systems Perspective. In Meyer, C.H. (Ed.). *Clinical Social Work in the Eco-systems Perspective*, pp 35–71. New York: Columbia University Press.

Habermas, J. (1985). *Der philosophische Diskurs der Moderne*. Frankfurt: Suhrkamp.

Haupert, B., and Kraimer, K. (1991). Die Heimatlosigkeit der SA/SP, Stellvertretende Deutung und Typologisches Verstehen als Wege zu einer Eigenständigen Profession. *Pädagogische Rundschau*, 45: pp 177–196.

Hollstein, W., and Meinhold, M. (Hrsg.) (1980). *Sozialarbeit unter kapitalistischen Produktionsbestimmungen, 5. Auflage*. Frankfurt/M: Fischer.

Horkheimer, M. (1984). Ideologie. In Lenk, K. (Ed.). *Ideologiekritik und Wissenssoziologie, Auflage*: pp 245–252. Frankfurt: Suhrkamp.

Horkheimer, M., and Adorno, T. (1973). *Dialectic of the Enlightenment*. London: Allen Lane.

Hudson, B.L., and Macdonald, G. (1986). *Behavioural Social Work. An Introduction*. Houndmills, Basingstoke: Macmillan.

Krumm, V. (1983). Kritisch-rationale Erziehungswissenschaft. In Lenzen, D. (Ed.). *Enzyklopädie Erziehungswissenschaft*, pp 139–154. Stuttgart: Klett.

Lorenz, W. (1994). *Social Work in a Changing Europe*. London. Routledge.

Merton, R.K. (1973). *The Sociology of Science*. Chicago: University of Chicago.

Meyer, C.H. (1983). The Search for Coherence. Clinical Social Work. In Meyer, C.H. (Ed.). *The Eco-Systems Perspective*, pp 5–34. New York: Columbia University Press.

Mollenhauer, K. (1973). Sozialpädagogik. Fischer Lexikon Pädagogik. In Groothoff, H.H., and Reimers, E. (Eds.). *Fischer Lexikon Pädagogik*, pp 291–300. Frankfurt/M: Fischer.

Nohl, H. (1933). *Die Pädagogische Bewegung in Deutschland und ihre Theorie*. (Unveränderte Auflage 1978). Frankfurt/M: G-Schulte-Bulmke.

Payne, M. (1997). *Modern Social Work Theory*. Houndmills, Basingstoke: Macmillan.

Pincus, A., and Minaham, A. (1973). *Social Work Practice: Model and Method*. Itasca: Peacock.

Roberts, A.R. (1991). *Contemporary Perspectives on Crisis Intervention and Prevention*. Englewood Cliffs. NJ: Prentice-Hall.

Rössner, L. (1977). *Erziehungs- und Sozialarbeitswissenschaft. Eine einführende System-Skizze*. München, Basel: Reinhardt.

Skinner, B.F. (1953). *Science and Human Behaviour*. New York: Macmillan.

Staub-Bernasconi, S. (1995). *Systemtheorie, Soziale Probleme und Soziale Arbeit. Lokal, National, International, oder: Vom Ende der Bescheidenheit*. Bern, Stuttgart, Wien: Haupt.

Turner, F.J. (1986). *Social Work Treatment. Interlocking Theoretical Approaches* (3rd Edn.). New York: Free Press.

Wendt, W.R. (1990). *Ökosozial Denken und Handeln. Grundlagen und Anwendungen in der Sozialarbeit*. Freiburg: Lambertus.

Chapter 4

Anderson, N. (1961). *The Hobo: The Sociology of the Homeless Man*. Chicago: University of Chicago Press.

Austin, J. (1962). *How To Do Things With Words*. Oxford: Clarendon.

Bateson, G. (1972). *Steps to an Ecology of Mind*. New York: Ballantine Books.

Becker, H.S., Blanche, G., Everett, C.H., and Strauss, A. (1961). *Boys in White: Students Culture in Medical School*. Chicago: University of Chicago Press.

Berger, P., and Luckmann, T. (1967). *The Social Construction of Reality*. London: Allen Lane.

Bourdieu, P. (1977). *Outline of a Theory of Practice* (trans. Nice, R.). Cambridge University.

Brown, G.W., and Harris, T. (1978). *The Social Origins of Depression: A Study of Psychiatric Disorder in Women*. London: Tavistock.

Cannan, C. (1994). Enterprise Culture, Professional Socialisation, and Social Work Education in Britain. *Critical Social Policy Issues*, 42: pp 5–18.

Cantell, T., and Pedersen, P.P. (1992). Modernity, Post-modernity and Ethics: An Interview with Zygmunt Bauman. *Telos*, 93: pp 133–145.

de Waus, D.A. (1994). *Surveys in Social Research*. London: UCL Press.

Dilthey, W. (1977). *Descriptive Psychology and Historical Understanding*. The Hague: Martinus Nijhoff (originally published in 1894).

Dominelli, L. (1996). Deprofessionalising Social work: Anti-oppressive Practice, Competencies and Postmodernism. *British Journal of Social Work*, 26: pp 153–175.

Douglas, J.D. (Ed.) (1971). *Understanding Everyday Life*. London: Routledge & Kegan Paul.

Durkheim, E. (1982). *The Rules of Sociological Methods*. Houndmills, Basingstoke: Macmillan (originally published in 1895).

Feyerabend, P.K. (1975). *Against Method*. London: Verso.

Foucault, M. (1980). *Power/Knowledge Selected Interviews and other Writings 1972–1977.* Edited by Gordon, C. Sussex: Harvester Press.

Frýba, M. (1995). *Psychologie zvládání ǎivota. (Psychology of Managing Life).* Brno: Masarykova Univerzita.

Garfinkel, H. (1967). *Studies in Ethnomethodology.* New Jersey: Prentice-Hall.

Giddens, A. (1993). *New Rules of Sociological Method* (2nd Edn.). Cambridge: Polity Press.

Gray, M. (1995). The Ethical Implications of Current Theoretical Developments in Social Work. *British Journal of Social Work,* 25: pp 55–70.

Habermas, J. (1981). *Theorie des Kommunikaven Handelns.* Band 1 und 2, Frankfurt: Suhrkamp.

Habermas, J. (1984). *The Philosophical Discourse of Modernity.* Cambridge: Polity Press.

Habermas, J. (1987). *The Philosophical Discourse of Modernity.* Cambridge: Polity Press.

Habermas, J. (1996). *Between Facts and Norms* (trans. Rehg, W.). Cambridge: Polity Press.

Heasman, P., and Adams, A. (1998). Reflecting Well on Social Work Practice: Professional Competence, Reflecting and Research. *Educational Action Research,* 6(2): pp 337–342.

Kuhn, T.S. (1977). *The Essential Tension: Selected Studies in Scientific Tradition and Change.* Chicago: Chicago University Press.

Laan, G. van der (1998). *Otázky legitimace sociální práce. (Legitimationsfragen der Sozialarbeit.)* Boskovice: Albert.

Lewin, K. (1951). *Field Theory in Social Science.* New York: Harper and Brothers Publishers.

Lewin, K. (1982). *Aktionsforschung und Minderheitenprobleme, Gesamtausgabe, Bd. 7.* Bern: Huber.

Lock, M. and Gordon, D. R. (1988) *Biomedicine Examined.* Kluwer: Academic Publishers.

Loučková, I., and Chytil, O. (1999a). *Sociální problémy klienů oddělení péče o rodinu a dětí v Ostravě.* Ostrava: výzkumná zpráva.

Loučková, I. and Chytil, O. (1999b). *Sociální reprezentace stylů a metod práce sociálních pracovníků OPD v Ostravě.* Ostrava: výzkumná zpráva.

Mayring, P. (1993). *Einführung in die Qualitative Sozialforschung.* Weinheim: Psychologie Verlags Union.

Merton, R.K. (1973). *The Sociology of Science.* Chicago: University of Chicago.

Morse, J.M. (1992). *Quantitative Health Research.* Newbury Park, CA: Sage.

Miles, M., and Huberman, A. (1994). *Qualitative Data Analysis.* London: Sage.

Miller, P., and Rose, N. (1988). The Tavistock Programme: The Government of Subjectivity and Social Life. *Sociology,* 22(2): pp 171–192

Pahl, J. (1992). Force for Change or Optional Extra? The Impact of Research on Policy in Social Work and Social Welfare. In Carter, P., Jeffs, T., and Smith, K. (Eds.). *Changing Social Work and Welfare.* Milton Keynes: Open University Press.

Parton, N. (1994). The Nature of Social Work Under Conditions of Post-modernity. *Social Work and Social Sciences Review,* 5(2): pp 93–112.

Potter, J. (1996). *Representing Reality.* London: Sage.

Raynor, P. (1984). Evaluation with One Eye Closed: The Empiricist Agenda in Social Work Research. *British Journal of Social Work,* 14: pp 1–10.

Reid, W.J., and Hanrahan, P. (1982). Recent Evaluations of Social Work: Grounds for Optimism. *Social Work Research and Abstracts,* 23: pp. 14–20.

Reid, W.J. (1994). The Empirical Practice Movement. *Social Services Review,* 68(2): pp 165–237.

Reid, W.J. (1997). Research on Task-centred Practice. *Social Work Research,* 21(3): pp 132–137.

Rein, M. (1976). *Social Science and Public Policy.* Harmondsworth: Penguin.

Rubin, A., and Babbie, E. (l984). *Research Methods for Social Work.* Belmont, CA: Wadsworth Publishing Company.

Shaw, I., and Lishman, J. (Eds.) (1999). *Evaluation and Social Work.* London: Sage.

Sheldon, B. (1983). The Use of Single Case Experimental Designs in the Evaluation of Social Work. *British Journal of Social Work,* 1(3): pp 477–500.

Sheldon, B. (1984). Evaluation with One Eye Closed: The Empiricist Agenda in Social Work Research: A Reply to Peter Raynor. *British Journal of Social Work,* 14: pp 635–637.

Sheldon, B. (1986). Social Work Effectiveness Experiments: Review and Implications. *British Journal of Social Work,* 16: pp 223–242.

Sheldon, B. (1987). Implementing Findings from Social Work Effectiveness Research. *British Journal of Social Work,* 17: pp 573–586.

Sheldon, B., and Macdonald, G. (1993). Implications for Recent Social Work. *Effectiveness Research Practice,* 6(3): pp 221–218.

Sibeon, R. (1989). Comments on the Structure and Forms of Knowledge in Social Work. *Social Work and Social Sciences Review,* 1(1): pp 29–44.

Skinner, B.F. (1953). *Science and Human Behaviour.* New York: Macmillan.

Smith, D. (1987). The Limits of Positivism in Social Work Research. *British Journal of Social Work,* 17 pp 401–416.

Spradley, J., and Mann, B. (1975). *The Cocktail Waitress: Woman's Work in a Man's World.* New York: Wiley.

Spradley, J. (1979). *The Ethnographic Interview.* New York: Holt, Rinehart and Winston.

Spradley, J. (1980). *Participant Observation.* New York: Holt, Rinehart and Winston.

Strauss, A., and Corbin, J. (1990). *Basics of Qualitative Research. Grounded Theory, Procedures and Techniques.* London: Sage.

Strom, K., and Gingerich, W. (1993). Educating Students for the New Market Realities. *Journal of Social Work Education,* 29(1): pp 78–87.

Taussig, M. (1992). *The Nervous System.* London: Routledge.

Taylor, B., and Devine, T. (1993). *Assessing Needs and Planning Care in Social Work.* Aldershot: Arena.

Thyer, B.A. (1989). First Principles of Practice Research. *British Journal of Social Work,* 19: pp 309–323.

Waus, D.A. (l994). *Surveys in Social Research.* London: UCL Press.

Whittacker, D.S. and Archer, J.L. (1990). Using Practice Research for Change. *Social Work and Social Science Review*, 2(1): pp 9–29.

Wolcott, H.F. (1973). *The Man in the Principal's Office: An Ethnography*. New York, Holt, Rinehart and Winston.

Zola, I.K. (1968). *Missing Pieces: A Chronicle of Living with a Disability*. Philadelphia: Temple University Press.

Chapter 5

A Child in Trust (1985). *The Report of the Panel of Inquiry into the Circumstances Surrounding the Death of Jasmine Beckford*. London: London Borough of Brent.

Abbott, A.A. (1988). *Professional Choices; Values at Work*. Silver Springs, MD: National Association of Social Workers.

Ahmad, B. (1990). *Black Perspectives in Social Work*. Birmingham: Venture Press.

Australian Association of Social Workers (1990). *Code of Ethics*. AASW.

Banks, S. (2001). *Ethics and Values in Social Work* (2nd edn). Houndmills, Basingstoke: Macmillan.

Barclay, P.M. (1982). *Social Workers: Their Role and Tasks (The Barclay Report)*. London: Bedford Square Press.

BASW (1975, revised l986 and 1996). *A Code of Ethics for Social Work*. Birmingham: British Association of Social Workers.

Biestek, F.P. (1961). *The Casework Relationship*. London: Allen & Unwin.

Braye, S., and Preston-Shoot, M. (1995). *Empowering Practice in Social Care*. Buckingham: Open University Press.

CASW (1983). *Code of Ethics*. Canadian Association of Social Workers.

CCETSW (1976). *Values in Social Work (Paper 13)*. London: CCETSW.

CCETSW (1991). *Rules and Requirements for the Diploma in Social Work (Paper 30)* (2nd edn.). London: CCETSW.

CCETSW (1995). *Assuring Quality in the Diploma in Social Work*. London: CCETSW.

Clough, R. (1987). *Report of the Enquiry into Nye Bevan Lodge*. London: London Borough of Southwark.

Cossom, J. (1992). What Do We Know About Social Workers' Ethics? *The Social Worker Le Travailleur Sociale*, 60(3): pp 165–171.

Davies, M. (1994). *The Essential Social Worker* (3rd edn.). Aldershot: Arena.

Department of Health (2000). *A Quality Strategy for Social Care*. http://www.doh.gov.uk/pdfs/gstrategy.pdf

Dobrin, A. (1989). Ethical Judgements of Male and Female Social Workers. *Social Work*, 34(5): pp 451–455.

Dominelli, L. (1997). *Anti-racist Social Work* (2nd edn.). Basingstoke: Macmillan.

Dominelli, L. (1998). Feminist Social Work: An Expression of Universal Human Rights. *Indian Journal of Social Work*, 59(4): pp 918–929.

Fook, J. (1993). *Radical Social Work*. London: Allen and Unwin.

Gould, N., and Harris, A. (1996). Student Imagery of Practice in Social Work and Teacher Education. *British Journal of Social Work*, 26(2): pp 223–237.

Hamalainen, J., and Niemela, P. (1993). *Sosiaalialan Etiikka (Ethics of the Social Sphere)*. Helsinki: WSOY.

Harding, S. (1980). *On Value Systems in Europe: Report on the Preliminary Values Studies Prepared for the European Values Systems Study Group*. London: Survey Research Unit, Polytechnic of North London.

Hare, D. (1997). *Skylight*. London: Faber and Faber.

HMSO (1988). *Report of the Inquiry into Child Abuse in Cleveland* (Cmnd 412). London: HMSO.

Holbrook, S.M. (1996). Social Workers' Attitudes Toward Participants' Rights in Adoption and New Reproductive Technologies. *Health and Social Work*, 21(4): pp 257–267.

Holland, T.P., and Kilpatrick, A.C. (1991). Ethical Issues in Social Work: Toward a Grounded Theory of Professional Ethics. *Social Work*, 36(2): pp 138–144.

Hollis, F. (1967). Principles and Assumptions Underlying Casework Practice. In Younghusband E. (Ed.), *Social Work and Social Values*. London: George Allen and Unwin.

IFSW (1988). *International Code of Ethics for the Professional Social Worker*. Vienna: International Federation of Social Workers.

IFSW (1994). *The Ethics of Social Work: Principles and Standards*. Oslo: International Federation of Social Workers.

IFSW (1995). *Principes Ethiques en Travail Social*. Oslo: International Federation of Social Workers.

IFSW (1996). *La Etica del Trabajo Social Principos y Criterios*. Madrid: Consejo General de Colegios Official de Diplomados en Trabajo Social y Asistentes de Eep.

Jones, C. (1983). *State Social Work and the Working Class*. London: Routledge and Kegan Paul.

Joseph, M.V. (1989). Social Work Ethics: Historical and Contemporary Perspectives. *Social Thought*, 3(4): pp 4–17.

Kugelman, W. (1992). Social Work Ethics in the Practice Arena: A Qualitative Study. *Social Work in Health Care*, 17(4): pp 59–80.

Landau, R. (1997). Ethical Judgements and Decision Making Orientation in Social Work. *Issues in Social Work Education*, 17(2): pp 66–80.

Maiherbe, M. (1980). Accreditation in Social Work: Principles and Issues in Context: A Contribution to the Debate (CCETSW Study 4). London: Central Council of Education and Training in Social Work.

NASW (1996). *Code of Ethics*. Silver Spring, MD: National Association of Social Workers.

Netherlands Association of Social Workers (1987). *Professional Profile of the Social Worker* (trans. Jansen, H.). s-Hertogenbosch, Netherlands Association of Social Workers.

NISW (1964). *Introduction to a Social Worker*. London: Allen & Unwin.

Parker, R. (1990). *Safeguarding Standards*. London: National Institute for Social Work.

Pearson, O. (1973). Social Work as the Privatised Solution of Public Ills. *British Journal of Social Work*, 3(2): pp 209–227.

Proctor, E.K., Morrow-Howell, N., and Lott, C.L. (1993). Classifications and Correlates of Ethical Dilemmas in Hospital Social Work. *Social Work*, 38(2): pp 166–177.

Reamer, F. (1993). *The Philosophical Foundations of Social Work*. New York: Columbia University Press.

Rhodes, M.L. (1986). *Ethical Dilemmas in Social Work Practice*. London: Routledge & Kegan Paul.

Segal, U.A. (1992). Values, Personality and Career Choice. *The Journal of Applied Social Sciences*, 16(2): pp 143–159.

Shardlow, S.M. (1998). Values, Ethics and Social Work. In Adams, R., Dominelli, L., and Payne, M. (Eds.). *Social Work: Themes, Issues and Critical Debates*. Basingstoke: Macmillan.

Solas, J. (1994). Why Enter Social Work? Why on Earth do they Want to do it? Recruits' Ulterior Motives for Entering Social Work. *Issues in Social Work Education*, 14(2): pp 51–63.

Teicher, M. (1967). Conclusion and Summary. In NASW (Ed.). *Values in Social Work A Re-examination*. New York: National Association of Social Workers.

Tissier, G. (1990). A Permit to Practice. *Community Care*, 14: pp 20–22.

Utting, Sir W. (1997). *People Like Us: The Report of the Review of the Safeguards for Children Living Away from Home*. London: Stationary Office/Department of Health.

Vecchiato, T., and Villa, F. (1995). *Etica e Servizio Sociale* (*Ethics and Social Work*). Milan: Vita e Pensiero.

Walden, T., Wolock, I., and Demonez, H.W. (1990). Ethical Decision Making in Human Services. Families in Society. *The Journal of Contemporary Human Services*, 71(2): pp 67–75.

Wells C.C., with Masch M.K. (1986). *Social Work Ethics, Day to Day*. Illinois: Waveland Press Inc.

Wilson, A.N. (1980). *The Healing Art*. Harmondsworth: Penguin.

Yelaja, S. (Ed.) (1982). *Ethical Issues in Social Work*. Springfield, IL: Charles C Thomas.

Chapter 6

See footnotes

Chapter 7

Bauman, Z. (2000). Am I my Brothers' Keeper? *European Journal of Social Work*, 3(1): pp 5–11.

Laan, G. van der (1996). Van geval tot geval. *Sociale Interventie*, 5(2): pp 51–60.

Laan, G. van der (1999). Social Casework: sociaal beleid van geval tot geval. *Sociale Interventie*, 6(3): pp 103–112.

Laan, G. van der (2000). Social work in the Netherlands. In Adams, A., Erath, P., and Shardlow, S.M. (Eds.). *Fundamentals of Social Work in Selected European Countries*, pp 83–102. Lyme Regis: Russell House.

Roebroek, J.M. (1999). Maatschappelijk werk en verzorgingsstaat, de terugkeer van een basisdiscipline van de sociale politiek. *Sociale Interventie*, 8(3): pp 104–134.

Schell, J.L.M. (1995). De algemene bijstandswet. Kluwer Deventer.

Schuyt, C.J.M. (1991). *Op zoek naar het hart van de verzorgings staat*. Leiden: Stenfert Kroese.

Swaan, A. de (1988). *Zorg en de staat*. Amsterdam: Bert Bakker. New York.

SZW (1997). *Ministerie van Sociale Zaken en Werkgelegenheid. Progress Report 1997 on the Implementation of the Multi-annual Programme Employment in the Netherlands*. Den Haag: Ministry of Social Affairs.

Veen, R.J. van der (1990). *De sociale grenzen van beleid*. Leiden: Stenfert Kroese.

Visser, J., and Hemerijck, A. (1997). *'A Dutch Miracle'. Job Growth, Welfare Reform and Corporatism in the Netherlands*. Amsterdam: Amsterdam University Press.

Waaldijk, M.L. (1996). *Het Amerika der vrouw. Sekse en geschiedenis van maatschappelijk werk in Nederland en de Verenigde Staten*. Groningen: Wolters Noordhoff.

Chapter 8

Didicher, W. (1987). *Sozialpolitische Perspektiven und freie Träger. Organisatorische und strukturelle Fragen einer funktionalen Verbandspolitik unter Berücksichtigung der Arbeiterwohlfahrt*. Konstanz: Hartung-Gorre-Verlag.

Evers, A. (1991). Pluralismus und Vermittlungsfähigkeit. Zur Aktualität intermediärer Aufgaben und Instanzen im Bereich der Sozial- und Gesundheitspolitik. In Heinelt, H., and Wollmann, H. (Eds.). *Brennpunkt Stadt, Stadtpolitik und lokale Politikforschung in den 80er und 90er Jahren*, pp 221–235. Basel, Boston, Berlin: Birkhäuser-Verlag.

Heinze, R., and Olk, T. (1981). Die Wohlfahrtsverbände im System sozialer Dienstleistungsproduktion. Zur Entstehung und Struktur der bundesrepublikanischen Verbändewohlfahrt. *Kölner Zeitschrift für Soziologie und Sozialpsychologie*, 33(1): pp 94–114.

Heinze, R., Olk, T., and Hilbert, J. (1988). *Der neue Sozialstaat: Analyse und Reformperspektive*. Freiburg: Lambertus-Verlag.

Klug, W. (1997a). *Wohlfahrtsverbände zwischen Markt, Staat und Selbsthilfe*. Freiburg: Lambertus-Verlag.

Klug, W. (1997b). Marktwirtschaft und Identität als Wohlfahrtsverband ein Gegensatz? *Theorie und Praxis der Sozialen Arbeit*, 48(10): pp 26–33.

Manderscheid, H. (1995). Freie Wohlfahrtspflege vor Ort: Vom Wertepluralismus zur fachlichen Differenzierung. In Rauschenbach, C., Sachße, C. Olk, T., and Backhaus-Maul, H. (Eds.). *Von der Wertegemeinschaft zum Dienstleistungsunternehmen*, pp 228–252. Frankfurt: Suhrkamp-Verlag.

Münder, J. (1993). Träger der Sozialhilfe. In Müller, W. (Ed.). *SelbstHilfe: ein einführendes Lesebuch*, pp 78–81. Weinheim - Basel: Beltz-Verlag.

Oppl, H. (1992). Zur 'Marktposition' der Freien Wohlfahrtspflege. *Soziale Arbeit*, pp 41(5): pp 152–158.

Sachße, C., and Tennstedt, F. (1988). *Geschichte der Armenfürsorge*, Vol. 2. Stuttgart Berlin Köln Mainz: Kohlhammer-Verlag.

Schulte, B. (1990). Das Verhältnis zwischen öffentlichen und freien Trägern in internationaler Perspektive. In Münder, J., and Kreft, D. (Eds.). *Subsidiarität heute*, pp 47–50. Münster: Votum-Verlag.

Chapter 9

Baratta, A. (1982). *Criminologia critica e critica del diritto penale: introduzione alla sociologia giuridico penale.* Bologna: Il Mulino.

Censis (Centro Studi Investimenti Sociali) (2000). *Le paure degli Italiani. Criminalità e offerta di sicurezza,* at http://www.censis.it/censis/ricerche/2000/pauresvileg/le_paure_degli_italiani.htm

Cesareo, V. (1987). *Socializzazione e controllo sociale: una critica della concezione dell'uomo ultrasocializzato.* Milano: Angeli.

Cowger, C.D., and Atherton, C.R. (1974). Social Control: A Rationale for Social Welfare. *Social Work,* 19(4): pp 456–462.

Donabedian, A. (1980). *The Definition of Quality and Approaches to its Assessment,* Vol. I. Ann Arbor: Health Administration Press.

Elmer, N., and Reicher, S. (1995). *Adolescence and Delinquency.* Oxford: Blackwell.

Fedele, M. (1993). Mass media e processo legislativo. *Sociologia e ricerca sociale,* XIV(41): pp 55–80.

Hess, H. (1983). Il controllo sociale: società e potere. *Dei delitti e delle pene,* 1(3): pp 499–525.

Higgins, J. (1980). Social Control Theories of Social Policy. *Journal of Social Policy,* 9(1): pp 1–23.

Hill, M. (1980). *Understanding Social Policy.* Oxford: Blackwell.

Hill, M., and Bramley, G. (1986). *Analysing Social Policy.* Oxford: Blackwell.

Lagrange, H., Peretti, P., Pottier, M., Robert, P., and Zauberman, R. (2000). Une enquête sur les risques urbains. Étude de préfiguration. Centre de Recherches Sociologiques sur le Droit et les Institutions Pénales. *Études & Données Pénales,* 81.

Mayhew, P., and van Dijk, J.J.M. (1999). Criminal Victimisation in Eleven Industrialised Countries. *Onderzoek en beleid,* 162. Amstelveen: Wetenschappelijk Onderzoek en Documentatiecentrum.

Mead, G.H. (1938). *The Philosophy of the Act.* Chicago: University of Chicago Press.

Melossi, D. (1990). *The State of Social Control: A Sociological Study of Concepts of State and Social Control in the Making of Democracy.* Cambridge: Polity Press.

Miethe, T.D. (1995). Fear and Withdrawal from Urban Life. *The Annals of the American Academy of Political and Social Science,* 539: pp 14–27.

Olivetti Manoukian, F. (1998). *Produrre servizi.* Bologna: Il Mulino.

Parsons, T. (1951). *The Social System.* Glencoe, Ill: Free Press.

Pitch, T. (1988). Che cos'è il controllo sociale. In De Leonardis, O., Gallio, G., Mauri, D., and Pitch, T. (Eds.). *Curare e punire,* pp 21–44. Milano: Unicopli.

Pitch, T. (1989). *Responsabilità limitate: attori, conflitti, giustizia penale.* Milano: Feltrinelli.

Scheingold, S.A. (1995). Politics, Public Policy, and Street Crime. *The Annals of the American Academy of Political and Social Science,* 539: pp 155–168.

Scott, R.W. (1992). *Organizations. Rational, Natural and Open Systems.* Englewood Cliffs: Prentice Hall.

Skogan, W.G. (1990). *Disorder and Decline.* New York: Free Press.

Taylor, R.B. (1995). The Impact of Crime on Communities. *The Annals of the American Academy of Political and Social Science,* 539: pp 28–45.

Chapter 10

Alvarez Uría, F. (1995). En torno de la crisis de los modelos de intervencion social a VV.AA. *Desigualdad y pobreza hoy,* Madrid: Talasa.

Bañez Tello, T. (1993). La formacíon en el Trabajo Social. Revista de Servicios Sociales y Politica Social, 30.

Beck, U. (1992) *Risk Society: Towards a New Modernity.* London: Sage.

Casado, D. (1988). *Introduccion a los Servicios Sociales.* Madrid: Acebo.

Castells, M. (1998). *La Era de la Información.* Madrid: Alianza.

Col.Legi Oficial de Diplomats en Treball Social i Assistents Socials de Catalunya (1997). *Els diplomats en Treball Social i Assistents Socials de Catalunya. Situació, perfil i expectatives.* Barcelona: Hacer.

Comité Espanol para el Bienestar Social (1981). *Memoria sobre los planes de estudios universitarios de Trabajo Social.* Madrid: CEBS.

Consejo General De Colegios Oficiales De Diplomados En Trabajo Social Y Asistentes Sociales (1993). *Dictamen sobre definición y objetivos profesionales.* Madrid: CGCODTSAS.

Consejo General de Colegios Oficiales de Diplomados en Trabajo Social y Asistentes Sociales (1995). *Propuesta de ampliación de los estudios de Trabajo Social.* Madrid: CGCODTSAS.

Domenech, R. (1989). *Panorámica de los Servicios Sociales y del Trabajo Social, 1939–1988.* Barcelona: Intress.

Escartin, M.J. (1992). *Manual de Trabajo Social.* Alicante: Aguaclara.

Estruch, J., and Güell, A.M. (1976). *Sociología de una profesión. Los asistentes sociales.* Barcelona: Península.

Friedson, E. (1986). *Professional Powers.* Chicago: University of Chicago.

Ii Congreso de Escuelas Universitarias de Trabajo Social (1998). *Globalizacion y Trabajo Social.* Madrid: EUTS-Universidad Complutense de Madrid.

Llovet, J.J., and Usieto Atondo, R. (1990). *Los trabajadores sociales. De la crisis de identidad a la profesionalizaciación.* Madrid: Popular.

Molina, M.V. (1994). *Las enseñanzas del Trabajo Social en España 1932–1983.* Madrid: Universidad Pontificia de Comillas.

Payne, M. (1996). *Teorías contemporáneas de Trabajo Social.* Barcelona: Paidos.

Red, N. de la (1993). *Aproximaciones al Trabajo Social.* Madrid: Siglo XXI.

Rubi, C. (1991). *Introducción al Trabajo Social.* Barcelona: Llar del Llibre.

Sabater, J. (1989). Configuración i crisi de Estat del Benestar a VV.AA. *Treball Social. Conceptes i eines bàsiques.* Barcelona: Euts-Icesb.

Sarasa, S. (1993). *El Servicio de lo social*. Madrid: Ministerio de Asuntos Sociales.

VV.AA. (1988). *Un cisma en la educación del Trabajo Social: ¿énfasis en el individuo o en la sociedad?* Barcelona: Hogar del Libro-EUTS Barcelona.

VV.AA. (1989). *La profesionalización del Trabajo Social en España*. Valencia: EUTS-Valencia.

Chapter 11

Adams, A., Erath, P., and Shardlow, S.M. (Eds.) (2000). *Fundamentals of Social Work in Selected European Countries*. Lyme Regis: Russell House Publishing.

Autès, M. (1983). L'identité de l'éducateur spécialisé ou les incertitudes du pouvoir de nommer in Cahiers D'E.C.A.R.T.S. (Espace Des Acteurs De La Recherche Pour Le Travail Social.) N°6, Publication de l'Association Francaise Pour La Sauvegarde De L'enfance Et De L'adolescence (A.F.S.E.A.).

Besnard, P. (1980). *Animateur socioculturel: une profession récente*. Toulouse: Privat, coll. Pratiques Sociales.

Bouamama, S. (1993). *De la galère à la citoyenneté. Les jeunes, la cité, la société*. Paris: éd. Desclée de Brouwer.

Castel, R. (1996). *Les métamorphoses de la question sociale. Une chronique du salariat*. Paris: éd. Fayard.

Demaziere, D. (1992). *Le chômage en crise? La négociation des identités des chômeurs de longue durée*. Lille: PUL.

Dingwall, R., and Lewis, P. (Eds.) (1983). *The Sociology of Profession*. London: Macmillan.

Dubar, C. (1970). *Idéologies et choix professionnels des éducateurs spécialisés, Thèse de 3 ème cycle*, Doctorat de sociologie, Paris VIII.

Dubar, C. (1980). Origine sociale et valeurs professionnelles des éducateurs. In Dutrenit, J.M. *Sociologie et compréhension du travail social*. Toulouse: éd. Privat, sciences de l'homme.

Dubet, F. (1987). *La galère: Jeunes en survie*. Paris: éd. Fayard.

Eloy, J., Gantier, P., and Samyn, E. (1984). Devenir professionnels de cinq promotions d'animateurs dans le Nord-Pas-de-Calais, *Les cahiers de l'animation*, N° 44/45.

Friedson, E. (1986). *Professional Powers*. Chicago: University of Chicago.

Jovelin, E. (1993). Les travailleurs sociaux d'origine étrangère. Destins professionnels et choix du métier, *Revue de l'Association Française de Sauvegarde de l'Enfance et de l'Adolescence*, N°4: pp 382–404.

Jovelin, E. (1998). *Les travailleurs sociaux d'origine étrangère.*

Vocation ou repli professionnel. Analyse sociologique d'un groupe professionnel. Thèse de doctorat en sociologie. Université de Lille.

Jovelin, E. (1998). Itinéraires des travailleurs sociaux d'origine étrangère. In Breuvart, J.M., and Danvers, F. (1998). *Migrations, Interculturalité et Démocratie*, pp 109–132. Lille: Presses Universitaires du Septentrion.

Jovelin, E. (1999). *Devenir travailleur social aujourd'hui. Vocation ou repli? L'exemple des Educateurs, Animateurs et Assistants Sociaux d'origine étrangère*. Paris; éd. L'harmattan.

Lapauw, R. (1969). *Educateurs…inadaptés*. Paris: éd. de l'Epi.

Larson, M. (1997). *The Rise of the Professions*. Berkeley, CA: University of California.

Morand, G. (1992). *Identité professionnelle et formation permanente des assistantes sociales*. Paris: éd. Bayard.

Muel-Dreyfus, F. (1983). *Le métier d'éducateur*. Paris: éd. Le minuit.

Munday, B. (1972). What is Happening to Social Work Students? *Social Work Today*, 3(6): pp 3–6.

Naville, P. (1957). *La théorie de l'orientation professionnelle*. Paris: P.U.F.

Paugam, S. (1995). *La société française et ses pauvres. L'expérience du revenu minimum d'insertion*. Paris: P.U.F.

Pearson, G. (1973). Social Work as the Privatised Solution of Public Ills. *British Journal of Social Work*, 3(2): pp 209–227.

Simonot, M. (1974). *Les animateurs socioculturels, étude d'une aspiration à une activité sociale*. Paris: P.U.F.

Verba, D. (1995). *Le métier d'éducateur de jeunes enfants*. Paris: éd. Syros.

Vilbrod, A. (1995). *Devenir éducateur, une affaire de famille*. Paris: éd. L'harmattan.

Postscript

Beck, U. (1992). *The Risk Society* (Trans. Ritter, M.). London: Sage.

Parton, N. (1994). The Nature of Social Work Under Conditions of (Post) Modernity. *Social Work and Social Sciences Review*, 5(2): pp 93–112.

Pillinger, J. (2000). Redefining Work and Welfare in Europe. In Lewis, G., Gewitz, S., and Clarke, J. (Eds.). *Rethinking Social Policy*. London: Sage.

Williams, F. (2000). Principles of Recognition and Respect in Welfare. In Lewis, G., Gewitz, S., and Clarke, J. (Eds.). *Rethinking Social Policy*. London: Sage.

Index

alienation 3, 37
Anglo-American 6–7, 13
assessment 21, 25, 47–49, 53, 58, 60, 97, 107, 111
authoritarianism 86

comparative
  studies 1–4
  analysis 1, 15, 105
capitalist 5, 8, 11, 22–23, 29, 63–64, 78, 86–87
care 7–8, 10, 12–13, 24–25, 27, 35–36, 40, 44–52, 54, 57–58, 60–61, 67, 70, 79–82, 92, 95, 103, 106, 108–110
case
  management 8, 24, 106
Church 7, 61, 86–87
civil rights 6, 53
citizens 5–13, 59–61, 67, 70, 73–74, 77, 81, 94, 103
clients 13, 18, 20–23, 34, 36, 39, 42–43, 49, 55, 57–63, 103
crime 35, 52, 77–79, 111
critical theories 18, 20, 22
code of ethics 40, 43, 45–46, 109
cognitive-behavioural 3, 19–21, 24, 77, 81, 107
collective
  responsibility 5, 9–10
communities 11–13, 23, 35, 40, 43, 80, 89, 92, 103, 111
community 8–12, 24–25, 31–32, 34, 37, 40, 44, 47–49, 52, 59, 69, 74–75, 77–83, 90, 96, 98–99, 106, 110
conservative 6–7, 69, 86
Continental 6–8, 13, 63–64
corporatist 2, 6, 11, 58, 64, 70, 72, 74

deregulation 69
demographic changes 91
democratic societies 6, 13, 22–23, 69, 87–88
deviance 77–82
dialectics 3, 23
difference 2–3, 13, 41–42, 54, 59, 64
disability benefits 63
discourses 2–3, 22, 29, 35, 37
diversity 2–3, 12, 29, 35, 40, 93, 96

eligibility 47–49, 53, 65
empiricism 20, 30
empirical-analytical 20–21, 25
Europe 1–2, 5, 8, 15, 39, 43, 45–46, 57, 69–70, 72–73, 75, 85–86, 88, 91, 93, 102–103, 105–107, 109, 112

European 1, 3, 6–8, 11, 13, 23, 25, 30, 32, 42, 47, 50–55, 63, 70, 75, 85–87, 91, 93, 105–106, 109–110, 112
ethnographic 3, 19, 25, 30–31, 108
ethical issues 21, 39, 42, 109–110
experience 3, 17, 19–20, 25, 27–30, 32–33, 35, 39, 63, 74, 85–87, 89–93, 96, 98–99, 101–102, 112
explanations 3, 17, 95
  behavioural 3
  causal 3, 17

families 3, 7, 9, 11–12, 18, 25, 44, 46, 58, 96–97, 105, 110

gestalt 3, 19
global 1, 3, 13, 69–70, 88, 93, 95, 105–106
globalisation 1, 13, 46, 92–93
groups 1–3, 8–13, 17, 23, 25, 27, 30, 32, 34–38, 40–41, 43, 60, 62, 64, 69, 71–72, 74–75, 77–80, 82–83, 88–90, 96, 101, 104
  vulnerable 3, 10–12, 37, 61–62, 81, 101
  disadvantaged 3, 10–11, 74

health care 8, 10, 13, 40, 60–61, 109
hermeneutics 17, 19, 29, 106

identity 3, 11–12, 18, 20, 22–24, 30, 57, 75, 89, 91–92, 95, 99, 103
immigrants 80
individuals 1, 3, 7, 11–13, 17, 23, 25, 34–35, 39, 41, 46–47, 49, 53, 55, 57–58, 61, 78–81, 83, 89, 92, 94–101, 103–104
individual rights 5, 69
infrastructure 2, 8, 78, 87
insurance scheme 7, 9–10, 57

judicial reviews 47

knowledge 1, 3, 12–13, 15–20, 22, 24, 27–33, 35–39, 41–42, 45–46, 51, 59–60, 81, 85, 89–90, 92–95, 108, 110

labour 7, 11, 37, 44, 57, 60, 62–67, 69, 71, 86, 91, 95, 97, 99
law 23, 39, 41, 43, 47, 49–57, 64–66, 71–72, 74, 77, 80, 86, 88–89, 91, 105
legislation 5, 7, 48–49, 51, 53–55, 57–59, 61, 66, 72, 90
life narratives 3

market forces 4, 11, 57, 66, 69–70, 91, 93, 95, 103
minors 79–80
minority groups 11, 37, 74
modern 3, 5, 22, 33, 103, 105, 107
morality 3, 11, 67, 86, 106

nation 3, 25, 43, 60, 67, 73, 93, 103
  state 3, 25, 43, 60, 93
  systems 25, 43, 93
  social movements 2, 8, 69, 74, 95
Nordic 5–11, 13
norms 5, 11–12, 20, 28, 30, 32, 35, 53, 61, 74, 78, 80, 96–97, 104–105, 108
not-for profit organisations 70

oppression 3, 23, 41, 98, 102

paradigms 3, 27–28, 30–31, 33, 44
personal responsibility 11, 40, 57
  safety 77
phenomenology 29, 32
philosophy 28–29, 41, 105–106, 111
prevention 10, 51–53, 81, 107
private 7–9, 11, 13, 39, 43, 50–55, 61, 70–71, 73, 87, 90, 93, 95, 103, 106
privatisation 9, 69, 103
professional
  codes of behaviour 39
  identity 20, 92, 95
  status 15, 44
policies 1, 5, 7, 10–13, 16, 25, 35, 49, 57, 59, 61–65, 67, 69–70, 72, 74, 77–78, 81, 85, 87–88, 94, 103, 106
population 6–7, 10, 12, 57, 62, 64–66, 86, 91, 96, 99
post modern 103
poverty 3, 25, 37, 61, 86, 98
psycho-social 17, 62, 86, 93

qualitative research 19, 30–34, 86, 108–109
quantitative research 30–31, 33–34, 37, 108

rationality 3, 20, 22, 30, 59–60, 67
regimes 1–3, 5–9, 12–13, 15, 51–52, 57, 75, 95, 106
religion 5, 86
research base 15
resources 6, 12, 17–18, 24–25, 47–49, 58, 74, 80, 82, 103
residential 48–50, 52, 54–55
  care home 52

sciences   2–3, 17, 19–20, 27–33, 37,
    87, 89, 91, 93, 108, 110, 112
  anthropological   2–3, 29, 32
  natural   19–20, 30, 32–33
self   19, 23, 35, 98
  understanding   3
  determination   43, 57, 102
  representation   3
social
  action   15, 23, 30, 59, 86–88
  assistance   65, 88–89
  institutions   2, 22, 87, 104
  groups   2, 34, 78–80
  organisation   4, 16
  participation   10, 60, 62–63
  policy   5–13, 21, 24, 57–60, 63–64,
      67, 70, 73, 75, 78, 86, 89, 91,
      105–107, 111–112
  services   6–8, 10, 21, 36, 44–48,
      51–55, 61–62, 71–74, 79–83,
      88–89, 91, 106, 108
  security   2–3, 5–13, 53, 58, 60–62,

64–66, 69, 74–75, 86, 106
  structure   12, 30, 91
work   1–9, 11–13, 15–25, 27, 29–47,
    49–51, 53, 55–63, 65, 67, 69–75,
    78–83, 85–95, 97–103, 105–112
  accountability   36, 54, 93
  education   86
  expertise   1, 12, 106
  interests   2–4, 8, 11, 17–18, 25, 30,
      33–38, 44–46, 50–51, 56, 64–65,
      70–71, 73–75, 82–83, 93, 99, 101,
      103
  international   1, 3, 13, 42, 46, 63–64,
      86–87, 94, 105–107, 109
  inter-cultural   1
  intervention   89, 91
  legitimacy methods   2, 8, 12–13, 28,
      59, 82, 103
  models of   5–8, 10–11, 15, 74, 85, 93
  motivation   27, 37, 95, 98–99,
      101–102
  occupation   10, 95–99

practice   1–3, 5, 8, 12–13, 15–25, 27,
    30, 32, 35–37, 39–47, 49–51, 53,
    55, 58, 63, 71, 78, 80–82, 86–87,
    90–93, 95, 101, 103, 105–110
purposes   4, 17, 27, 29, 34–35, 83,
    93, 103
responsibilities   2, 23, 39, 69, 71, 74,
    104
role   40, 98
tasks   2, 5, 13, 15, 19, 24, 35, 63, 65,
    67, 72, 74, 93, 109
theory   20, 22, 41, 103
socially excluded   79–80, 98, 103
solidarity   9–13, 58–59, 61, 75, 81
standards   36, 39, 43–46, 52, 54, 67,
    71, 73–74, 78, 94, 103, 109
subsidiarity   7, 69–70, 72, 74

third sector   69–71, 73–75

wealth   6, 67
welfare mix   5, 8–9, 13, 106